WOMEN OF GRACE

Also by Kathleen Parbury

The Saints of Lindisfarne.
The Star of the North.
The Hermits of the House of Farne.

WOMEN OF GRACE

A Biographical Dictionary
of British Women Saints,
Martyrs and Reformers

by
Kathleen Parbury

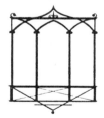

ORIEL PRESS
STOCKSFIELD
BOSTON . MELBOURNE . HENLEY,
LONDON

BX
4659
.G7
P375
1985

First published in 1984
by Oriel Press Limited
Stocksfield, Northumberland,
England, NE43 7NA.

9 Park Street, Boston,
Mass. 02108, U.S.A. and

6th Floor, 464 St. Kilda Road,
Melbourne, Victoria 3004, Australia.

Set in Plantin and
printed by Knight & Forster, Leeds.

Trade enquiries to
Routledge & Kegan Paul PLC
Broadway House, Newtown Road,
Henley-on-Thames, Oxon, RG9 1EN.

ISBN 0 85362 213 2

Dedicated
In Memory of My Sister
CONSTANCE
a
Woman of Grace

ACKNOWLEDGMENTS

I wish to thank Mrs Ruth Crossman for the very great help and time that she gave me in the research work for this book; without her aid it would not have been written.

The late Theodore Nicholson, F.S.A., supplied me with facts about the nunneries in Yorkshire. I am grateful to him for all the trouble he took.

I thank the Rev. Canon G. R. Parke and Mrs Parke for the loan of many books, and also Miss Simpson of the Berwick-on-Tweed library and Mr. Hall of the Alnwick library.

I wish to acknowledge the information that I received from the following:

Miss W. Loader, from the West Midlands,

The Rev. C. E. Woolstenholmes, Rector of Shadforth, Co. Durham,

The Rev. Peter Hartley, one time Rector of Elstow Abbey Bedfordshire,

The Rev. Peter Moore, one time in Norfolk,

The Rev. Canon Grice-Hutchinson, vicar of North Sunderland,

The Rev. Ian R. Lovell vicar of Minster in Sheppey, Kent,

Sister Concordia O.S.B. of Minster Abbey, Thanet, Kent,

The Rev. G. E. Wood, Rector of Sempringham, Lincolnshire,

The Mother Superior, The Bar Convent York,

The Rev. W. Bentley, Rector of St. Hilda's Hartlepool,

Mrs Betty Prentice for the loan of the Life of St. Margaret Clitheroe.

Also I wish to thank Mrs C. Bosanquet, Mr. Bruce Allsopp, F.S.A., and Miss Christine Cowham of Oxford University Press for their encouragement.

CONTENTS

PUBLISHER'S NOTE

Miss Parbury has devoted a great deal of time over many years to patient research but the first edition of a reference book, such as this, can only depend upon the material accessible to the author. Moreover, in later times the selection of entries must depend, to some extent, upon opinion.

The publishers would be grateful to any readers who might care to send comments, emendations or additional entries for the next edition. These should be addressed to: The Editor, Oriel Press Ltd. c/o Routledge and Kegan Paul PLC, 14 Leicester Square, London, WC2H 7PH.

INTRODUCTION

In the following pages I have endeavoured to write about the Holy Women of Great Britain who were of the Christian Faith. In some cases a misty veil of legendary tales obscures their history, but I have sought to pierce that veil to reveal something of their virtuous lives, employed in the service of God and their fellow men. There are countless numbers whose names are unknown to us, but those whom we do know of, are worth remembering, and so that they will not be forgotten, I have striven to turn back the pages of history.

In this introduction is given a short summary of the way in which the nunneries and the different Orders came into existence, and the names of the men and women who founded the Orders; the majority of which were of foreign origin.

In the infancy of the Christian Church there was much persecution, and to escape from it, many of the early Christians gathered together into communities, and some sought solitude in the Egyptian desert.

It was there that a form of monastic life first started among the followers of Christ. Under the influence of two great men, St. Anthony, who lived from 251 to 356, and St. Pachomius, who lived from 290 to 346, the life of these people began to develop with an organized plan and a simple set of rules.

From these beginnings in the desert, religious communities gradually spread over the Eastern Mediterranean, and then on towards the west of Europe. St. Martin of Tours, who died in 397, was one of the founders of a monastery in France, and inspired by his example, other men built religious houses, and in a short time there appeared such dwellings in Britain.

There is a tradition that St. Joseph of Arimathaea in very early times founded the Monastery of Glastonbury:

> "In a cave under ground, over which a chapel was afterwards built in Honour of this saint, was also found the following Epitaph of great antiquity:
>
> 'Ad Britones veni postquam Christum Sepelivi, Docui, requievi.'
>
> That is, 'After I had buried Christ, I came to the Britons, I taught them and rested.'

Dugdale's *Monasticon*, English edition, 1718.

The monks at Glastonbury always believed in this legend, but too much is veiled in mystery to give a definite date to the coming of Christianity to Britain.

It is only when the fourth and fifth centuries were reached that a few real facts begin to emerge out of the past, and we can state positively that St. Ninian built in 397 a monastery in Wigtonshire and called it Candida Cassa. Another monastery was built at Menevia by St. David, who was born about 446. Many great saints were educated at these two places, among them was St. Finnian of Clonard, whose pupils included the Twelve Apostles of Ireland, St. Columba being one of them. From Ireland came St. Columba to Iona in 563, and from Iona came missionaries to Northumbria to convert the Anglo-Saxons to Christianity in 634.

Almost certainly the rule varied in the different monasteries. St. Columba composed a rule, which would be the one followed at Lindisfarne at the beginning of its foundation. The early Christians in Britain and Ireland had been cut off from the rest of Europe for a long time, and it was only gradually that new ideas began to filter in. When St. Augustine was sent by Pope Gregory, then the Anglo-Saxons first heard of the Rule of St. Benedict.

St. Benedict built a monastery at Monte Cassino in Italy in 530. His Rule became the norm for the rules for the majority of the Orders of Monks and Nuns from the sixth century down to the present day, and was known as the "Holy Rule".

At what date communities for women were first formed is not exactly known, probably in the early days of Christianity. St. Anthony's sister followed his example in the fourth century, and with a number of other women lived a religious life, and St. Bridget in Ireland founded the nunnery of Kildare before 525. There may have been nunneries among the Britons before the Saxons came; in the tales told about King Arthur, his queen retired to a nunnery.

It is after the advent of St. Augustine in 597 and of St. Aidan in 635 that we have definite information about houses for women being built in England. At first the majority of the Anglo-Saxon women who wished to become nuns belonged to royal or noble families, and went over to nunneries in France, where there were a number of flourishing houses for women, such as Brie and Chelles. St. Hilda's sister, Herewith, went to Chelles; King Eorcenberht of Kent sent his daughter Eorcingota to Brie, and it was there that King Anna of East

Anglia sent his daughter Ethelburga and his stepdaughter Saethryth. Fara of Burgundofara founded the monastery of Brie, inspired by the Celtic saint Columban. It was a double monastery, under the control of the Abbess, like so many founded soon afterwards in England. The Rule they followed was probably a mixture of a Celtic and the Benedictine Rule.

Bede states that the first woman to take the habit and vows of a nun in the Northumbrian kingdom was the Abbess Heiu, and she was ordained by St. Aidan, and took charge of the Monastery of Hartlepool. St. Hilda succeeded her there as Abbess, after having spent a year at a place near the river Wear, given to her by St. Aidan to form a community for women. St. Aidan died in 651. The double monastery of Whitby was founded within a few years of his death.

Towards the end of the seventh century, and after the Synod of Whitby, which was held in 664, many of the monasteries adopted the Benedictine Rule. Both Benedict Biscop of Monkwearmouth and St. Wilfrid of Hexham were mainly responsible for its introduction. It began to be recognised as the ideal way of life for all the religious to follow, at first still retaining the spirit of the Celtic tradition by individual abbots and abbesses.

There were about eighteen houses for women founded among the Anglo-Saxons before the century came to a close. The life led by the women is well described by Bede in his account of Whitby. They were well educated, having as much learning and knowledge as there was known in the world in those days. They learnt to read and write, and in the Scriptorium to copy and illuminate the books. Above all the nuns had to study the scriptures, and the Psalms they learnt by heart.[3] They were to observe "the virtues of justice, devotion, and chastity, and other virtues too, but above all to continue in peace and charity. After the example of the primitive Church, no one was rich, no one was in need, for they had all things in common, and none had any private property." Bede, when he writes of the Abbess Etheldreda of Ely, relates how austere the life was; the nuns spent a long time in prayer on their knees, and attended all the Offices, night and day.

Occasionally there were abuses, such as at Coldingham; the nuns there became too worldly and fond of extravagances in dress, and were not always as chaste as they should be, but the scandal of their behaviour was an exception at that time and was the cause of a rebuke

[3]Bede: *Ecclesiastical History*, Book IV, C 23.

3

by the bishop.

The age of the Anglo-Saxons from the beginning of the seventh century to the end of the tenth century produced more women saints in England than in any other period of our history; an era of Christianity that lasted nearly three hundred years, until this great epoch of faith finally came to an end under the persecutions by the Danes.

During the last two decades of the eighth century, the first sight of strange sails was seen advancing from over the eastern horizon, causing alarm among the people on the eastern side of England. Then these pagan raiders came and attacked all the coastline from the Forth down to the southern shores of the land, eventually pushing their way inland until they occupied more than half of what is now England, having driven the inhabitants towards the south west. These Danish pirates had no reverence for anything sacred, and swept away nearly every holy building they could find and left them all in ruins.

After such a holocaust, and the country utterly devastated, it is surprising that a recovery did take place. In the fastnesses of south west England King Alfred tried to rally his fighting forces. He ascended the throne in 871, and for most of his life waged a war against the Danes, gradually driving them towards the north and east. Horrified by the ignorance of his people and of many clergy who were left after the destruction of all places of education, he determined to bring back sanctity and learning to the life of the nation.

In trying to restore the religious communities,[4] "he had greater success with the women than the men." He and his queen founded two monasteries for women: St. Mary's Winchester and Shaftesbury. But the king had great difficulty in finding any of the clergy educated enough to be of any assistance and he had to ask for help from abroad.

It is said that in spite of all that had happened "the traditions of the early monasteries, old sites, the names of saints, lingered on and moulded the minds of Alfred, Dunstan and other men of his time".[5]

Monasteries of men and women, living a regular, in contrast to a secular, religious life, do not seem to have been properly re-established after their destruction by the Danes until Dunstan came and took over the leadership of the Church. In 939 King Edmund appointed Dunstan Abbot of Glastonbury. There, the new

[4]Lingard's *Anglo-Saxon* Church.

[5]Dom David Knowles — *The Monastic Order In England.*

4

Abbot placed monks who followed the Rule of St. Benedict. From that time onwards Dunstan, with the cooperation of two other great men, Ethelwold and Oswald, was responsible for starting the Great Revival of monasteries filled with regular monks and nuns in England.

These three men sought advice from abroad, especially from the monastery of Fleury, which came under the direct influence of Cluny in 930. Cluny was founded in 910. Berno was the first Abbot and the monastery observed the Rule of St. Benedict. But what distinguished the Cluniac monasteries from other Benedictine monasteries was the emphasis on a ceaseless round of liturgical services with great ceremony, leaving very little time for any manual work.

A number of men from Fleury came to the court in England, and many discussions took place between them and St. Dunstan concerning the management of religious houses.

Under St. Dunstan's influence and that of his two colleagues, Ethelwold and Oswald, the monasteries rose again out of the ashes of the former houses burnt by the Danes. There is something innate in the Anglo-Saxon race that enables it to rise above the deepest disaster. During the tenth century at least ten houses for women sprang up.

In 959, when King Edgar came to the throne, the English rule over the whole country was restored, and so came to an end "the first great episode in the Viking history of England. A hundred and twenty years had passed since the impact of the Vikings had smitten the island". King Edgar became the first king of all the English. He and his queen took many monasteries under their direct patronage.

In 972 a great Synod was held at Winchester, at which bishops, abbots and abbesses were present. There was drawn up the code known as the Regularis Concordia Anglicae Nationis Monachorum Sanctimonialiumque (in short Regularis Concordia.) All the monasteries, male and female, undertook to observe its rules.

In 973 at Bath, the king was crowned. A great gathering of abbots, abbesses, monks and nuns assisted at the Coronation.

Both Dunstan and Ethelwold did a great deal towards ministering towards the welfare of the women. Ethelwold translated the Rule of St. Benedict into English especially for the nuns.

While these three men were in charge of the Church in England the monasteries of men and women continued to flourish and they

Winston S. Churchill; *A History of the English Speaking Peoples.*

5

continued to expand even after the death of St. Dunstan. Though there was a certain amount of influence from abroad, this was only slight and not considerable during the tenth century.

At the beginning of the eleventh century a fresh Danish invasion caused a slight setback, but under the strong rule of King Cnut there were no ravagings of the monasteries as in the earlier invasions. The king allowed no interference with the Church, and he became a benefactor of the religious houses.

With the return of the Anglo-Saxon dynasty under Edward the Confessor in 1042, a change began to develop of great significance in the government and structure of the monasteries; Edward brought in Norman monks and installed several secular clerks or canons. These canons were formed from a new movement, which had started in Italy.

But the old Anglo-Saxon regime still had a certain hold over the Church, even though there were only two men left who held high office who were not of Norman blood: St. Wulfstat of Worcester, and St. Aethelwig of Evesham.

The form of government which came in with the Normans was the same as in the Cluniac houses, with their impressive choral worship, but with the difference that the English houses still retained something of the Benedictine Rule in its love for learning and the arts.

At the time of the conquest by William of Normandy in 1066, there were, as Knowles states, only nine fully organised monasteries for women, six of these being of old Wessex foundations. Most of them were founded by royal ladies, and the nuns came from the upper classes. It is only after 1066 that the abbesses appear to have Norman names. The houses for women clung to past traditions longer than did those for men. In spite of this the nunneries did become great centres of culture and several of the nuns gained excellent proficiency in letters; quite a number became known for their poetry; Wilton, Shaftesbury, Romney and Winchester all produced talented women.

St. Anselm, who before he became Archbishop of Canterbury, was at the great Benedictine monastery of Bec in Normandy, wrote a considerable number of letters to the English abbesses and nuns. He called them his spiritual daughters. Knowles mentions that the "most beautiful of all his letters, perhaps, is that in which he recalls a fallen nun to her better self".

When Henry I came to the throne in 1100 the number of nunneries started to increase. But in the north there was a complete absence of even one foundation; all the old houses were lying in ruins. It was not until that venerable saint, Gilbert of Sempringham drew up his Rule for seven holy women that the northern part of the land started to recover.

The houses in the south during the first few years of Henry's reign followed the Rule of St. Benedict. This Rule was designed to show the duties of the religious to be performed at every moment of the twenty four hours of the day: six hours for sleep, the nocturnal service to be chanted soon after midnight; to be summoned to the Church seven times for the day Offices; seven hours in manual labour; two in study, and the rest of the twenty four hours in refreshment. All the Orders bound themselves to observe the same threefold vow; that of Obedience, Chastity and Poverty.

The Benedictines were known as the black monks and nuns, because of their black habits. They and the Cluniacs came into England some time before the Norman Conquest. Other Orders were founded abroad during the late eleventh and twelfth centuries. In 1098, Robert of Molesmes and Stephen Harding, an Englishman, founded at Citeaux a monastery in which they wished to restore the simple life that the early communities had practised, and unlike the Cluniacs, who concentrated on their choral services to the detriment of manual labour, they wished to bring back manual work to its original position in monastic life; this manual work included all the arts and crafts as well as working in the fields.

In 1112 St. Bernard joined the two founders of Citeaux. He left them in 1115 and became the founder Abbot of Clairvaux, where he carried out their ideas. From that centre he established sixty eight houses of Cistercians, and so became the real founder of that Order. Those who joined these houses became known as the white monks and nuns. The Cistercians first came to England under Henry I, and two of the first houses were Waverley in 1128 and Rievaulx in 1131.

Another Order whose members lived a regular life was that of St. Augustine. Strictly speaking they were not monks but clerics — ordained priests. At the Council of Rome in 1059, the fourth canon recommended that the clergy should adopt a regular life. Communities of clergy in Italy started to live by the so called Rule of St. Augustine. A few monasteries of these regular canons, known as the black canons, were in England before 1100. Many were attached to nunneries to assist in the church services and to minister to the nuns.

In 1120 St. Norbert founded the Premonstratensian Order of White Canons. These canons resembled the Cistercian monks in the simplicity of their way of living and their ideals. In England there were very few before 1170.

An Order founded mainly for women by St. Bridget of Sweden, also known as the Order of Our Saviour, because Our Lord is supposed to have dictated its Rule to St. Bridget, came to England in 1415 under the patronage of Henry V. St. Bridget was of Royal blood and was born in 1302. Her mother was saved from shipwreck while she was pregnant, and the child was dumb until she was three years of age, and then began to talk with great wisdom and clarity. At thirteen she was married to Alpho, Prince of Nericia in Sweden. For the first year they both lived in continence and took the habit of the Order of St. Francis. Afterwards they had eight children. They took many pilgrimages, and on returning he entered the Order of the Cistercians, but soon after died. She is known for her mystical writings: her "Revelations". In 1344 she built the monastery of Vadstena in Sweden and there founded the Order of Brigittines, principally for women. Each house of the Order was to be composed of 60 nuns, 13 priests representing the Thirteen Apostles (including St. Paul), 4 deacons — the four Doctors of the primitive Church, and 8 lay brothers; the total depicting the Thirteen Apostles and Seventy two Disciples of Christ.

All these Orders of monks and nuns in England after the Norman Conquest, had their origins abroad. There was only one which had its birth and growth on English soil, and that was the Order of St. Gilbert of Sempringham in Lincolnshire. I am giving a fuller account of the Gilbertines than of the other Orders because it was especially of a national character, and demonstrates the way in which a monastery for women was organised in medieval times.

It was founded by a remarkable man who had a great concern for women, and for those who came under his care.

Gilbert was born in 1083.[7] His father was a Norman with estates in Lincolnshire. His mother was English. She dreamt she saw the moon descend into her lap, a presage of the light her son was to spread

[7]Much of this information is from the English Abridged edition of Dugdale's *Monasticon*.

abroad. During his first years he was misshapen in body and so uncouth that he became contemptible, so that even the servants would not eat with him. He improved on going to school, till being severely corrected, he ran away to France.

A change came over him and he seriously applied himself to learning and spiritual exercises, and after obtaining the title of Master, he returned home and taught literature and how to live a regular life. His father gave him the livings of Sempringham and Tirington, where he lived in company with a virtuous priest named Geoffry, but both finding the beauty of the daughter of the master of the house where they lodged too great a temptation, they built themselves a dwelling in the churchyard. Gilbert gave much away to the poor. His sanctity was conspicuous and he refused all honours. He was made priest by Alexander, Bishop of Lincoln.

Seven virgins came to him to seek his advice about how they could live a more sublime kind of life. He shut them up from all worldly contact and conversation so that they might devote themselves entirely to the Service of God. This was the beginning of his Order.

With the advice and assistance of the Bishop of Lincoln, he built the women a habitation and cloister adjoining to the north side of the Church of St. Andrew at Sempringham, with only one door to it, the key to which he kept himself. A window gave access to other young maids from without so that they could provide the nuns with the necessities of life. Those young maids who desired to serve in the religious habit as lay sisters, he made undergo a year of trial, or novitiate, and then they also were shut up. St. Gilbert found it necessary to appoint lay brothers to supply all the provisions from outside, and to do the rough labour.

When the Order was constituted in its final stage about the year 1139, it consisted of canons, nuns, lay brothers and lay sisters. In each house the nuns were in the majority. The larger houses had a minimum of thirteen canons, and the smaller at least seven. The canons were chosen for their learning and piety, but to avoid any fear of scandal, their habitation was placed some distance from the nuns', and the priests only entered the nuns' dwelling to administer the Sacraments and in the presence of many witnesses. The nuns were always veiled in the presence of the priests. In view of the growing reputation for piety of this Order, great landowners were so impressed that they gave land to the founder, and many monasteries were erected in Lincolnshire and other counties. The number increased so rapidly that St. Gilbert felt he was unable to keep them all under his control, and he requested the Cistercians to take the Order under their authority; but they refused. Pope Eugenius decided that Gilbert himself should become sole director, and eventually confirmed him in the office and title of Master.

At St. Gilbert's death these houses had pride of place among all the houses for women in England. He died in 1189 at the great age of one hundred and six, "Perfect in all respects except his eyes." In 1202 he was canonised by Pope Innocent III. He left behind a great Order of about two thousand and two hundred women, living dedicated holy lives. The Rule they followed was that of St. Benedict, which St. Gilbert wrote out for them himself, adding something of his own. The men followed that of St. Augustine.

Such was the foundation of the Order of St. Gilbert, and it all started because he took under his care seven holy women, whose names have not even come down to us.

When I write about the Priory of Sempringham I will mention some of the Rules of the Order. Sempringham became its Mother Church.

Apart from the Order of St. Bridget, which I have mentioned, no more Orders for women came to England between the twelfth and sixteenth centuries, except the Preaching Order of St. Dominic, of which there seems to have been only two houses for women, and the Minoresses, founded by St. Clare with the help of St. Francis.

St. Dominic was born about the year 1170. His followers were known as the Preaching Friars. His object in founding the Order was to fight against the heresy of his time. He is said to have taught the use of the Holy Rosary as a special defence against heresy and vice.

St. Francis was born in Italy in 1182. He founded the Order of Friars Minor; its members all vowed to live in poverty and to give away all that they possessed. His Rule was approved by Pope Innocent III in 1210. He founded a second Order for women, who became known as the Minoresses or Poor Clares. St. Clare was born in 1194. She came of a noble family, and when she was sixteen she first heard St. Francis preach. She was determined to follow his example. Much against her family's will, she left her home and joined him. There was no physical love between them but a union of souls. St. Francis found a retreat for her at a hermitage called after St. Damien, where a number of other women joined her. Within seventy or eighty years, houses of Minoresses were being founded in other countries, and there were four in England.

Besides those who formed communities, there was another group of women who dedicated their lives to serve God, living as hermits. They were known as Solitaires or Ancresses. Such was Juliana of Norwich, who died in 1423. Some of these women had formerly been in a nunnery, but wishing to live a more contemplative life of prayer and meditation, chose some isolated retreat.

As the Middle Ages drew to a close, life in these nunneries of holy women began to deteriorate, and there were many abuses. Some kept up their high standard of living and went on their tranquil ways unaware of the arguments and upheavals among churchmen outside their cloistered walls.

These monastic houses, many with great treasures of art, and some with fine libraries of books, which were irreplaceable; some of outstanding architecture; serving the nation with their hospitality; looking after the poor, were, under Henry VIII, to be all swept away, or taken over for profane purposes.

Psalm 74: — They have set fire upon thy holy places: and have defiled the dwelling-place of thy Name, even unto the ground.

Yea, they said in their hearts, Let us make havoc of them altogether: thus have they burnt up all the houses of God in the land.

The Cathedrals and parish churches were spared, but in place of monks, secular clergy took the services. The rest of the houses being evacuated, those dedicated men and women, belonging to any sort of regular religious Order, were cast out into the world to fend for themselves. They must have been bewildered, and found life very strange. Some, if they would acknowledge Henry as the supreme head of the Church, were given pensions; a mere pittance. Those who refused to give up their vows were given nothing, and some were put to death.

There was only one exception to this wholesale destruction and that was the Royal Foundation of St. Katherine in the east end of London, which had been founded by Queen Matilda in 1148. The Offices that had been recited formerly were replaced by reading from the Book of Common Prayer, but the works of charity and mercy were still carried on, as they are to this present day.

The nation suffered a great loss in the dissolution of these houses as it did away with satisfying an innate need in mankind to worship God, and did not replace enough in the form of worship for those who wished to devote the whole of their lives to prayer.

What of the women themselves? Many went abroad; some lived their lives hidden away in secret places, in great fear that they should be found out, and get into trouble any friend who had assisted them. Some women were martyrs for their faith; such were Margaret, Countess of Salisbury in 1541, Margaret Clitherow in 1586, and Margaret Ward, hanged at Tyburn for rescuing a priest in 1588. No doubt there were a great many other women who suffered for their religion, some belonging to the Reformed Church and some belonging to the Old Faith, and both accused the other of atrocities.

Did no one raise any objection? Yes; the North rose up in arms in 1536 against the suppression of the monasteries. This revolt was known as the Pilgrimage of Grace. It was ruthlessly put down with hangings, heads falling and burnings of abbots, lay lords, their ladies, and others who had been concerned.

When Mary came to the throne in 1553 there was a slight revival of monastic life, but with the succession of Elizabeth I, there was no further trace of communal life until we hear of a remarkable family, who in the first half of the seventeenth century lived a regular religious life according to the canons of the Church of England. Nicholas Ferrar and his mother bought a manor house at Little Gidding in Huntingdonshire. Here a number of the rest of the family joined them, and the whole house contained about thirty persons. They made no rule but kept up a continuous round of praise and worship for twenty four hours of the day. They lived very simply but were hospitable to the poor and rich alike. Many influential people, including King Charles I visited them. But among a lot of people there was a good deal of prejudice, they feared that this family was bringing back papal ritual.

Nicholas died in 1637, and his brother John took over the running of Little Gidding. One night in the year 1646, Charles I fleeing from his enemies, sought shelter at Little Gidding. The Puritans in revenge came and destroyed everything in the community, and so ended a very wonderful venture. I will write more about this place when I am giving an account of the separate houses and their inmates.

After this unique family had been dispersed there were no real imitators of such a household for about two hundred years. Those who controlled the nation under Cromwell saw that the Church was stripped of all its trappings and all ritual that had any resemblance to the Roman Church. They suppressed all who had any leanings towards life lived under a Rule.

At the restoration of the monarchy in 1660, there was a change in the manner in which the Church was run; those who favoured more ritual came back into power. Quite a number of Churchmen had ideas about reviving some kind of religious houses. Some women drew up schemes on paper about how such houses should be run, but they never materialised; there was still a great deal of prejudice. One or two women lived a life of devotion and prayer in secret. A number, who really wished to follow a Rule and take vows, went abroad.

A feeling for worship that goes deep down into the roots of human nature was not being given any encouragement, except among a few; the past still haunted them; memories of ancient shrines still lingered on. They lingered for the next hundred years and that was probably the reason that when the French Revolution started and monks and nuns came as exiles into England about the year1793, that the English opened their gates and welcomed them with open arms.

Because of the persecution by the French government, those English women, who had formerly fled abroad from antipapal feeling in their own land, now fled back again. No feeling of intolerance was raised against them, and no cry of — "No Popery!" — and by 1794 several houses of Benedictine nuns and of other Orders were being established.

The example of these nuns inspired some members of the Church of England to agitate for houses of Anglican Sisters of Mercy. One of the most influential people to encourage this idea was the Poet Laureate, Robert Southey in 1829, the year of Catholic Emancipation. He advocated an urgent need for Protestant Sisters of Mercy.

' "Why then have you no Beguines, no Sisters of Charity? Why in the most needful, the most merciful form that charity can take, have you not followed the example of the French and the Netherlands? No Vincent de Paul has been heard in your pulpits; no Louis Le Gras has appeared among the daughters of Great Britain. Piety has not found its way into your prisons; your hospitals are imploring it in vain; nothing is wanted in them but religious charity, and what a want is that.' "[8] Southey continues for several pages in the same strain — a
Peter F. Anson; *The Call of the Cloister.*

13

veritable call to the Cloister.'

In the year 1833 the Oxford Movement started, and the first of the "Tracts for the Times" was published. The movement was formed by a group of high churchmen in the Anglican Communion including Newman and John Keble. One of the Tracts they published dealt with Canonical Worship and the reciting of the Offices. They were not all well received by the authorities. Many of the members of this movement had great sympathy with Southey's idea of having Sisters of Mercy to visit the poor, and to do general work of charity, and it was their wish to found a community of such women.

Dr. Pusey, a great controversial figure in the church at the time, also had the same desire and he wrote to Newman about it. He had made a great study of Church history, and he became obsessed with medieval traditions, but he was a man of determination and capable of putting ideas into practice.

Many of those who would have been willing to give their support to founding some sort of sisterhood within the Church of England were frightened of offending the majority of Protestants.

In 1844, a few courageous clergy and laymen held a meeting in the rooms of Lord John Manners at the Albany, where they discussed the introduction of the first Sisters of Mercy into the Church of England. They wanted to find a house in a parish where the incumbent would give his support. They found one in the parish of Christ Church, St. Pancras, where Mr. Dodsworth was the vicar.

On the 26th of March 1845, the Sisterhood of the Holy Cross was opened at 17 Park Village West; the first Sisterhood the Church of England had since the Reformation. It was started as a memorial to the Poet Laureate, Robert Southey.

There were two houses of Sisters of Mercy belonging to the Roman Catholic Church at this time, besides several enclosed nuns. When the Crimean war was started in 1854, and Florence Nightingale called for volunteers to nurse the wounded soldiers, Anglican Sisters from Park Village and Devonport and Plymouth joined with the Catholic Sisters from Bermondsey, and together they did splendid work. Surely one of the first Ecumenical Movements?

It is not the purpose of this book to write about the Holy Women who were active in the service of God from 1845 onwards, as a number of authorities have written excellent accounts of them. This book is divided into two sections; the first is a list in alphabetical order of the women of the Celtic and Anglo-Saxon races, who led saintly lives since the coming of Christianity to Britain down to the year 1845; the second part gives an account of all those monasteries and nunneries which were founded for their habitation. It may not be a complete list as there were probably many unknown foundations which have disappeared leaving no trace, and many women whose names and lives are known only to God.

There are great variations in the spelling of the names of the women; I have used that which is most commonly adopted nowadays; in some cases I have showed the different variations in brackets. I have given the feast days when they are known, and if any of the women have been found in any Calendar of Martyrology, I have used the following abbrevations:

R.M. — Roman Martyrology
A.C. — Approved Cult
P.C. — Popular Cult (unofficial).

PART ONE

A BIOGRAPHICAL DICTIONARY
FROM EARLY TIMES
TO 1845

St. Aelfflaed (Elfleda). Died c.714, February 8th. A.C.

Her life reveals the influence that women had in the affairs of the country in her time. She was the daughter of King Oswy and Queen Eanflaed of Northumbria.

Just before the battle of Winwaed, which took place in 665, Oswy tried to pacify the old savage King Penda of Mercia with gifts, but Penda would not accept them. Then Oswy realised that he would have to go to war with him. He made a vow that if he gained the victory against Penda, he would dedicate his daughter to the Lord as a holy virgin. Oswy won the battle, and his daughter, Aelfflaed, who was hardly a year old, was sent to the monastery of Hartlepool and placed in the care of the Abbess Hilda.

Two years later, when St. Hilda built the Monastery of Whitby, Aelfflaed went there with her, as a pupil. She received a very high education for that time, and when she was older she undertook the teaching of the students herself.

Her father died in 670, and her mother then joined her at Whitby. On the death of St. Hilda in 680, Aelfflaed became the Abbess with the help of her mother. Bede says she had very great assistance in the government of the monastery from Trumwine, who had been the bishop of the Picts, but because of trouble in the north, had to leave Abercorn, and came to retire in the monastery of Whitby.

Aelfflaed seems to have risen to moral greatness among her fellow-men; she had many friends among the bishops, and joined them in their conferences. Archbishop Theodore of Canterbury once wrote to her asking her to help to make friends with St. Wilfred. She is said to have been "one of the most influential personages of her time".

One of her great friends was St. Cuthbert, and she often called on him for advice, which he never failed to give her. At one time she was seriously ill and the doctors did not seem able to cure her. At last she made a turn for the better, but found she was unable to stand because of the great pain in her legs. She began to think "How I wish I had something belonging to my dear Cuthbert". Her thoughts must have been transmitted to him, as Bede says, by heavenly means, because soon afterwards a linen girdle arrived from him. She wrapped it round herself and the next morning could stand upright, and within a few days was completely cured.

On another occasion, during the time that St. Cuthbert was living as a hermit on the Farne islands, she sent for him to discuss some matter which deeply affected her. He took a boat and sailed south, and she sailed north, and they met on Coquet Island. After telling him a few things about which she was worried, she came to the subject which was really on her mind: her brothers, and especially King Ecgfrith, and who would succeed him if he were killed. Bede gives a very clear and vivid account of this meeting in his prose Life of St. Cuthbert, and of how the saint prophesied that some brother would come from overseas to ascend the throne, and he describes how Aelfflaed's emotions were affected by her thoughts of what would happen to her brothers, of whom she appears to have been very fond.

At the same meeting Aelfflaed told Cuthbert that in her opinion he was the right and most worthy person to become the Bishop of Lindisfarne.

One day the Abbess Aelfflaed entertained St. Cuthbert at dinner when he came to consecrate a church on one of her estates, and while they sat at table, the bishop suddenly had a vision; he saw some holy man being borne to heaven. He told the Abbess that it was someone from her monastery. She afterwards found that one of her shepherds had fallen from a tree at the exact moment that St. Cuthbert had his vision.

To show the regard for the wisdom of Abbess Aelfflaed held by the bishops of the land, they invited her to join a full gathering of bishops, abbots and men of importance and rank in the kingdom, to a Synod held in the north near the river Nidd, to discuss the problem of St. Wilfrid's claims. She rose and spoke to them all and told them of her brother, King Aldfrith's last Will and Testament, and that he wished the judgements of the Holy See to be carried out. At the end of the Synod on her advice they all made their peace with St. Wilfrid. She must have been a remarkable woman to have been able to sway with her words a whole company of men.

She died about the year 714.

Alice Rich. Died 1270, August 24th. P.C.
She was the sister of St. Edmund, Archbishop of Canterbury. Alice and her sisters were brought up by her mother, her father having left them all penniless. Her mother died while Edmund was away in Paris. His sisters being then left in his charge he returned to England, hoping to find some convent to take over the responsibility of looking after them. But because of the sisters having no dowry, he had

19

difficulty in persuading any convent to take them. Eventually the Priory of Catesby consented to have them without payment. It appears he did not wish to spend money on them, but kept plenty for his own needs.

Alice later became Prioress of Catesby Priory. Her name does not appear in any Calendar, and she was never called a saint, but was given the title of Blessed.

St. Alkelda. Late 8th or early 9th century. P.C.
She was said to have been an Anglo-Saxon princess. Very little is known about her, but tradition says she was strangled by two Danish women about the year 800 A.D.

There are two churches in Yorkshire dedicated to her, one at Middleham and the other at Giggleswick. The church at Middleham, part of which was built in 1280, contains a window at the west end of the north aisle depicting St. Alkelda's martyrdom, and in it there are fragments of medieval glass. She is said to have been buried on the site of this church, and in 1878, in the presence of the vicar and two church wardens, a female body was discovered near a pillar at the south east corner of the nave. A brass plaque has been placed above the spot under which these remains were found. A stone, which can be seen near the font may be part of her tombstone.

The church at Giggleswick shows signs of Saxon stones in its fabric. Major restorations were carried out between 1890-1892, and underneath the present building there was evidently a very ancient church.

Near each of these churches there is a holy well, and legend says St. Alkelda baptised her converts in their flowing waters. Even in these days people come to bathe their eyes, hoping to cure them from any trouble.

The name Alkelda may have been derived from the old English word Haeligkeld, which means a holy spring or well.

St. Alkelda's feast day is March 27th.

St. Almedha (Elyned, Tayned). 6th century. A.C.
She was the grandaughter of King Brychan of Brecknock, whose numerous sons, daughters and grandchildren came to be known as one of the Three Holy Families of Britain, as they nearly all became Christians and founded many churches.

St. Almedha was martyred by heathen Saxons on a hill near Brechnock. A chapel was erected on the site and dedicated to her. It was still standing in 1698, but only a few ruins can now be seen, and in the last century an ancient yew tree was seen growing out of the ruins, with a well near by.

A feast in her honour was held on August 1st, and Giraldus Cambrensis in the twelfth century, gives a description of this feast, and of how a great number of people gathered on the site of her martyrdom and danced around, nearly all in a great frenzy, some falling down in a trance, and only when being brought into the church did they come to themselves.

There are several churches in Wales with a corruption of her name, which may originally have been dedicated to her.

St. Amabilis. Died c.634, July 11th. P.C.
Tradition says this saint was the daughter of an Anglo-Saxon king, whose name is not given. All we know about her is that she went abroad and became a nun at a convent in Rouen.

St. Anne Line. Died, February 27th.
She was born in Essex, and with her husband became a convert to the old faith. In 1586 a priest was discovered celebrating Mass in their house, and Anne's husband was imprisoned and then banished and died abroad soon afterwards, leaving Anne to fight for herself alone. Father Gerard, a priest in London helped her; he put her in charge of a house for priests which had been started in London, and she spent her time looking after children and doing needlework, and she was known there as Mrs Martha.

Despite what appeared to be her innocent occupation, the authorities were suspicious, and on February 2nd, Candlemas Day in 1601, they raided the house and found the inhabitants at Mass. The priest managed to escape, but Anne was arrested, and at her trial she was condemned to death for harbouring priests. She was hanged at Tyburn on February 27th.

Anne was one of the Forty Martyrs who were canonised on October 25th 1970. Her feast day, with the other martyrs is held annually on October 25th.

St. Arilda A.C.

Her date is unknown, and all that is known about her is that she met her death defending her chastity. Baring-Gould says she was a maiden of Kingston near Thornbury in Gloucestershire, and that a man named Muncius murdered her. Her body was buried in the Abbey at Gloucester, and a church at Oldbury-on-the-Hill is dedicated to her. Her name is a Saxon name, not British. Her feast day is given as October 30th.

Mary Astell 1668-1731.

She was one of the first women of the Protestant faith to suggest that there should be a house for women to live in retreat and under discipline, since the dissolution of the monasteries in the sixteenth century. She wrote a book in 1696 entitled "A Serious Proposal to the Ladies for the Advancement of their True and Greatest Interest". She was supported by Queen Anne, but the bishops were not in favour, and were prejudiced against such a proposal, and so nothing came of her idea.

St. Bathildis. Died 680, January 30th. R.M.

Although this saint lived most of her life abroad, she was of the Anglo-Saxon race and lived her early girlhood in England. Her story reads as a Cinderella romance. She was sold as a slave to the Mayor of the palace of Neustria. Because of her beauty she attracted the attention of the Mayor himself, and he decided to take her out of the kitchen and make her his wife. But she, being most alarmed at the prospect, clothed herself in rags, disguised her beauty and hid herself from his view, so that eventually he forgot her.

Bathildis had a very humble but pleasing disposition, and willingly waited on her fellow servants, "cheerfully obeying them, ministering reverently to her elders, often taking off their shoes for them, scraping and cleaning them, and bringing them their washing water, and mending their clothes also".

As a servant, Bathildis would wait on her master at table, and it must have been on one such occasion that the King, Clovis II, noticed her. He fell passionately in love with her and married her; so it came about that Bathildis, the little servant girl, at the age of nineteen, in 649, became the Queen of France.

She had a great influence for good over her husband, and persuaded him to do away with all harsh laws, and also, remembering that she herself had been a slave, she became the benefactress of slaves and tried to abolish slavery.

Bathildis bore the king three sons, and after they had been married six years, the king died, and the eldest son being under age, Bathildis became Regent of France. She founded the Abbeys of Chelles, Corbie and Jumieges. When her son came of age, she retired to Chelles and lived as a simple nun.

Chelles, founded by one, who, from being a humble English maid, rose to the highest position in the land of France, became the Abbey to which a great number of English women resorted before there were houses of religion provided for them in England.

St. Baya. 9th or 10th century. November 2nd. A.C.
She was a recluse who lived on the Island of Cumbrae, off the coast of Ayrshire in Scotland, where her pupil, St. Maura, visited her. She was a friend of Donald, King of Scotland, who reigned from 893 to 904. There has been some confusion between this saint and St. Bees of Cumberland. St. Baya died on her lonely island, where the ruins of a chapel can be seen, which was built over her remains.

St. Bees (Bega). 7th Century, September 6th or October 31st. A.C.
This saint, although Irish, lived most of her life in England. She was the daughter of an Irish king, and she wished to become a Bride of Christ, and she is said to have received from an angel a bracelet as a sign of her betrothal. Her father wished her to marry a King of Norway, and on the night before the proposed wedding she escaped while the whole household was feasting and holding revels. She was miraculously taken across the sea to a promontory on the Cumberland coast, where she built a monastery. She became greatly venerated in the north west of England, and was known as the Patroness of those who laboured.

There has been a dispute, which both Butler and Baring-Gould mention, as to whether she was the nun whom Bede calls Hieu, to whom St. Aidan gave the first monastery for women in the north of England, and the question has never been settled.

There are two churches in the Diocese of Carlisle dedicated to St. Bees.

Dame Julian Berners (Barnes). 15th century.
Dame Julian in her work, illustrates the high education which some of the nuns received in the Middle Ages. She was a prioress of Sopwell, which nunnery was under the rule of the Abbot of St. Albans. She was the authoress of a book on hunting called "The Boke of St. Albans", and one on fishing called "Treatyse of Fysshynge with an Angle". These were both printed in the Abbey of St. Albans about 1484, and the printing press there, was the third to be set up in England.

St. Breaca. 5th century, June 4th. A.C.
She is supposed to have been the disciple of St. Bridget or St. Patrick. She came to Cornwall about 460, and there she lived a solitary holy life. There is a church dedicated to her at Breage in Cornwall.

St. Bridget (Bride). 450-525 February 1st. R.M.
She was an Irish saint, and is mentioned here as there are a number of churches dedicated to her in Britain; six in the northern Province of York, and six in the Province of Canterbury, which includes St. Bride's in London, and also a number in Wales.

She was the first woman to build a nunnery for the women in Ireland, and next to St. Patrick, is the patron saint of Ireland.

Bugga. 7th century.
She was the daughter of King Centwine of Wessex, who reigned from 676-685.

Aldhelm, who was Abbot of Malmesbury, wrote a poem about the church at Withington at which Bugga was Abbess, and which she is said to have built. The poem describes the beautiful coloured glass, most rare in these days, the gold cross and chalice studded with jewels. Nothing else is known about her. E.S. Duckett says she must not be confused with the Bugga who was the friend of St. Boniface, or with the Bugga who was daughter of Abbess Dunne of Withington.

Bugga 8th century December 27th.
An abbess of a monastery in Kent, known through her correspondence with St. Boniface. She asked for his advice in her troubles, and she would try to supply him with the books which he requested her to send him. Quite a number of letters passed between

Bugga in Kent and Boniface in Germany, and in one letter she told him of her desire to make a pilgrimage to Rome, which she did undertake about the year 738, and St. Boniface met her there.

There is a letter from Bregwin, Archbishop of Canterbury to Bishop Lul in Germany, written between the years 759-765, announcing Bugga's death, in which he says they were keeping the day, December 27th in memory of her.

St. Burian. 6th century, May 29th. A.C.

She is known as a Cornish saint, but she was evidently Irish in origin, as she was foster sister to St. Kieran. King Athelstan built a church in her honour on the spot where she is said to have lived as a recluse — four miles from Lands End.

St. Buryan in Cornwall is named after her.

Ceolburga. Died 805 or 807.

According to a document, which still survives, she was the mother of Ealderman Aethelric, son of Aethelmund, a thegn of King Offa of Mercia. Aethelric granted to his mother on his death land at Westbury and Stoke. This he did so that she should be protected from the people at Berkeley, as evidently she had been having trouble with them, and he wished her to be provided for, in case she was turned out of Berkeley after he was no longer there to help her.

Coelburga must have been an important person as two of the old chronicles mention her death; the chronicle of Florence of Worcester calls her the Abbess of Berkeley, and records her death under the year 805, but the Anglo-Saxon Chronicle gives the year 807.

Christina. 11th century.

She was the granddaughter of Edmund Ironside, King of England in 1016. She was born in Hungary, where her father had gone to seek shelter when Cnut, the Dane, came to the throne of England. After the battle of Hastings, she and her brother and sister, Edgar the Atheling and Margaret of Scotland, came to Britain, and Malcolm the King of Scotland gave them shelter.

Christina later retired as a nun at the Abbey of Romsey, where she took charge of Queen Margaret's two daughters, Edith (Matilda) and Mary.

St. Christina of Huntingdon. Died 1160, December 26th. A.C.
Her parents were of a family in a good position, and she could have enjoyed many of the luxuries which they could have provided for her, but she decided to give up all the riches of this world, and devote her life in solitude in the service of God. She became a recluse at Markyate near the Dunstable road.

Roger the Hermit was her spiritual adviser, and she was enclosed in a cell adjacent to his cell. Roger, at one time, had been a monk at the Abbey of St. Albans.

Both Thurstan, Archbishop of York and Geoffry, Abbot of St. Albans, were immensely impressed with Christina's wisdom and sanctity; she was a woman of great talent and highly educated.

After Roger the Hermit's death, she took over his cell and was joined by several companions. Abbot Geoffry then founded a nunnery at Markyate, and placed her in charge under his direction. There is evidence that the nuns wrote poetry and were very skilled in doing embroidery; in both these, Christina's work was always beautifully executed. In 1155, Abbot Robert, who succeeded Abbot Geoffrey, went to Rome and took with him many presents for the Pope, but the Pope refused all the gifts except "three meters and some sandals of exquisite workmanship, which had been most carefully prepared"; these were the work of Christina.

St. Claudia. 1st century. August 7th. A.C.
She is mentioned by St. Paul in his second letter to Timothy, chap VI, verse 21. There is a legend that she was the daughter of Caractacus, a British king, who opposed the invading army of the Roman Emperor Claudius, when he tried to conquer Britain. Caractacus was captured and taken to Rome with his wife and daughter in A.D. 51. After he was set free, he became a Christian, and returned to his own country in A.D. 58. Tradition says that he was the first to bring Christianity to Britain. His daughter Claudia also became a Christian, and is supposed to have married Senator Aulus Pudens, and both St. Peter and St. Paul visited her house in Rome. There is no positive proof whether there is any truth in these legends.

Susanna Collet . . . . . . See under Mary Ferrar.

St. Columba. November 13th. Year unknown.

She was a Christian maiden murdered by a Cornish king. Nothing else is known about her, but the two parishes of St. Columb Major and St. Columb Minor in the diocese of Truro are dedicated to her.

Dame Alice Croft.

A nun in the monastery of Wrexhall, which was founded in the 12th century by Hugh, Lord of Hatton and Wrexhall.

Dugdale in the Monasticon mentions this nun and describes how she built a chapel. He must have copied this account from some old manuscript as it is in very archaic language. I quote in the following what he has written:—

"Sometime nun and Lady of this place, poore of worldly goods, but rich of vertues, desired heartily of God and Our Lady, that she in her dayes might see here a Chappell of Our Lady. To that intent she prayed oft time and on a night there came a voice to her, and bad her in the name of God and Our Lady, beginn and performe a Chappell of our Lady. She remembred her thereof, and thought it but a dreme, and toke noe heed thereof. But not long to, another night following, came the same voice to her againe, and gave her the same charge more sharplye. Then she wakened and bethought her, and fell in a grete weping, for she had not wherewith to make it, and as soone as she might she came to her prioress dame — and informed her of all the processe, but she set little by it, and said it was but a fantasye, and she dryve it off as for tyme. But at last Our Lady appered to the same dame Alice Croft, blaming her why she was negligent in fulfilling her commandement, and so vanished away from her. Then she in grete fears came and told the prioresse. Then askyd she what she had towards it. And she seyd XV.d. Then said the prioresse, though it be little Our Lady may encrease it full well: and then she gave her leave to set upon it.

Then this Dame Alice Croft gave herself to prayers, and besought Our Lady to give her knowledge where she should build it, and how much one should make it. Then she had by revelation to make it on the north side her church, and there she should find markyd the quantity. This was in harvest and between the two feasts of Our Lady; and on the morrow earlye she went into the place assigned her, and there she found a certeyne ground covered with snow, and all the churchyard else bare without snow; and there the snow abidde from foure of the clocke in the morning until noone. She glad of this, had masons ready and marked out the ground, and built the chappell and performed it up. And every saturday whilst it was building she would say her prayers in the allyes of the church-yard, and in the playne pathe she should and did finde weekely, sylver sufficient to pay her workmen, and all that was behooful to her worke, and no more.

This good Lady, Dame Alice Croft, dyed the VII calends of Feverel, on the morrow after the conversion of St. Paul, and she is buryed under a stone in the same chappell afore the dore, entring into the quire. She, as beseming of her bones was a woman of greate stature. There was a young Lady bury'd in the same grave, and there we see her bones."

St. Cunera. June 12th. Date uncertain. A.C.
The legends about this saint are impossible. She is venerated in Rhenen in Germany, but her father is supposed to have been the King of Orkney and she is said to have been born in York. She went over to Germany where she attracted the attention of King Radbod, who took her into his household in Rhenen, and she is said to have been strangled by his wife out of jealousy. She is also said to be connected with St. Ursula, which is unlikely because their dates do not coincide, as Radbod lived nearly three hundred years later than St. Ursula.

St. Cuthburga. Died 725, August 31st. A.C.
Sister of Ine, King of Wessex. She is said to have been very beautiful and attracted the attention of King Aldfrith of Northumbria, who asked her brother Ine for her hand in marriage. She became Queen of Northumbria, but begged King Aldfrith to annul the marriage, as she wished to dedicate her life to the service of God. When he consented, she entered the Abbey of Barking under the Abbess Hildilid, who was the second to take command of this double abbey of men and women, and who was very conscientious in instructing her charges in the way of a religious life.

It was while St. Cuthburga was at Barking that her famous kinsman, Aldhelm of Malmesbury wrote his letter to the nuns on the virtues of the virgin life. He addressed several of the nuns by name, including Cuthburga; the letter was written about the year 686.

After Cuthburga had been at Barking for only a year or two, her brother Ine, gave her land at Wimborne in Dorset to found a double monastery. Her sister Cuenburga assisted her. This monastery later became famous for sending nuns as missionaries to help St. Boniface in converting the pagans in Germany.

St. Cuthburga is commemorated in the Sarum Breviary.

Cuenburga (Queenburga). Late 7th and early 8th century.
All we know of her is that she was the sister of St. Cuthburga and King Ine of Wessex, and assisted her sister to found the monastery of Wimborne, and that she became a nun there. It has been suggested that she was St. Cuneburga, an abbess to whom Bishop Lull wrote from the continent.

Cuthswith. Late 7th century.
I can find very little about Cuthswith except that she was an abbess, and had been given a grant by Oshere, King of the Hwiece in 693 to build a monastery, the site of which is unknown. But the very interesting thing is that her name is on the flyleaf of a manuscript recording that it belonged to her. It is a 5th century copy of Jerome's "Commentary on Ecclesiastes", and is at present in Wurzburg. It may have been Jerome's own copy and is one of the earliest books to have found its way into England, and it is surprising that it should have been owned by an English Abbess.

Cwenburgh. 7th century.
A nun at Watton and daughter of the Abbess Hereburh . . . See under Hereburh.

Margaret Clitherow . . . See under St. Margaret.

Devorguilla (Derveguld). 13th century.
She was the daughter of Alan, last king of Galloway, who married Margaret daughter of David, Earl of Huntingdon, who was the grandson of David I, King of Scotland.

Devorguilla married Sir John de Baliol, son of Hugh Baliol of Bernard's Castle in County Durham. Sir John became in 1251 the guardian of the royal couple, Margaret, daughter of Henry III, and her young husband Alexander III, King of Scotland. Sir John endowed in 1263, Scholarships in Oxford, and after his death in 1269, his wife founded the college which bears his name.

Devorguilla died in 1289, and yet six centuries afterwards she is still said to be "a lovely memory in Galloway" and "left the world a love story under the broken arches of an abbey". The abbey is Sweetheart Abbey, which she founded so that even in death she and her husband would not be parted and they could be buried together in the same tomb under the high altar. For years after his death she carried about his heart enclosed in an ivory casket; hence the name Dulce Cor, Sweetheart Abbey, which perpetuates by its name the great love she bore her husband.

She spent the last years of her life at her castle at Buittle near Dalbeattie, and during that time she founded the black friars monastery at Wigtown, and the grey friars monastery at Maxwelltown near the river Nith, and because she was distressed when she heard how the friars got soaked to the skin when they crossed the river, she had a bridge built over the Nith especially for them. In the name of the present bridge: the Devorguilla Bridge, her memory lingers on to the present day.

Her son, whose rival for the throne of Scotland was Robert the Bruce, reigned as king from 1292–1296.

St. Domneva (Ermenburga). Died November 19th 690. A.C.
She was also called Donna Ebba, the Lady Ebba, which was shortened into Domneva. Ebbsfleet in Kent perpetuates her name.

She was the daughter of Ermerid, Prince of Kent, and great granddaughter of Ethelbert, King of Kent. She married Merewald, son of Penda, King of Mercia. She and her husband were very active in spreading the Christian religion. She became the mother of three saintly daughters, Mildred, Milburga and Mildgytha.

Domneva had two brothers, Ethelbert and Ethelred, who while still youths aroused the jealousy of their cousin Egbert, King of Kent. In his court there was a man named Thunur, who whispered evil suggestions into the king's ear concerning these two young men. One day this sinful man murdered them, and the king was conscience stricken, as he felt partly responsible for their deaths. He sent for Domneva to come to Kent. Baring-Gould says that he offered to pay what is known as Blood-geld, a fine which a murderer had to pay to the next of kin of anyone who had been murdered.

Domneva arrived in Kent, and it was decided between her and

30

King Egbert that she should be given such land as her tame doe could run round in the course of a day. The whole court set off for the Isle of Thanet, where the doe started off to encompass the ground. Thunur tried to prevent the king from carrying out the deal, and then a thunderbolt struck him and he was buried in a crack which opened up in the ground. The king ordered the spot to be covered with a great heap of stones, and the place was henceforth called Thunerhleap.

The land which the doe surrounded was about ten thousand acres, and this Egbert willingly gave to Domneva. There she built a monastery in 669, and it became known as Minster in Thanet, and of which she eventually became abbess, and her daughter Mildred after her. The monastery was consecrated by Archbishop Theodore.

St. Dwynwen. Died c.460, January 25th. A.C.
She was the daughter of King Brychan of Brecknock, whose family was one of the Three Holy Families of Britain. After she had founded a church in Anglesey, she went to Cornwall, where she settled at Ludgvan. She is called by the Welsh bards, the patron saint of true lovers, and the saying "nothing wins hearts like cheerfulness" is credited to her.

The legend about her says that she and a young man, Maelon Mafodril, fell violently in love with one another. But she, in a facetious mood laughed at him, and he became deeply offended, and spread malicious tales about her. This greatly distressed her, as she still loved him. She sought help and prayed that she might be cured of her love for him. An angel came and gave her a heavenly draft, which should rid her of her lovesickness. The angel then turned Maelon into stone. Then again she was upset as she wished him no harm, and so she prayed to God, and He granted her three wishes:— one, that Maelon should be turned back into his natural state, two, that all maidens who invoked her should obtain their desired husbands or become indifferent to them, and three, that she, herself might be free of her own desire for marriage. She is said to have founded several churches in Cornwall.

St. Ebba. Died 683, August 25th A.C.
She was the sister of King Oswald and Oswy of Northumbria, and great-granddaughter of King Ida. When King Edwin won the throne from her father Ethelfrith, she and her brothers took refuge in

Scotland and received the Christian religion in the Island of Iona. Her brother Oswy wished her to marry a Scottish prince, but she rejected his suit. When the prince pursued her, she escaped to the rocky headland on the south east coast of Scotland, where later the monastery of Coldingham was built. She was miraculously defended from him for three days by the swelling of the stream in the valley between her and the mainland.

Wishing to devote her life to the service of God, she received the veil from Bishop Finan, who succeeded St. Aidan at Lindisfarne. King Oswy gave her land on which to build a monastery near the river Derwent at a place called Ebchester. Then she became the abbess of the double monastery of men and women at Coldingham. The remains of a small chapel are still seen on the promontory, which rises 500 feet out of the sea, and are all that is left of this great house. On a similar situation on the coast at Beadnell the ruins of a small chapel dedicated to St. Ebba can be seen.

Although St. Ebba ruled over both the men and women she did not seem to have any great control over them, and she often sought the advice of St. Cuthbert, who was a close friend of hers. He went and stayed at her monastery when she was in any trouble.

One of her monks, realising that she was ignorant of the worldly conduct of the monks and nuns taking place in the cells, warned her that the vengeance of Heaven would descend on the inmates unless they reformed their ways. She was very shocked and asked him why he had not reported the matter to her before. He calmed her by telling her that the punishment would not happen in her lifetime. It was after her death that the monastery was burnt to the ground.

St. Ebba was an admirer of St. Wilfrid. When King Ecgfrith, her nephew, imprisoned St. Wilfrid, he was released through her intercession. It happened at the time that the king and queen were staying at Coldingham that one night the abbess went to the queen's apartment and found her in great pain and obviously at the point of death. She rushed to the king and rebuked him, saying the queen's illness was as a punishment because of his hardness of heart over St. Wilfrid, and she made him make his peace with the bishop.* She said, "Do this and, as I see it, you will live and your queen will recover. Disobey and, as God is my witness, you shall not escape punishment." The king obeyed her and freed St. Wilfrid, and the queen recovered.

St. Ebba lived to a good old age and died in 683 A.D. There is an old poem about St. Ebba and two others, said to be her sisters, but I do not know who they were:—

St. Abb, St. Helen and St. Bey
They a' built Kirks, whilk to be nearest the sea;
St. Abb's upon the Nabs,
St. Helen's on the lea,
St. Bey's upon Dunbar's sands
Stands nearest to the sea,

There are four churches dedicated to St. Ebba in England, two in the diocese of Oxford, one in the diocese of Durham and one in the diocese of Newcastle.

*Eddius *Life of St. Wilfrid.*

St. Ebba. Martyred 870. April 2nd. A.C.

Abbess of Coldingham. She should not be confused with the former St. Ebba, Abbess of Coldingham, who lived two hundred years earlier.

Who the parents of the younger Ebba were, is not known. After the fire which burnt down the abbey in 685, it was rebuilt but without the house for men, and a more orderly community of nuns existed than in former times.

When the Danes came and ravaged the coast, Ebba mutilated her face and ordered her nuns to do the same, so that these maidens would be repulsive to behold and they could thus preserve their virginity. The Danes, when they entered the monastery and saw these nuns with lips and noses cut off, were so furious that they burnt down the place and the Abbess Ebba and the sisters all perished.

St. Eadburga. Died 751, December 12th. A.C.

Abbess of Minster in Thanet, Kent, succeeding St. Mildred. She was a very cultured woman and educated her nuns in the art of writing, illuminating and embroidery. One of her pupils was Leoba, who sent to St. Boniface some verses, of which she said she had learnt the art from Eadburga.

Boniface, while he was in Germany often communicated with Eadburga. He greatly admired her, and addressed his letters "to his most beloved Sister Abbess Eadburh".* She supplied him with gifts of books and vestments. In one letter he asked her "to write for me in gold the epistles of my lord, St. Peter the Apostle", and in another, thanking her for sending gifts of Sacred books, "you have consoled with spiritual light an exile among the Germans."

St. Eadburga built a new church for the abbey in Thanet, which was dedicated to St. Peter and St. Paul by Cuthbert, Archbishop of Canterbury, and where she translated the body of St. Mildred.

Historical Documents. Ed. Whitelock.

St. Eadburga. Late 7th century, June 20th. A.C.

She was a daughter of King Penda, the heathen king of Mercia, most of whose children became Christians. She became a nun at Caister (Dormundecastre) in Northamptonshire where her sister Kyneburga was abbess. She was buried at Caister, but later, with the bodies of her sisters, was translated to Peterborough (Medehampstede), the Abbey toward whose foundation her brother and sisters had contributed, and where their shrine stood. The Danes destroyed the Abbey of Peterborough in 870. Eadburga's relics were transferred to Flanders.

St. Eadburga. Died June 15th 960. A.C.

She was the daughter of King Edward the Elder.

When she was three years old, her father called her to him and offered her a choice of sparkling jewellery with a selection of brilliant female adornments, or a book of the Gospels with a Chalice. The small child chose the Gospels with the Chalice; her father was so astounded at this, that he assumed that she was pre-ordained to be a nun, and while she was still young he sent her to St. Mary's convent at Winchester, where she was in the charge of her grandmother, King Alfred's widow, and where for the rest of her days she led a holy life.

St. Ealswitha (Ealsitha). Died July 20th, 903. A.C.

She was the wife of King Alfred the Great and daughter of Ethelred, Ealdorman of Mercia. She and her husband tried to restore the old religious communities which had been devastated by the Danes, and with her help, the king brought to the English people a new spirit of hope and pride in their own nationality.

Ealswitha was directly responsible for founding the convent of St. Mary's at Winchester, and on Alfred's death she retired there.

St. Eanflaed. Died November 24th, c.700-704. A.C.

She was the daughter of King Edwin and Queen Ethelburga of Northumbria. She was born in 626 on the night that King Edwin had been saved from the knife of an assassin. The king was so delighted at the birth that he began to give thanks to his heathen gods, when Bishop Paulinus, who had come to Northumbria as escort to the queen, told him that the safe delivery was really due to his own prayers to the true God. The king then promised that if God would give him life and save him from the hands of the king who had sent the assassin, he would give up his heathen gods and give his daughter to be consecrated to Christ. The child was baptised at Pentecost by St. Paulinus, and, as Bede says "the first of the Northumbrian race to be baptised".

There is a very vague rumour that Edwin, his daughter and ten thousand of his people were baptised by Rhun, son of Urien. This is only found in Nennius, a Welsh source, and certainly not mentioned by Bede or any other English writer. It has been suggested that the British did not like to think that Christianity came to the North in any other way than through their own influence. But it is almost certainly a fabulous story, otherwise Bede would have heard of it.

In 633 King Edwin was killed and there was a great massacre among the people of Northumbria. St. Paulinus, fearing for the safety of the queen and her children, fled with them by boat to Kent, where the queen's brother was reigning.

Eanflaed spent her childhood in Kent, then about 643, when she was seventeen, she returned to Northumbria to marry King Oswy. She brought her own chaplain with her; his name was Romanus. She and her priest, having been brought up under Canterbury, celebrated Easter at a different time to that of the court of King Oswy. This caused great confusion, which was not resolved until 664 at the Synod of Whitby, when the Roman observances were adopted by the Church in the North. Queen Eanflaed might have had some influence on her husband's final decision. She certainly influenced him by making him give a grant of land at Gilling on which to build a monastery, to atone for his part in the death of King Oswine of Deira.

The queen helped St. Wilfrid when he was a youth, and it was on her advice that he became a pupil at Lindisfarne, and later with her encouragement he was able to make his first journey to Rome.

As King Oswy was married twice, it is difficult to say which of his numerous offspring were the children of Eanflaed. Certainly Aelfflaed was her daughter. On the death of Oswy in 670, the queen retired to the monastery of Whitby, where her daughter was a nun, and on the death of Abbess Hilda in 680, the two royal women became joint Abbesses. Eanflaed was responsible for bringing her father King Edwin's bones to be buried at Whitby, where a shrine was built for them near the altar of St. Gregory.

The exact date of Eanflaed's death is not known, but it was probably sometime between 700 and 704.

St. Eanswitha. Died c.640, August 31st or September 12th. A.C. She was the daughter of King Eadbald of Kent, and grandaughter of Ethelbert, first Christian king of Kent. Her father wished to marry her to a Northumbrian prince, but she preferred to become a nun. When the prince came to press his suit, Eanswitha pointed to a log of wood and said she would marry him if he could lengthen it by one foot. Although he persevered, he was not successful. Then King Eadbald gave his consent to his daughter's desires, and he built her a nunnery on the coast near Folkestone, of which she became the abbess.

As well as artistic and literary work, her community of nuns did their own farming. She is said to have tamed flocks of geese because they tried to destroy her harvest. She provided the town with a supply of fresh water by striking her crozier on the ground, and showing where the water flowed. This incident is very similar to what water diviners do at the present day. There is still a spring called St. Eanswitha's Spring, which supplies water to a reservoir. Among other wonders, she is said to have given sight to the blind, cast out devils and cured many people of their infirmities.

The church and convent were later washed into the sea. A new church was built several centuries afterwards dedicated to St. Mary and St. Eanswitha, and in 1885 a lead casket was found, believed to contain her relics. Baring-Gould gives her feast day as August 31st, but Butler gives it as September 12th.

Eangyth. 8th century.
She was an abbess, but it is not stated of what monastery. She corresponded with St. Boniface about the troubles in her monastery; the failure of the harvest, the taxes she found difficulty in paying, her

worries over looking after her nuns and also her own sins.

St. Boniface seems to have been a confidant of quite a number of the nuns at that time. Eangyth asked him whether he thought it would be beneficial for her to make a pilgrimage to Rome. She wrote to him in despair saying she had no one to advise her but only a daughter. This daughter might have been the Abbess Bugga or Healburg, who also corresponded with St. Boniface.

Ecgburga. c. late 7th century.

She was the daughter of King Aldulf (Ealdwulf) of East Anglia, and she became a friend of St. Guthlac, the Hermit of Croyland. Felix in the "Life of St. Guthlac", calls her "the most honoured virgin of the virgins of Christ, the Abbess Ecgburga, daughter of King Aldulf". She made for Guthlac a lead coffin with a shroud, and shaped it in the form of Our Lord's Cross, with arms extended in the likeness of a suppliant at prayer. She sent it to him and asked that he should be laid in it after his death. In her letter she requested him to tell her who would inhabit the place where he dwelt after he was gone.

Guthlac replied thanking her for her gift and to the question asked of him, "that the heir to that spot was of pagan race and had not yet entered the waters of baptism, though he would soon". Guthlac was prophesying future events, as the man who occupied his cell after his death, was called Cissa and was a heathen during Guthlac's lifetime, and was baptised some years later.

The genealogical tables give the daughter of King Ealdwulf as Abbess of Repton, but I cannot find out for certain whether this was Ecgburga, and I can find no reference to the date of Ecgburga's death.

St. Edith (Eadgyth). July 15th, ? 925 or after 962. A.C.

To distinguish this saint from any other of the same name she is known as St. Edith of Polesworth.

She was the daughter of Edward the Elder and granddaughter of King Alfred. Her brother Athelstan, when he became king, married her to Sihtric, who was king of Northumbria and was a Dane. Sihtric, because of his great love for Edith, became a Christian, but reverted back to paganism, and died, it is said miserably as an apostate.

St. Edith remained a virgin and became a nun at Polesworth, where she died on July 15th 925, and because of her great piety and of her many good works, miracles were afterwards performed at her tomb.

This information is given by Roger of Wendover and Matthew of Westminster. But William of Malmesbury gives her date of marriage to Sihtric as 925 and that she was then fifteen years of age, and lived until she was more than fifty two; so her death would be after 962.

The story that St. Edith of Polesworth was the daughter of King Egbert and was put in charge of St. Modwenna is a myth by Capgrave, according to Baring-Gould, and Dugdale, when he repeated the story was misled by Capgrave.

St. Edith (Eadgyth). September 16th 984. R.M.

Known as St. Edith of Wilton. She was the illegitimate daughter of King Edgar and Wilfrida, who was a nun at Wilton. Edith was born in 962, and was brought up by her mother in the monastery at Wilton, and remained there all her life. She received the veil from Ethelwold, Bishop of Winchester, who reproved her for her gaiety in dress; she replied to him that "the mind might be modest under fine clothes as well as under a drab serge habit, as God looks at the heart and not the dress".*

Her father wished her to be abbess at both Winchester and Barking, but she preferred to remain at Wilton with her mother.

She seems to have had the gift of prophesy, for she foretold the death of Edward, the son of Edgar, who was murdered at Corfe Castle. The nobles then tried to persuade her to ascend the throne, but she refused, wishing to remain in a humble position.

At the time she was living, St. Dunstan was Archbishop of Canterbury. He consecrated the church which she built at Wilton, dedicated to St. Denys. It was while they were at Mass that St. Dunstan noticed that St. Edith frequently crossed herself, and as she did so, he caught hold of her thumb, and he prophesied that it would never decay because of the holy sign she gave with it.

St. Edith was only twenty two at the time of her death. There is a tale that a nun heard some angels singing as she went to enter the door of the church. One of the angels stopped her from entering saying "go back, the angels await the good maiden."*

Some years earlier St. Edith had promised to stand as godmother to the child of a lady at Winchester. This lady did not have a child until three years after the death of St. Edith; then she had a daughter. The Bishop of Winchester baptised the child, and the lady was sorrowful as she remembered St. Edith's promise, but in the middle of the ceremony, and as the bishop handed the lighted taper to the child, he looked up and saw St. Edith was present, holding the child in her arms, and she stretched out her hand towards him, and took the light from him, and there she remained for the rest of the ceremony, and when it was finished she vanished out of sight.

* Baring-Gould, quoting from a Life of St. Edith.

Edith. 7th century.

This Edith was a nun at Barking, who looked after a young boy when he suffered from the plague, which attacked a great many of the inmates of the monasteries during the seventh century. In spite of her devoted nursing she was unable to save him. Just before he died he called out for her, "Edith, Edith, Edith." *She, unfortunately, had contracted the disease, and followed him who had called for her, and so they both died on the same day.

*Bede-*Ecclesiastical History.*

St. Edith

This saint is mentioned by Butler as being in the calendars. He mentions no dates, but that she was the daughter of Earl Frewald, and that she died a nun at Ailesbury.

St. Ela. Died 1261, February 1st. P.C.

She was the only child of William Devereux, 2nd Earl of Salisbury. On the death of her father, she was left an heiress, and was secretly taken to Normandy, where she was closely guarded, presumably by her relations. An English knight, William Talbot, is said to have searched for her, wandering about disguised as a troubadour for two years. When he found her, he presented her to Richard I, who gave her in marriage to his half brother, William Longespée. William was the natural son of Henry II and Fair Rosamund. Ela at the time was only ten years old.

Through this marriage, de jure uxore, Longespée became Earl of Salisbury, Ela being a countess in her own right. The Earl was present at the signing of the Magna Charta, and he assisted in founding the new Cathedral at Salisbury. He died in 1226.

At his death, the Countess placed herself under the direction of St. Edmund Rich, Archbishop of Canterbury, and it is said directed by visions, she founded a monastery of Carthusians at Hinton, and a convent of Augustinian nuns at Lacock, where in 1236 she became the first Abbess.

She died at the age of seventy four and was buried in the church at Lacock. One of her sons died in a battle in the Holy Land, and legend says that Ela saw his soul ascending into heaven as she was seated in her abbatial stall at Lacock.

St. Elfleda (Ethelfleda). Died c.936, October 23rd. A.C.

She was a lady of royal blood. On the death of her rich husband she became a recluse at Glastonbury, where she had her cell to the east of the abbey. Elfleda was very fond of St. Dunstan when he was a schoolboy at Glastonbury, and he became a great admirer of hers as he grew up.

There is a tale that King Athelstan visited her, and the king's servants were anxious to see whether she had enough to entertain him in a suitable manner. They found that she had plenty of cups and plates, but not enough to drink. But she assured them that the Virgin Mother would supply the need. She prayed for help in an ancient oratory dedicated to St. Mary.

When the king arrived there appeared to be only enough beer in the barrel to give each of her guests one full cup, but miraculously the barrel never seemed to run dry, and they all had as much as they wished to drink.

St. Dunstan spent a great deal of his time with St. Elfleda when she was ill. One evening after he had veen visiting her, it was too late to enter the church for Vespers, so he remained outside the door and as he waited there he saw a dove rising into the sky from the roof of the abbey and flying in the direction of Elfleda's house. Filled with wonder at the sight, he hurried back to her. When he entered her cell he heard her voice carrying on a conversation behind the bedcurtains. He was surprised, and enquired of those attending on her if they knew who could be with her. The attendants did not know of anyone, but they had seen a light shining around her bed. St. Dunstan concluded that she must be speaking with angels; her spirit being so close to them, and that they were preparing to take her with them. The next morning her end in this world came, and she departed to a more Heavenly Realm.

St. Elfleda. Died 1030, October 29th A.C.

She was the daughter of Earl Ethelwold, a friend of King Edgar, and her mother was related to the queen. She had many brothers and sisters. Her father died while she was very young, and her mother neglected her, so the king took her under his care. He sent her to the monastery of Romsey in Hampshire, where St. Merwenna was the abbess.

Elfleda was consecrated a nun by Bishop Ethelwald of Winchester sometime before 975. She became famous as a saint and all sorts of tales, some of a miraculous nature were told of her.

One windy night when she was reading the lesson at Matins, the light from the candle was blown out. To try and stop the draught from the wind she held up her hand, and as if it were a torch, a glow of light radiated from her hand so that she could see to continue reading. She loved to sing praises to God and she was known to stand in a cold pond the whole night through singing psalms.

After St. Merwenna died in 993 and her successor in 996, Elfleda became Abbess of Romsey. She is said to have such a generous nature that she depleted the funds of the abbey by giving a great deal away as charity to the poor.

When she died she was buried in the abbey.

St. Elfgiva (Aelfgifu). Died 971, May 18th A.C.

She was the wife of King Edmund I, and the mother of Kings Edwy and Edgar. Both the Anglo-Saxon Chronicle and the Chronicle of Florence of Worcester name her as a saint. She was left a widow when quite young; her husband having been murdered, and she was greatly troubled over the morals of her sons. William of Malmesbury says of her, "She was a woman intent on good works, and gifted with such affection and kindness that she would even secretly discharge the penalties of those culprits whom the sad sentences of the judges had publicly condemned." He goes on to say that she even gave away her beautiful clothes to any poor person she saw.

She eventually ended her life as a nun at the monastery of Shaftesbury.

Earcengota (Earcongotha). Died 660, July 7th A.C.

The above dates are from the "Book of Saints" compiled by the monks of St. Augustine's Abbey, Ramsgate, but Baring-Gould gives

February 23rd, 700. I think the date 660 is more likely to be the correct one.

She was the daughter of King Erconbert of Kent and his Queen Sexburga. As there were few monasteries for women in England at the time, she was sent to Faremoutier-en-Brie in Gaul, to be under her aunt Ethelburga, who was the abbess there.

On the day that she died, she had a vision revealing that her end was near; she saw a crowd of men all dressed in white, entering the monastery. They came, they stated, to take back the golden coin which had been brought thither from Kent. After seeing these celestial beings, she went round all the cells in the monastery, visiting the infirm, those of great age, and those who had especially led holy lives. She asked them all to pray for her.

That night she departed this life, and the sound of angels singing was heard by monks in other buildings in the monastery. Wondering to hear what the sound could be, they hurried out of their cells, and saw a great light shining down from above, which gathered up the holy soul of the maiden and bore it away to heaven.

Her body was buried in the Church of St. Stephen, and three days later it was decided to raise the stone covering her grave. While this was being carried out, the brothers and sisters standing by all sensed a sweet fragrance as of balsam rising from the tomb. This sweet smell, which is said to have come from many of the saints's graves, was often looked on as a sign of Sainthood. It quite possibly might have been due sometimes to spices that were used for embalming.

St. Ermengytha. Died 680, July 30th. A.C.

She was the daughter of Ermenred King of Kent, and sister of St. Domneva, in whose monastery at Minster in Thanet she became a nun. "The Book of Saints" calls her a saint, but Baring-Gould says she does not appear in any Calendar.

St. Ermenilda (Ermengild) Died 703, February 13th. A.C.

She was the daughter of Ercombert and St. Sexburga, King and Queen of Kent. She married King Wulfhere of Mercia, who was son of the old pagan King Penda. Ermenilda and her husband both became Christians, and together they did their best to stamp out the last traces of the old heathen religion in the kingdom of Mercia. It was during that time that St. Chad became Bishop of Lichfield.

The royal couple had a daughter, Werburga, who became a great saint. On the death of King Wulfhere in 675, his widow became a nun in the convent which her mother had founded at Minster in Sheppey, and when St. Sexburga left Sheppey and went to join her sister at Ely, Ermenilda became Abbess at Sheppey. Later she followed her mother to Ely, and succeeded her there as abbess.

Ermenilda was renowned for her great sanctity. When she died she was buried beside her mother and her aunt, Etheldreda, in the church of the great abbey of Ely.

St. Ethelburga. Died c.664, July 7th. R.M.

She was one of the four saintly daughters of Anna, King of East Anglia. She went abroad and became a nun at the double monastery of Faremoutier-en-Brie, and eventually succeeded the founder, St. Fara as abbess. She began to build a church for the monastery, and had chosen the position in it where she wished to be buried, but she died before the building was completed. Work on it was never continued, and after seven years it was decided to translate her bones to another church, which had been finished. On opening her tomb they found her body with no sign of decay and lying there as fresh as if it had just been buried. This being against the usual course of nature, was considered a miracle.

Colgrave, in a note in his edition of Bede's Ecclesiastical History, says that Ethelburga has been wrongly described as illegitimate.

Ethelburga (Aethburgh, Tata). Died c.647, April 5th. A.C.

Daughter of King Ethelbert and Queen Bertha of Kent. When Edwin, King of Northumbria sent ambassadors to Kent to ask for her hand in marriage, her brother, Eadbald was king, and he replied that no Christian maiden was allowed to marry a heathen, which Edwin and all his kingdom were at that time. But Edwin promised that he would put no obstacles in the way for her to worship in a Christian manner, and all her attendants might freely do the same. He even hinted that he might consider and examine the Christian religion himself.

On these conditions, Ethelburga, in 625 was sent to Northumbria to become the wife of Edwin. She was accompanied by St. Paulinus, who acted as her chaplain. Before they left Kent, Paulinus was consecrated bishop, so as to give him authority in his efforts to preach and convert the heathen Northumbrians.

Ethelburga became the mother of Eanflaed, and the child was born on the night that Edwin was saved from an assassin. He was delighted at the birth and gave thanks to his heathen gods. Paulinus rebuked him and said the safe delivery was due to his own prayers to the one true God.

Ethelburga must have had a civilising influence on the rather wild Northumbrian court, as the court in Kent where she was brought up was much more cultured. She was encouraged to help in the conversion of her husband by a letter written to her from the Pope, addressed thus: "To his daughter the most illustrious Lady, Queen Aethelburh, Bishop Boniface, servant of the servants of God." At the end of the letter he mentions a gift which he sends the queen, which seems to be just the sort of gift a woman would appreciate. "As well as the blessing of St. Peter, chief of the apostles and your protector, we send a silver mirror and an ivory comb adorned with gold. We beseech your Majesty to accept it in the same kindly spirit as that in which it is sent."

The palace at Yeavering, built under the shadow of the Cheviots, was the usual residence of the king and queen. It had a long wooden hall with the fire in the centre and doors at both ends. Just the setting for the lovely story of the bird, which, when they heard it, influenced the king and his council to make up their minds to become Christians. One can imagine the queen in her eagerness praying that some miracle might help their decision, and when in the flickering firelight she saw the tall old thegn rising to give his opinion in favour of joining the new religion, she knew that her prayers had been answered. How delighted she must have been when she heard him saying, "O King, when you and your nobles are sitting feasting round a fire in the midst of winter, while stormy gales of snow and rain are raging outside; and a sparrow flies in through the door from the darkness and cold, it flutters around for a brief time in light and warmth and then quickly passes out through the other door into the darkness again, and is seen no more. So does the life of man appear for a short time; of what went before or what is to follow, we are in utter ignorance. If this new religion can bring us more information, I think it is right we should accept it."

It is strange that the name of this old man, whose words were responsible for making Northumbria a Christian nation for the first time, is not even known.

In the year 633 King Edwin was killed by Penda, King of Mercia. The kingdom was left in chaos, but with the help of one of the king's thegns, whose name was Bass, Paulinus managed to escape with the queen and the children by boat to Kent. There, the queen's brother, King Eadbald, gave her land on which was founded the monastery for men and women at Lyminge, where the queen retired with her chaplain Paulinus, and she became the first Abbess. Paulinus eventually became Bishop of Rochester.

There is a church in York dedicated to St. Ethelburga, and there are several in the south of England dedicated to a St. Ethelburga, but as there are a number of saints of this name, it is difficult to say to which one the churches are dedicated.

St. Ethelburga. Died c.678. October 11th. A.C.

She was the sister of St. Earconwald, who was Bishop of London. Baring-Gould gives an account of her when she was young. He says that her father was named Offa, and that she was born at Starlington in Lindsey. She was baptised, but her father still remained a heathen. He was angry with her for her piety, so she used to steal away to church unbeknown to him, and the path which she trod was always green. It was because her father wished to marry her to a man of wealth, that she ran away to Barking in Essex, and was given shelter by a farmer on condition that she helped him with the harvest. The story goes on to say that while she prayed, angels with sickles cut down the golden corn for her. I can find no other authority that mentions this account of her childhood.

Her brother built her a monastery at Barking, and placed her there as the first Abbess, and as she was inexperienced, he sent abroad for Hildelith to come and instruct St. Ethelburga in the running of the monastery; Hildelith had been a nun at Chelles of Faremoutier. Barking is said to have been the first house in England that took women. It was a double monastery, and had separate buildings set apart for the men. The community had its sorrows, as during the plagues, which ravaged the country in the 7th century, many of the inmates died.

A few days before the abbess departed from this world, one of her nuns, whose name was Torhtgyth, had a vision. It was evening at dusk when she saw a human body wrapped in a shroud, which shone brighter than the sun, and appeared to rise from the building where the nuns slept; golden cords were drawing it up into heaven. The nun realised that it must mean that a member of their community would shortly be going to enter the gates of heaven. It was not long after this vision had been seen, that the soul of St. Ethelburga, their abbess, was taken from them.

In the monastery there was a nun who was very disabled, and when the body of the abbess was taken into the church, she asked if she might be carried in and placed beside the coffin. She spoke to Ethelburga as if she was still there, and begged her to plead that she might be delivered from her cruel pains, which she had had for such a long time. Twelve days later she was set free from her agony and departed to eternal rest.

St. Etheldreda (Aethelthryth, Audrey). Died 679, June 23rd or October 17th. R.M.

She was one of the four daughters of Anna, King of East Anglia. These daughters were all known as saints, and Etheldreda was probably the best known and most popular of them all. She was first married to Tonberht, an Ealdorman of the South Gyrive, but he died soon afterwards. She remained a widow for five years, and then married Ecgfrith of Northumbria, son of King Oswy. She became Queen of Northumbria when Ecgfrith succeeded to the throne in 670. Their marriage was never consumated, although Ecgfrith was desirous that it should be, and he sought the cooperation of Bishop Wilfrid to persuade her, as he knew that she greatly admired the bishop, feeling that he might be able to influence her. It was the queen who gave St. Wilfrid land on which to build the church at Hexham.

Etheldreda, however, wished to enter a monastery, and become a nun. After twelve years of being frustrated, the king reluctantly gave his consent, and she entered the monastery of his aunt Ebba, at Coldingham. She received the veil from Bishop Wilfrid. The king never really forgave Wilfrid for his part in assisting her to become a nun, and he always suspected him of encouraging her in her resistance to his demands.

I think some explanation is needed here to understand her conduct, as well as the conduct of a great many other women who entered monasteries during the age known as the Anglo-Saxon period of our history. It was not a fear or disgust of sex; I do not think that in the majority of cases that feeling entered into it. At the end of the sixth century and the beginning of the seventh century, the kingdoms of the Anglo-Saxons nearly all became Christian. It was an age of great faith, and many desired to devote their lives to God, including the women, who in their enthusiasm wished to become brides of Christ. The monasteries gave them this opportunity, and also enabled them to become educated, the women as highly as the men. They learnt Greek and Latin, wrote prose and poetry. No wonder those women of great ability felt as they did: such were St. Etheldreda, St. Aelfflaed, St. Eadburga of Thanet, St. Hilda of Whitby and St. Tetta of Wimborne, to mention just a few. They took the advantage offered them to develop their talents, and nowhere but in a monastery could they do so. Quite a number did marry and entered afterwards, when they became widows.

I do not think that the idea of fleeing from the world had anything to do with their motive for wishing to live a religious life, or, that parents, not knowing what to do with their daughters, who were unable to obtain husbands, put them into convents to get rid of them. Most of those we hear of were outstanding women, who, if they had lived at the time when the majority of the peoples were still heathen, would have been a loss to the world. Christianity raised the quality of living of men and women alike.

St. Etheldreda is said to have been a very beautiful woman and certainly had no lack of suitors, but she appears to have had a genuine call to the religious life. The king regretted having let her go and still tried to make her come back him, and it was the Abbess Ebba who suggested that she should flee from his pursuit.

After having spent a year at Coldingham, she set out, disguised as a poor woman, accompanied by two nuns, towards her own homeland. On the journey south, they came to a spot called Colberts Head, which was a promontory washed by the sea, and here the three women were safe because the tide rose so high for seven days that it rendered it a refuge against pursuit.

There is another version of this journey, which is given in Dugdale's Monasticon:— Etheldreda fled from Coldingham with two servants of God named Sewenna and Sewera, and they ascended a high hill and God poured down plenty of water which encompassed the place and they were protected there for seven days. Prints of their feet are shown on the side of the hill as if on soft wax.

Baring-Gould tells another tale, how, nearing the end of her long journey, being exhausted by the length of her walk, she stopped and lay down at the roadside and fell asleep. She had thrust her staff into the ground, and when she awakened, she found it had taken root. A very large ash tree is pointed out to be the spot where this happened. The same authority, Baring-Gould, says the ash became the emblem of the great monastery of Ely, which she founded.

Bede, who gives a great deal of her life in his Ecclesiastical History, says that she led a most austere life; never wearing fine linen, but only garments made from rough wool, and seldom taking a hot bath, and then only before the great feast days, having first assisted her nuns to wash themselves. As a rule she took only one meal a day, and would continue praying in church after the night Office, until dawn broke.

Ely was a double monastery and St. Etheldreda ruled over both the men and women. Her sister Sexburga joined her there, and after she had been abbess for seven years, she died and was succeeded by Sexburga. Whether her death was due to the plague or to a malignant tumour, which developed in her neck, the evidence is not clear. There was a doctor in the monastery named Cyndrith, whom Etheldreda ordered to lance the tumor beneath her jaw to let out the poison. This being done, she had relief for several days, but the swelling returned and appears to have been the cause of her death. She is said to have welcomed the pain in her neck as a penance, as she could then be absolved from the vanity that caused her, when a young girl, to adorn her neck with necklaces of gold and pearls, which she had loved to do. She was buried by her own wish in a plain wooden coffin among the graves of her nuns.

After sixteen years, her sister Sexburga, who was then abbess, decided that St. Etheldreda's bones should be raised and placed in a place of honour in the church. The abbess sent some of the monks to seek for a suitable stone for the coffin. As the monastery was built among fens and marshes, they had to take a boat to go some distance to search for the stone, as there were none in the vicinity. They arrived at last at a deserted place where now stands the University of Cambridge, and there they found a coffin, "beautifully made of white marble, with a close-fitting lid of the same stone" which they took back to the monastery.

When the wooden coffin of the saint was opened, they found her body to be uncorrupt. The doctor who had attended her during her last illness, gave a description of the scene when they elevated her body. He told how she looked as if she was peacefully asleep, and when he examined the incision that he had made in her neck, he found that it appeared to have healed, leaving hardly any trace of a scar.

The nuns wrapped her in new vestments and placed her body in the marble coffin, which fitted her perfectly, and carried her into the church, where in the future her tomb became held in great veneration. There are twelve dedications of churches to St. Etheldreda.

St. Etheldrith (Alfreda) of Croyland. Died 834, August 2nd. A.C.
Daughter of King Offa and Queen Cynethryth of Mercia. She was betrothed to the young King Ethelbert of East Anglia. Her father had invited the young man to come to his court, where he was received at first with great hospitality. One night he was foully murdered, and the queen is generally said to have been guilty of the deed.

Etheldritha was so horrified at this crime that she could no longer stay at her father's court, and fled to the island of Croyland among the marshes of Lincolnshire, where she sought sanctuary as a recluse. She spent the next forty years of her life in a cell beside the church of the monastery of Croyland.

When King Witlaf of Mercia was driven from his throne by King Egbert of Wessex he sought refuge for four months in the cell of Etheldritha, until Abbot Siward of Croyland made peace between the two kings. King Witlaf then again ascended his throne. He was ever afterwards generous to the monastery of Croyland, and was griefstricken when he heard of the death of Etheldritha. She was buried in a tomb near Tatwin, who was the guide and boatman of St. Guthlac of Croyland many years before.

Ethelgifu (Ethelgiva, Elgiva). Died 896, December 9th. A.C.
She was the third child of King Alfred of Wessex. She took religious vows, and the king built for her the Abbey of Shaftesbury, in which she became the Abbess of a community of nuns, and where she seems to have led an uneventful life, as nothing else is written about her, except that she was thought of as having been of great sanctity and was venerated as a saint.

Mary Ferrar. Died 1634.
Mother of Nicholas Ferrar, who was the founder of Little Gidding.

She was the daughter of Laurence Woodnoth of Shavington Hall, Cheshire, and she married Nicholas Ferrar, a merchant of London. She helped her son Nicholas, the fourth of her seven children to found a devout Community, the first of its kind in the Anglican Church since the dissolution of the monasteries in the sixteenth century. She bought her son the manor house at Little Gidding in Huntingdonshire in 1625, and it was there that Nicholas and his mother with other members of the family agreed to live a religious life in accordance with the principles and rites of the Church of England. The mother herself paid the expenses for repairing the church.

Mrs Ferrar never failed to rise about five o'clock in the morning, at which time the family started their daily devotions. Bishop Linsel, her contemporary, said of her "Few were equal to her in charity towards man, or piety towards God",* and her eldest son, John, when he spoke of his mother after her death, said, "In her person she was of a comely presence, and had a countenance so full of gravity that it drew respect from all who beheld her. In her words she was cautious, in her actions obliging. She was a pattern of piety, benevolence, and charity. And thus she lived and died, esteemed, revered, and beloved by all who knew her."

Further information about the Ferrar family can be found under the heading "Little Gidding" in the accounts of the religious houses in the second part of this book.

* *Little Gidding* by Henry Collett, 1925.

St. Frideswide. Died c.735, October 19th R.M.

She was known as the patroness of the City and University of Oxford. There are many legendary tales about her, and it is not easy to sort out fact from fiction.

The following passage is a translation from the historian, William of Malmesbury:— "There was formerly in Oxfordshire a monastery where Frideswide a very holy maiden found her consolation. The daughter of a king, she despised a royal marriage, professing her whole trust in the Lord Christ. But her would-be bridegroom, since he had set his mind on marriage with the virgin and entreaties and flatteries had made no effect, determined to take her by force. When Frideswide heard of this she determined on flight into a wood. But neither was her hiding place able to conceal her from her lover nor the weakness of her own desire able to prevent him from pursuing her in her flight. Therefore the virgin, a second time, aware of the ardour of the youth, by hidden paths, God accompanying her, came into Oxford one stormy night. There, when in the morning her ardent lover would have hastened to her, the maiden now desperate in her flight and unable through weariness to go any further, prayed to God for protection for herself and punishment for her persecutor, and he, when he had come with his companions to the gates of the town, by a stroke sent down from heaven was afflicted with blindness. And when the result of his obduracy was known and Frideswide had expressed her entreaties through the messengers who came to her, with the same speed with which he had lost his sight he regained it. For this reason a fear was implanted in the kings of that time to be wary of entry into that Anglican town or of receiving hospitality there because this might be the way of destruction, whilst on the other hand each one fleeing from the peril of danger experienced the justice of the matter. There therefore the young woman strong in the triumph of her virginity established a convent and betrothing herself to God passed the rest of her life there".

Baring-Gould gives the name of her father as Didan, a prince of a territory near Oxford, and that she had a governess named Algiva, a very religious woman, who greatly influenced her life.

Baring-Gould also gives the name of the suitor as Alfgar, who was a powerful neighbour of her father, and more details of her flight. He says that Frideswide escaped with two nuns, and they were rowed up the river Isis to Abingdon by an angel disguised as a white robed youth. At Abingdon she hid herself in a sty built for swine near the edge of an oak forest. Alfgar was hot in pursuit, and Frideswide in her distress invoked the aid of St. Catherine and St. Cecilia, both of whom had had to defend their virginity. At that moment Alfgar was struck with blindness. There seems to be some confusion in the two accounts as to where he was struck with blindness, but a third account by Butler, says that this happened as Alfgar entered the City of Oxford.

Butler and Baring-Gould both say that Frideswide built herself a small oratory in the wood at Thornbury near Oxford, so that she could live in greater retirement, and when she wanted a drink, a fountain of water sprung up at her prayer. The fountain and oratory both became places of pilgrimages.

There is a tale that one day as Frideswide was on her way back to her monastery at Oxford, she met a leper, from whom she shrank in

51

horror, but the leper asked her in the name of Jesus Christ to kiss him. Overcoming her fear, she did as he requested with a sisterly kiss on the lips. Straight away the leprosy left him, and he became fresh and perfect in body.

During the Danish invasions the nuns of Frideswide's monastery were dispersed, and later Canons of St. Austin took over the building.

On the site of the monastery now stands Christ Church, built by Cardinal Wolsey. In the Cathedral is the tomb of St. Frideswide. There are three dedications of Churches to her.

Elizabeth Fry. 1780-1845.

Eminent philanthropist. Chief promoter of prison reform in Europe. She belonged to a Quaker family. Her father was John Gurney of Earlham Hall and her mother was Catherine Bell, grandaughter of Robert Barcley, who was a friend and companion of George Fox, founder of the society of Friends.

Elizabeth was never a fanatical Quaker, but her religion meant a great deal to her. In 1800 she married Joseph Fry and lived for some years in St. Mildred's Court in the City, where she took a great interest in the poor around her; afterwards she and her family moved to Plasket House in Essex.

In 1813 she first started visiting Newgate Prison, and four years later she founded "The Association for the Improvement of the Female Prisoners in Newgate". In 1818 she travelled all over the north of England and Scotland, inspecting the conditions in the prisons, accompanied by her brother. It was due to her exertions that great improvements were made in the prison systems. She also visited prisons in many countries on the Continent, and had discussions with a number of prison officials there.

Elizabeth was a woman with a love of humanity, especially those unfortunates who had sunk so low as to be incapable of profiting by any help, and so remained neglected in their misery. Elizabeth took pity on them and did her best to relieve their sufferings. She certainly did her utmost to keep the Second Great Commandment — "Love thy Neighbour".

She died on October 12th, 1845, and left behind a numerous family.

Margaret Godolphin (Blagge). 1652-1678

She was the fourth daughter and one of the co-heirs of Thomas Blagge (Blague) esq, groom of the bedchamber to Charles I and II. At the age of eleven she began to live according to a religious rule of life, even though there were no Communities at that time in England that she could join. She maintained it strictly all through her life, even when she was attached to the courts of Charles II and James, Duke of York. She became Maid of Honour to Anne Hyde, Duchess of York, and in spite of being very beautiful, and living in a dissolute court, she became known as one of the most virtuous young women.

She married Sidney, third son of Francis Godolphin esq, M.P. for St. Ives (who secured the Isles of Scilly for Charles I). Sidney was groom of the bedchamber to Charles II in 1660. When he was very young he fell violently in love with Margaret Blagge and married her.

They lived in a house in Scotland Yard, near Whitehall, and it was there, in 1678 that Margaret gave birth to her son Francis, and a week later she died. She was a close friend of John Evelyn, the diarist, and he took charge of Francis's education. Evelyn also wrote a life of Margaret.

It was not until after his wife's death that Sidney was raised to the peerage; he became a minister of State in 1684 and was created a baron and in 1704, he became Earl of Godolphin, and Lord High Treasurer of Great Britain. He died in 1712, thirty four years after his wife. Margaret's son Francis married the daughter of John and Sarah Churchill.

There is a portrait of Margaret painted by Mary Beale, who is known as England's first professional woman painter and was very active painting portraits during the seventeenth century.

St. Gwen (of Wales). Died c.492. October 18th. A.C.

She was said to be the grandaughter of Brychan of Brecknock, whose numerous family was called one of the Three Holy Families of Britain. She was murdered at Talgarth by heathen Saxons. The church at Talgarth is dedicated to a St. Gwengoline; probably another name for this saint.

St. Gwen (of Cornwall). 5th century. A.C. Her day is given October 18th, on the same day as the former St. Gwen.

She married Selyf, Duke of Cornwall, and was the mother of St.

Cuby. She was also the sister of St. Non, who was the mother of St. David. The name Gwen means white, and is the same as Wenn in Cornwall, and the village of St. Wenn is named after this saint.

Heiu. 7th century.
She was the first woman to take the vows and habit of a nun in the Anglo-Saxon kingdom of Northumbria, and was consecrated by Bishop Aidan of Lindisfarne, while he occupied the northern See during the years 635-651. She founded the first monastery to admit women in the north at Hartlepool. Soon afterwards she retired to Tadcaster, where she may have built another monastery, but there is no definite evidence of her having done so, but she probably dwelt there with one or two companions. She was succeeded at Hartlepool as abbess by St. Hilda. Nothing is known of her family or when she died.

St. Helena. Died c.330, August 18th. R.M.
It is very difficult to sort out fact from fiction in the life of St. Helena. The ancient chroniclers are not in agreement as to whether she was the wife or concubine of Constantius, who died in York in 306. The historian, Henry of Huntingdon says she was the daughter of the British King of Colchester, named Coel. This King Coel was the monarch of the old nursery rhyme.

She was the mother of Constantine the Great, who is said to have been proclaimed Caesar in York. When her son adopted Christianity in 312, she also became a Christian. She was then sixty four years of age. In 325 she went on a pilgrimage to the Holy Land, where she erected two churches. Tradition says that she discovered the True Cross, and there is an old Anglo-Saxon poem written probably in the eighth century by one named Cynewulf about the legend of St. Helena going to Jerusalem to search for the Cross. This legend was very old and began to take form soon after the events described in the poem.

St. Helena died at the age of eighty in 330. The Emperor Constantine conveyed her body to Constantinople, where she was buried with great pomp.

There are one hundred and nineteen churches dedicated to this saint in England; an extraordinarily large number.

Hereburg. 7th century.
She was Abbess of Watton. Nothing much is known about her except

that she was a friend of St. John of Beverley, who came to visit her at Watton when he was made Bishop of York. At this time Hereburg's daughter Cwenburh, who was a nun at Watton, was greviously ill with a poisoned arm and had recently been bled. Hereburg asked St. John to see her, but the bishop asked when exactly the bleeding had taken place. When told that it was done on the fourth day of the rising moon, he said, "I remember how Archbishop Theodore of blessed memory used to say that it was very dangerous to bleed a patient when the moon is waxing and the ocean tide flowing. And what can I do for the girl if she is at the point of death?"* The abbess besought him to come to her daughter, and he relented and prayed over her, and she recovered.

Hereburg was training her daughter to succeed her as abbess; it was the custom at that time for those in high position to be succeeded by their relatives, but one that was beginning to be disapproved of by many, among them the historian, Bede.

St. John's story of Archbishop Theodore reveals how much medicine was governed by superstition in those days.

* *Bede's Ecclesiastical History*, Book V, chap. 3.

St. Hilda. Born c.614, died 680. November 17th. A.C.
She was one of the most outstanding women of the seventh century. She belonged to the royal family of Northumbria. Her father was Hereric, grandson of Aelle, the first known Anglo-Saxon king of Deira. Her mother was named Breguswith.

When Ethelfrith united the kingdoms of Bernicia and Deira, and became king of the whole of Northumbria, Hereric and his wife sought refuge at the court of the British King Cerdic (Ceretic) of Elmet, which was a small Celtic kingdom near Leeds, and it was there that Hilda and her sister Hereswith were most probably born.

Hilda's father was traitorously murdered, either by Cerdic or a member of his court. At that time, which was just before Hilda's birth, her mother Breguswith had a dream; she dreamt that her husband was taken away and she could not find him. While she was searching for him she found under her a garment a necklace of precious stones, which began to shine while she gazed at it, and the light from it gradually increased, until it filled the whole of Britain with its brightness. This dream according to Bede, was a prophesy which was fulfilled in her daughter Hilda's life.

Hilda joined her uncle Edwin when he became king of Northumbria in 617. She was then only about three years old, and her mother and sister were probably with her. She was baptised by St. Paulinus with Edwin and his whole court on Easter Day in 627.

Exactly what happened to her when Edwin was killed by Penda in 633 is not clear. It has been suggested that she went with her mother and sister to East Anglia. Her sister married a king of East Anglia, and became the mother of King Ealdwulf.

Hilda returned to Northumbria; this must have been after Oswald defeated Penda at the battle of Heavenfield and became king. Oswald was a Christian, having been converted on the Island of Iona, and Hilda appears to have been on friendly terms with the new royal family. St. Aidan, when he came from Iona at the request of King Oswald to be Bishop of Lindisfarne, was one of many who admired St. Hilda for her wisdom and ability.

Bede says that she led a secular life until she was thirty three years old, and then she decided to became a nun. She withdrew to the kingdom of East Anglia about the year 646, and she remained there for about a year, hoping to follow her sister, who had taken the veil in a monastery at Chelles in Gaul. Her wish was not granted, as she was recalled home to Northumbria by St. Aidan, who gave her land near the river Wear, on which she and a few companions lived a monastic life for just over twelve months.

She was consecrated a nun by St. Aidan, and he then made her Abbess of Hartlepool, where she succeeded Heiu, the first Abbess, who had retired. St. Hilda established a Rule of life at the monastery which won praise from all the leading men devoted to the service of God, including St. Aidan, who instructed her in all the virtues of the Christian religion. It was while she was at Hartlepool that she took into her care the young princess Aelfflaed, the daughter of King Oswy.

When St. Finan was Bishop of Lindisfarne, sometime after 655 St. Hilda was sent to take over the charge of the great Abbey of Streaneshalch, which is now called Whitby. She may have been the founder of this double monastery of monks and nuns. There the men and women lived in separate quarters, but they worshipped together in the same church. Under the supervision of St. Hilda they studied the scriptures, and were given what was considered a high education for those days. They were taught to look after those in need; they shared all things in common, no one having more possessions than another, and in the majority, they lived lives showing the virtues of justice, devotion and chastity.

The Abbey of Whitby under St. Hilda produced many men who became famous saints and scholars, and one great poet. She was probably the only woman in our history under whose training five men became bishops: Bosa, bishop of York, Aetla, bishop of Dorchester, Oftfor, bishop of the kingdom of the Hwice, John of Beverley, bishop of York, and Wilfrid II, bishop of York. The first English poet to write in the vernacular, Caedmon, was a simple cowherd, whom St. Hilda took into her care, and encouraged.

St. Hilda was the hostess at the Synod of Whitby, which was held in 664, when the king and clergy assembled to decide on the date at which Easter should be held. Although she had been baptised by St. Paulinus, she had been for most of her life brought up in the Celtic tradition, so all her sympathies were on the side of St. Colman, the Bishop of Lindisfarne, but when King Oswy decided in favour of the Roman dating, she obeyed his ruling.

Six years before her death a burning fever attacked her which continued for the rest of her life and gave her great pain, but she never complained, but went on looking after her charges, giving them instructions and seeing to their welfare. She died when she was sixty-six years old. That night, as Bede says, she joyfully saw death approach, and in the words of St. John, she "passed from death unto life."

There are two stories of nuns having a vision of a soul being borne to heaven by angels. One was seen by a nun in the monastery of Hackness, which was built by St. Hilda, and was situated about thirteen miles from Whitby. The nun was named Begu, and had lived a monastic life for over thirty years. She was resting that night in the nun's dormitory, when she thought she heard a bell ringing, as if for one who had departed. Then it seemed to her as if the roof was rolled away, and a light from above filled the whole place. As she gazed upwards she saw the soul of St. Hilda being assisted by angels winging its way to heaven. In her wonder and fear, Begu hastened to the nun Frigyth, whom St. Hilda had placed in charge of the monastery at Hackness. Frigyth immediately summoned all the nuns there to the church, and they spent the night in prayer for the soul of their abbess. When the messengers came in the morning to tell them the news, they said that they already knew.

Another nun had a similar vision while she was in the remotest part of the Abbey of Whitby, long before anyone brought her the news in the morning, she was able to tell those around her.

I have found there are thirty five churches dedicated to St. Hilda, in England, thirty one of these are in the Province of York.

Hildelith (Hildilid). Died 717, March 24th. A.C.

She was one of the earliest Anglo-Saxon women to become a nun. As there were no houses for women wishing to live a monastic life at that time in England, she went to Chelles or Faremoutier in Gaul where she took the veil.

St. Erconwald founded the Abbey of Barking for his sister Ethelburga. He became Bishop of London in 675, and he is said to have founded the Abbey sometime before then. He sent for Hildelith to come back to England to instruct Ethelburga and the nuns at Barking in the monastic Rule of life.

Hildelith came and remained a simple nun under the abbess, but after Ethelburga's death in 678, she succeeded her as the second abbess. Bede says she was a devoted servant of God, and ruled the abbey well.

She arranged for the bones of the former monks and nuns, who had been buried in the grounds, to be taken up and transferred to the church of the abbey and interred there in one place, as there was very limited space for any further burials outside.

It was while Hildelith was abbess of Barking that she corresponded with St. Aldhelm of Malmesbury, and about the year 685 he wrote to her and her nuns a long letter on the virtues of virginity. This letter is addressed:- "Hildilid, abbess; Justina, Cuthburga and Osburga, Aldgitha and Scholastica, Hidburga and Derngitha, Eulalia and Tecla, adorning the Church in renown of holiness."* St. Aldhelm ends his letter bidding them farewell and calling them "flowers of the Church, sisters of the convent, disciples of learning, pearls of Christ, Jewels of Paradise and heirs of our home-to-be in Heaven."

The nun addressed in this letter as Cuthburga, was the former Queen of Northumbria, who studied under Hildelith and later became Abbess of Wimborne.

Sometime Hildelith must have been in touch with St. Boniface as he says in a letter to the Abbess of Minster in Thanet that he had been told a story by Abbess Hildelith about a monk who had been dead and raised to life again. Whether she told him in a letter or met him at one time he does not say.

Hildelith ruled the monks and nuns of Barking for about forty five years, and is said to have extremely old when she died.

*Letter of St. Aldhelm, . . . translated by E. S. Duckett.

Mrs. Hopton. 17th century.

One of the many women, who after the restoration of the monarchy in 1660, felt the need for a more formal liturgy in the Church of England. Assisted by George Hickes, Dean of Worcester, in 1683 she re-edited a Roman Catholic manual entitled "Devotions in the Ancient Way of Offices" by John Austin. She intended it for Anglican readers.

Hugeburc. 8th century.

She was an English nun who went abroad to the monastery of Heidenheim in Bavaria. She was probably one of those many women who went to Germany at the request of St. Boniface. In 775 she wrote the "Life of St. Willibald", an Englishman, who was made Bishop of Eichstatt by St. Boniface. After St. Willibald's travels to Rome and the Holy Land, he came back and told Hugeburc all about his adventures, so that she was able to get first hand knowledge of his experiences. Her Latin was not very good, and she was very humble about it, and apologised for her lack of wisdom.

Julian of Norwich. 1342- c.1423.

The fourteenth century was an age when there flourished in England a number of celebrated mystics, and among them was Julian of Norwich, probably one of the greatest women mystics of all time.

She became a recluse, and was enclosed in the churchyard of the Church of St. Julian, which was under the rule of the Benedictines. She was probably getting on in years when she entered her anchorage, but the exact date is unknown. As was the custom with anchoresses, she was called by several titles, such as Dame, Lady and Mother.

Not very much is known of her life, and most of the details come from her own writings. She was the author of a book entitled "Revelations of Divine Love". In it she has written the account of sixteen visions, which she described herself as having received.

The style and manner in which Julian wrote show her to have been a highly intelligent and reasonable woman, who genuinely felt that she was telling the truth when writing down on paper what she believed she really saw. She was extremely orthodox in her faith, and well grounded in the teaching of the Church.

These showings, as they have been called, came to Julian when she was very ill on May 8th in 1373, and she thought she was lying at the point of death, and was then only in her 31st year. A priest was sent for to give her Extreme Unction. At the time of her illness it appears she had not yet become a recluse, as she was surrounded by companions and also her mother.

In her book Julian vividly and simply describes what happened to her. She insists the Revelations were not dreams as she was wide awake, and the first fifteen were revealed to her during five hours, starting at five o'clock in the morning and going on until nine o'clock, and as they appeared all the pain and misery that she had endured left her material body, leaving her with nothing but to gaze on the Passion and Glory of God, as these visions passed in front of her eyes. It was not until the next evening that she had her sixteenth revelation, and then she realised that what she was being shown was the great Lasting Love and Goodness of God.

There are two versions of the book, one very much longer than the other, and Julian mentions that she wrote it, probably the longer version, twenty years after she had received the revelations, and when she had had time to meditate on her experiences. She felt that she was compelled to write and tell the world the unique things that she had seen; not for her own glory, but so that she would not be the only one to benefit from such a wonderful vision of the sight of God. It is reasonable to date the book to the year 1393, and to this day in the twentieth century, nearly six hundred years after it was written, it is still read with immense pleasure.

At that time, 1393, she may have been enclosed in her cell at Norwich. Some of these dwellings where recluses lived were quite comfortable and consisted of more than one room. They were not the living death or hole in the ground, so often conjured up in the modern mind when one thinks of these medieval mystics. It is known that the Lady Julian was visited by several people seeking her advice, and one of these was Margery Kempe, who wrote a book describing her interview with the anchoress.

The Lady Julian is also mentioned in several wills; it was a custom to leave money to these anchoresses, asking them to pray for the souls of the donors. In one of these wills, dated 1416, Julian is called the "Recluse atte Norwyche", so we know that she was still alive at that date, when she was well on into her seventies. The date of her death has been given as c.1423.

Katherine Audley. 14th century.

According to a legend quoted by Baring-Gould, there lived at Ledbury at the end of the fourteenth century a holy woman whose name was Katherine Audley, and she was called St. Katherine. He is not at all clear as to who she was.

In the Close Rolls of Edward II in the Public Record Office, it is stated that a large annuity was given to "Katharine de Audele" described as the "Recluse of Ledebury".

Baring-Gould in his "Lives" wonders why she was given so munificient a grant, as he suggests she was a lady who had lands and wealth, and he goes on to quote from another Close Roll of Edward II, "Katharine de Audeleie granted to James de Ferrers and Ela his wife, her daughter, the castle and town of Thlanandeuery". Then he says, having settled her daughter comfortably, the lady would seem to have adopted the profession of a recluse.

From these Rolls we know the fact that she was a recluse during the reign of Edward II, 1307-1327. There was a Lady Audley of Helegh who lived at that time, and whose mother was Lady Maud de Longespée, whose first husband's mother was named Ela; Katherine Audley may have named her daughter after this Ela, who was considered a saint and founded the Abbey of Lacock.

The following information I quote from "Burke Extinct and Dormant": "In 1271 Maud de Longespée, widow of William Longespée, son of William Earl of Salisbury, and Ela his wife, having by letter complained to the King (Henry III) that John Giffard had taken her by force from her manor house, and carried her to his Castle of Brimsfield, where he kept her under restraint, he was summoned before the King, when denying the charge, but confessing his marriage to the lady without the royal license, he made his peace by paying a fine of 300 marks.

The Lady Maud had three daughters; by William de Longespée she had Margaret, commonly called Countess of Salisbury, ...By John Giffard, Lady Maud had Katherine, who

married Nicholas Aldithely, or Audley, 1st Baron Audley of Helegh
. . . ."

This Katherine, Lady Audley of Helagh was most probably the "Recluse of Ledbury".

There are legends about Katherine Audley, and according to one she was told that she should go to a spot where she could hear the bells ring of themselves. Accompanied by her maid she found it at Ledbury, and there she became a recluse.

One day her mare with its colt was stolen, and she prayed that she might be able to find it by following the tracks of its feet. The tracks went across a brook, the thief hoping that they would be lost in the stream, but the imprints were left on the stones under the water, and so the thief, who turned out to be the maid, was discovered. These marks on the stones were shown until recently, and the legend that they were made by a mare's feet was firmly believed by the local people.

St. Lioba (Leofgyth). Died c.779, September 28th. R.M.

She was one of the leading women whom St. Boniface asked to leave her monastery in England and to go abroad to Germany to assist him in his missionary work. She was a relation of his, and he had known her when she was young before he left his home in the west country to go to the continent.

Lioba's father was named Dynna and her mother Ebba. Both were advanced in age when their daughter was born. According to tradition, her mother had a dream before the birth. In quite a number of these saint's lives some tale is told about a miraculous happening before they were born. In this dream, Ebba found a bell of the church. As she drew it out, it was ringing. When she awakened she told her nurse, and the nurse prophesied that the daughter that would be born to her would be like Samuel, whom Hannah had offered to the service of God in the temple.

Lioba was baptised Thrugeba, but was soon called Lioba, which means dear or beloved one. She was first placed in the convent of Minster in Thanet under the Abbess Eadburga. It was from there in 733 that she wrote to St. Boniface. She asked him to remember the former friendship with her father and mother, and she hoped that he would hold her in his memory. She also asked him to correct the rude style of her letter, and she sent him some verses and hoped he would help her with them. She mentioned that she had learnt the art from the Abbess Eadburga.

Later on she left Thanet and went to Wimborne: which was a double monastery ruled over by the Abbess Tetta at that time. Tetta was a great disciplinarian, keeping the women entirely separated from the men, never allowing them to have any contact with each other.

About the year 748, St. Boniface wrote to the Abbess Tetta requesting that she should send his cousin Lioba to assist him in his work of the evangelising of the pagan Germans. St. Boniface made Lioba the Abbess of Tauberbischofshaim near Mainz, and she became his leading woman helper.

Her Life was written by Rudolf, a monk of Fulda, which he compiled about sixty years after her death from information supplied by her nuns and pupils, who had all loved her. She was a model pattern for any abbess, tolerant and full of charity, and devoted herself to her work in a foreign land.

On his way to Friesland, St. Boniface called on her, for the last time, as he was soon afterwards martyred. He placed her and her nuns in the care of Bishop Lull, whom he wished to succeed him. He told Lioba that he hoped that after death, her body should be placed in the same grave as his own bones at Fulda.

When Lioba was old and ill she was visited by Hildegard, the wife of the Emperor Charlemagne, who had become a great friend of hers. Hildegard was shocked at her appearance, and realised that it would be the last time that she would see her. Lioba died soon after this visit, and was buried beside the body of St. Boniface at Fulda as he had requested.

St. Margaret, Queen of Scotland. Born, c. 1046. Died 1093, November 17th. Feast Day June 10th. R.M.

She was the daughter of Edward, who was the son of Edmund Ironside, King of England. Edmund had two sons, and when he was murdered and succeeded on the throne by Cnut the Dane, the children were sent into exile to Stephen King of Hungary. Edward, the second, eventually married Agatha, who was said to be the niece of the Emperor Conrad. The young couple had three children, Edgar Atheling, Christina and Margaret.

After the battle of Hastings, some of the English nobles wished to place the young Atheling on the throne. He was the only remaining male left of the old royal Saxon family. He came to England with his mother and sisters to claim the throne, but William of Normandy proved too powerful.

There are two accounts of what happened to the family; one, that Margaret with her mother and brother were taken to Scotland by Earl Gospatrick when they were fleeing from the wrath of William, and they sought refuge with Malcolm, King of Scotland.

The other account says that Malcolm, while he was harrying the north of England, found the royal refugees on board ship at the mouth of the river Wear and offered them a welcome in his kingdom. They sailed up the east coast to Scotland, where he found them when he returned. It was then that he offered to marry Margaret.

Malcolm was the third of that name, and was known as Malcolm Canmore. He was the son of Duncan, who was murdered by Macbeth. Margaret was twenty four years of age when they married. The marriage took place in the royal castle of Dunfermline, and there she was crowned queen of Scotland in 1070. History says that she brought a great fortune to her husband, including the famous Black Cross, or Black Rood of Scotland, which was said to have a piece of the True Cross set in an ebony crucifix. It disappeared at the time of the Reformation.

The royal couple had eight children, six sons and two daughters. Three of the sons succeeded to the throne of Scotland, Edgar, Alexander and David, in that order. One of the daughters, Maud (Edith) married Henry I of England.

Margaret had a great influence for good over her husband: she softened his nature and calmed the ferocity of his temper, especially in works of justice and mercy. It was not only in her husband that she made great improvements but in the character of the whole state of the Scottish nation. She did her best to raise the standard of living among the poor. We read of her piety and of how she spent long hours in prayer, but she did far more in a practical way, and by her example; she fed any she found starving, she adopted orphans, she released captives and assisted debtors.

Many abuses that were being carried on in the church, she corrected. She saw that the holy days and the feast days were properly observed, and that a fast was kept during Lent.

The great Church of the Holy Trinity at Dunfermline was built by this queen. It became the burial place for several of the Scottish kings and queens, including Robert the Bruce. St. Margaret also refounded the monastery of Iona.

Malcolm and one of his sons were killed at Alnwick in Northumberland while besieging the castle in 1093. The queen at the time was very ill, and she died four days after her husband. Her life was written by Theodoric, a monk of Durham, who was with her in her last illness. She asked him to remember her in his prayers, and to look after her children and teach them to fear and love God. She died on the sixteenth of November, and was canonised in 1251, when her feast day was moved to June the tenth. She was buried in the Church at Dunfermline, and the bodies of her husband and son were removed from Tinmouth to be placed beside her.

At the Reformation their remains were rescued from the mob and taken by Philip II of Spain to Spain, and placed in a chapel in the Escurial. Over their graves is the Inscription —

St. Malcolm King, and St. Margaret Queen.

Butler, in his *Lives of the Saints* says that the head of St. Margaret was taken separately to Douay and kept in the church there in a silver case.

St. Margaret Clitherow. Born 1556, Died 1586, March 25th.
She was the youngest daughter of Thomas and Jane Middleton of York. All the family were parishioners of St. Martin's church in Coney Street, whose vicar had great sympathy with those who still wished to follow the old faith, but trying to conform to the authority of the land, he found it difficult to keep a foot in both camps.

Margaret's father was a wax chandler and had vested interest in the continuance of the old Catholic services. When Elizabeth I came to the throne, he had to suppress his feelings, but in his will he asked for prayers for his soul, which were not allowed in the reformed religion. He died in 1567 when Margaret was eleven years old. Four months after his death, his wife Jane married Henry May, who was an innkeeper and a very ambitious man.

At the age of fifteen in 1571, Margaret married John Clitherow, a butcher, and much older than she was. They went to live in the Shambles in York, and as her husband away a great deal, Margaret had charge of the shop.

She was said to be a lovely woman, skilled in all housewifery, duties and nursing, with a sharp and ready wit and possessed of an unconquerable gaiety, and very popular with her neighbours.

In 1572, Thomas Percy, 7th Earl of Northumberland, was publicly executed in York for refusing to conform to the reformed religion. His martyrdom for the old faith deeply affected Margaret, and she was secretly received into the Roman Catholic Church when she was eighteen years of age. Her name was on a list of recusants who refused to attend the services of the Established Church, and with some of her friends she was sent to prison.

Her house had a secret communication with the house next door, where priests and vestments for the Mass were hidden. Margaret was always very careful not to involve her husband, and he most probably knew nothing of what went on in his house and next door.

There were a great number of priests in York, who if they were caught, were put to death. Many of them were friends of Margaret's, and she often with a few other women, made a pilgrimage to the place where they suffered, and would kneel at the foot of the gallows. The route they took was over the Ouse bridge and up Micklegate; the same route, as years before they followed doing the old Mystery Plays.

She became great friends with Doctor Vavasour and his wife, and was horrified when they were arrested and she found that her stepfather was responsible. Henry May found his stepdaughter a great source of embarrassment. He was anxious to find favour with his fellow citizens because he wished to become the Lord Mayor of York, and so he did not wish for any scandal in the family. He hoped to scare her by sending officers to search her house.

In the end it was a young boy who gave away the secret of the door leading to the next house. An Act of Parliament was passed in 1585 which gave the death penalty to anyone who harboured priests, and although no priest was found in Margaret's house, the authorities were suspicious and arrested her.

Margaret had been in prison several times before for being a recusant, but this was the first time she had come before the judges for a crime for which the penalty was death if she was found guilty. She was accused of having "harboured and maintained Jesuit and seminary priests, traitors to the Queen's Majesty and her Laws", and when asked whether she was guilty, she realised that whatever she said she must not involve her neighbour. She kept her wits and thought to herself that these priests were not traitors, and so she answered, "I know no offence whereof I should confess myself guilty". Then she was told that they knew that she had harboured priests, but she maintained that she had not, knowing that the priests had been in her neighbour's house. The judge asked her how she would be tried, and she answered, "having made no offence, I need no trial".

She realised that whatever she said the judges were determined to sentence her to death. But it was suggested to her that she might save herself if she gave away the names of her friends and would consent to attend the reformed church. Whatever happened to her she felt she must save her neighbours, and so in the end this saint really gave her life for her friends. She was sentenced to a most cruel and horrible death, and on March 25th, she was crushed to death between heavy stones. She was one of the "Forty Martyrs" selected for canonisation and on October 25th 1970, four hundred years after her death, she was canonised.

Her son Henry, who had been sent abroad to be educated, became a priest and her daughter Ann, a nun.

Margaret Plantagenet (Pole) Countess of Salisbury. Born 1473. Died 1541 May 28th.

The last of the Plantagenets. She was great granddaughter of Edward of Langley, 1st Duke of York — (5th son of Edward III). Her father was George, Duke of Clarence (murdered in the Tower, 1477), brother of Edward IV. Her mother was the Lady Isabel Neville, daughter of Richard, Earl of Warwick and Salisbury, son and heir of Alice, daughter of Thomas Montacute, Earl of Salisbury.

In 1499, Lady Margaret's brother, Edward Plantagenet, was executed on Tower Hill by Henry VII, and she petitioned Parliament to be restored to the honours of her maternal family, whereupon in 1513 she became Countess of Salisbury in her own right.

She married in 1494 Sir Richard Pole K.G. (died 1514), son of Sir Jeffrey Pole, Kt. of Bucks, and his wife Edith, daughter of Sir Oliver St. John, and aunt of Henry VII.

The Countess was one of Catherine of Aragon's chief friends among the nobility of England. In 1525, Princess Mary, aged 9, was separated from her mother and sent to Ludlow Castle, accompanied by the Countess of Salisbury as governess. When Mary was ill treated by her father, Henry VIII, the Countess always supported and comforted the princess, and this caused her to be dismissed from the post of governess.

Henry was afraid of the Countess, partly because he was suspicious of anyone who might have a prior claim to the throne and also because she refused to acknowledge him as supreme head of the church, and supported Queen Catherine in her fight against the divorce.

Thomas Cromwell, when he became Henry's chief minister, to please his master, worked to bring about her downfall. He was able to do this through the activities of her sons.

Margaret had four sons, and to understand how their deeds eventually destroyed her, it is necessary to give a brief account of each one:—

1. Henry Pole, given the title of Lord Montacute in 1522 by Henry VIII and created Baron in 1533. Allied himself with those who took part in The Pilgrimage of Grace, 1536–7, and was accused by his own brother, Sir Jeffrey Pole, of a design to elevate his youngest brother, Reginald Dean of Exeter, to the throne. He was convicted of high treason and beheaded on Tower Hill in 1539.

2. Sir Jeffrey Pole was taken to the Tower, and there put under pressure and made wild accusations against his brother and his mother. He received sentence of death himself, which was however not carried out.

3. Arthur, the third son does not seem to have joined with his brothers in any conspiracy at that time, but he was charged in the reign of Elizabeth, with plotting for the release of Mary, Queen of Scots, and was sentenced to death, but the execution was not carried out, by reason of his near alliance to the crown.

4. Reginald, who was made Dean of Exeter by Henry VIII, went abroad when the king abolished Papal Authority in 1534, and because he refused to return to England, he was declared a traitor, and divested of his deanery. In 1536 the Pope made him a Cardinal, and when Queen Mary ascended the throne in 1553, he returned to England, had his attainder reversed, and became Archbishop of Canterbury in 1556, and in 1558 he died.

The Countess of Salisbury was accused of assisting her sons, but she denied it. Copies of Papal Bulls were found in her house, probably placed there by her enemies, and she is said to have scorned the accusation of conspiracy. She was arrested and sent to the Tower. The Earl of Southampton, who visited her in prison, admired her courage and said: "We may call her rather a strong and constant man than a woman".

The king became exasperated with her, longing to be rid of her, and so an opportunity was seized upon to destroy the only remaining branch of Plantegenets in this illustrious lady, and who would rather suffer death than give up her old faith. In 1540, her ladyship was condemned to death, unheard by Parliament, and beheaded on Tower Hill on May 27th 1541.

The Countess of Salisbury was beatified by Pope Leo XIII in 1886.

St. Margaret Ward. Died August 30th 1588.
She lived at Congleton in Cheshire.

She visited a priest, Father Watson, in Bridewell prison, and took pity on him and tried to help him; she felt all his friends had deserted him. She made friends with the gaoler's wife, and thus was able to get into the prison. At first she was very careful, as on entering she was searched, but finding nothing on her, the authorities gradually ceased to bother about her and grew careless. That was what she had been aiming for, and she then seized the opportunity to smuggle in a rope, with which the priest managed to escape from the goal. Unfortunately he left the rope behind, and Margaret was immediately suspected of being responsible, and was arrested.

Her punishment was very cruel; she was put into irons and hung up by her hands and beaten. This continued for eight days. When she was tried, she said she never repented anything less "than the delivery of that innocent lamb from the hands of those bloody wolves." She refused a pardon which would be given to her if she would go to a protestant church. In the end she was executed at Tyburn.

She was one of the Forty Martyrs who were canonised on October 25th 1970.

St. Merwenna. 5th century. May 13th. A.C.
She was the saint of Marhamchurch, near Bude in Cornwall.

One of the twenty-four daughters of Brychan of Brechnock.

St. Merwenna. Died c.970, May 13th. A.C.
She became Abbess of Romsey in Hampshire, after it was remodelled by King Edgar in 967. She was probably British, but there is no further information given about her.

St. Milburga. Born c.662. Died 722, February 23rd. R.M.
The eldest daughter of Merewald of Mercia and St. Domneva of Thanet, and great-great-granddaughter of Ethelbert King of Kent. From a very early age she had dedicated herself to the service of God. She founded a monastery for virgins at Much Wenlock in Shropshire and was consecrated as abbess by Theodore of Canterbury. She is said to have had the gift of working miracles, such as giving sight to the blind and raising the dead to life. There is a tale that one day a woman brought her dead child and besought the saint to restore him to life. St. Milburga told the woman that she should submit to the Divine Will, and said "Go and bury thy dead". But the woman was very persistent, and so Milburga knelt by the child and prayed. Immediately fire appeared to descend from heaven, and all those nuns who were in the vicinity were terrified. But the fire suddenly disappeared and St. Milburga rose from her knees and restored the child alive to his mother.

A son of a neighbouring king wished to marry Milburga and planned to carry her off by force. When she was visiting a village now called Stoke St. Milburga, he pursued her, but she fled from him, and as she crossed a stream, the waters rose so high that he was unable to follow her.

At Stoke St. Milburga there is a well which, legend says, appeared when she commanded her horse to strike his hoof upon a rock, and immediately water flowed, where before there had been a shortage of water, and the local people had begun to suffer from the drought. From that time the waters of the well flowed on increasingly and never dried up, and many ailments were cured by its miraculous properties.

St. Milburga seems to have had an exceptionally lovable character; even the birds of the air loved and obeyed her.

In her last illness she called all her nuns to her bedside and advised them to choose as her successor the most pious of their sister nuns, and told them always to remember the two sentences: — "Blessed are the pure in heart, for they shall see God," and "Blessed are the Peacemakers, for they shall be called the children of God."

The monastery of Much Wenlock was destroyed by the Danes in the 9th century. It was restored many years later, and in 1084 Cluniac monks took over the building. They discovered in the foundations of where the altar once stood, some human bones, and in the tomb where they reposed a wonderful fragrance issued forth. They were presumed to be the relics of St. Milburga. In 1501 they were enclosed in a chest and placed in a prominent position. They disappeared in the time of Henry VIII.

I have found three churches dedicated to St. Milburga, in the dioceses of Coventry, Hereford and Worcester.

St. Mildgytha. Died c.676, January 17th. A.C.

She was the youngest sister of St. Mildburga and St. Mildred. Nothing much is known about her except that she became a nun and entered a convent, probably Thanet. It is said she migrated to a convent in Northumbria, where she died, but Butler says she retired to the monastery of Estrey, which, he says, was built by King Egbert of Kent, and that it was there she died.

St. Mildred. Died c.700 (or 725). February 20th, or July 13th.

The second of the three daughters of Abbess Domneva of Thanet. She was sent by her mother to Chelles in France to be educated. The abbess there did her best to persuade her from taking the veil, and threatened her with all kinds of ill treatment, as she wished to compel Mildred to marry one of her relations. But St. Mildred stood out against such a proposal, and escaped back to England, where she received the veil from Archbishop Theodore of Canterbury.

When her mother retired, she took over the government of the Abbey of Minster in Thanet.

St. Mildred became one of the most popular saints in South East England, even though not very much is known about her life. There do not seem to have been any miraculous tales told about her, as with a great number of other saints who lived at that time. Her popularity in Kent was even greater than St. Augustine's, and the rock on which he first stepped ashore, is called St. Mildred's Rock.

Soon after she died her body was translated to Canterbury. There is some confusion about which is the date of her death. It was probably February 20th, and July 13th the date when she was translated to Canterbury. Later her body was removed to Holland, and recently part of her relics have been brought back to Minster in Thanet.

Seven churches are named after St. Mildred, three dedications in the Diocese of Canterbury, two in London, one in Southwark, and one in Portsmouth.

St. Modwenna. Died c.695, July 6th. A.C.

She was Irish in origin, but I have included her as she founded monasteries in Great Britain as well as in Ireland. She was the daughter of Mochta, Prince of the Sept of the Conalls.

The Irish King Conall wished to make a present to Aldfrith, son of King Oswy of Northumbria. While his brother , Ecgfrith, was alive, Aldfrith had been living in Ireland, but on his brother's death, he was recalled to Northumbria to ascend the throne. Conall told one of his nobles to go and rob a church; the noble happened to choose a monastery of St. Modwenna, and Conall gave King Aldfrith the spoils.

St. Modwenna is said to have taken ship in pursuit of her property, and crossed over to England, and she found Aldfrith at Whitby. He promised to return all her possessions, but first he placed her in the Abbey at Whitby to instruct his sister Aelfflaed in the Rule of St. Benedict.

Baring-Gould says St. Modwenna succeeded St. Hilda as Abbess of Whitby, but Bede states that Aelfflaed succeeded St. Hilda as second abbess, and he never mentions St. Modwenna.

This is the St. Modwenna, who is most likely to have founded monasteries in Scotland and Burton-upon-Trent, not the following saint of the same name. The young child, St. Osyth, was placed in the care of the abbess, probably at Burton.

St. Modwenna of Polesworth. Died c.900. A.C. July 5th.

She is given the title "of Polesworth" to distinguish her from the other St. Modwenna, who lived about two hundred years earlier; their two lives are hopelessly confused.

This saint came from Ireland and was the daughter of the King of Connaught. She was very skilled in healing all manners of diseases.

King Egbert of Wessex sent his son, Arnulf, who was a leper to her and she cured him. Whereupon King Egbert invited her to England, and she is said to have become Abbess of Polesworth. That he sent his daughter Edith to be in her charge certainly is a myth, because Edith of Polesworth was the daughter of Edward the Elder.

Butler says this saint established two nunneries in Scotland, one at Stirling and the other in Edinburgh. He also says that she lived as an anchorite on an island in the river Trent, but Baring-Gould says this is a mistake; it was the other St. Modwenna who founded nunneries in

Scotland, and whose remains were placed in the Abbey of Burton-upon-Trent.

St. Modwenna. 5th century. July 6th or 8th?

She was one of the family of King Brychan of Brecknock, and came to Cornwall from Wales. She settled on the high cliffs on the north Cornish coast near Bude. The village of Morwenstowe commemorates her name, and her remains are supposed to lie there.

St. Nennoc (Nennocha). Died 467, June 4th. A.C.

Legend says she was the daughter of King Brychan, who, when his other children had all left him, promised all his gold and land to God if he would give him another child. His wife, Menedue then had a daughter who was christened Nennoc.

When she was fourteen, a Prince of Ireland sought her hand in marriage but she, being influenced by St. Germanus, Bishop of Auxerre, was longing to embrace the religious life. St. Germanus had come to Britain to fight against the heresy of Pelagianism. When he returned to Gaul, St. Nennoc followed him with a number of those who wished to join her, including four bishops, several priests and virgins. They eventually arrived in Brittany, where Nennoc was given some land at a place called Ploermel.

There she founded a large monastery, and passed the rest of her life within its walls.

St. Non (Nonnita, Nonna). 5th-6th century, March 3rd. A.C.

Mother of St. David. Her father was Gynyr of Caer Gawch in Pembrokeshire, and she is said to have been a granddaughter of King Brychan of Brecknock.

In the Life of St. David by Rhygyfaech, written in 1090, it is recorded that she was a nun at a convent at Ty Gwyn which was situated near the present city of St. Davids. A young prince named Sandde, grandson of Ceredig of the House of Cunedda, was so smitten by her beauty that he seduced her. This happened about the year 520.

When the time drew near for the birth of her child, she withdrew to a lonely place, high above the cliffs overlooking the sea near St. Davids. Here there was a circle of prehistoric standing stones. A violent thunderstorm was raging overhead, but inside the stone circle the sun shone. St. Non lay down under one of the great standing stones, and as she lay there a sudden flash of lightning split the stone in two. One half was hurled right over her head and landed at her feet, where it stood upright. She suffered no harm, but in her agony she gripped the stone so hard that her hands left their imprint on its surface. This stone was afterwards made the foundation stone of the altar for a chapel which was erected on this spot, the ruins of which can still be seen. Near by is a well which bears her name. Her child was christened David, who became the patron saint of Wales.

It is said that afterwards St. Non "continued in chastity of body and mind and led a most faithful life". From Wales she went to Cornwall where two churches are dedicated to her: Altarnum and Bradstone. There is also a well at Altarnum and one at Pelynt which bears her name. At Bradstone there is a local legend that she was martyred by Druids on a large stone, which was part of a cromlech.

St. Non is patroness of Dirinon in Brittany, where she founded a retreat and the local legend says she died there. A miracle play is performed in her honour, and a rock is shown there with the imprint of her knees. There is in the church at Dirinon a tomb, which is said to be St. Non's and it shows a representation of her trampling on a dragon and holding a book in her hand. But Altarnum in Cornwall also claims that her grave is there.

St. Osythe. Died c.675, October 7th. A.C.
She was the daughter of Frithewald, who, according to one account, was a Mercian prince who assisted St. Erconwald, Bishop of London, in founding the monastery of Chertsey in 675. Another account gives Osythe's father as Frithwald or Redwald, the first Christian King of East Anglia. St. Osythe's mother was Wilteburg, a daughter of Penda, King of Mercia.

When Osythe was a young child she was put into the care of St. Modwenna. Capgrave says St. Modwenna of Polesworth, but he has confused the saints; the saint of that name of Polesworth lived two hundred years later than St. Osythe. It must have been St. Modwenna of Burton-upon-Trent into whose care she was placed. There is also confusion about the story of St. Osythe being nearly drowned crossing a footbridge and falling into the water. She was said to have been taking a book to the abbess, having being told to by either St. Edith or St. Aelfflaed. St. Edith's date is certainly wrong, and there is no record of St. Aelfflaed being at Burton.

When later on St. Osythe returned to her parents, she was betrothed to Sighere, King of the East Saxons. She had a desire to live a religious life, but her parents were determined on the marriage. During the wedding feast a magnificent stag was seen bounding past the hall. King Seghere was a great sportsman and the temptation was so great that he immediately left the banquet, and went in pursuit of the stag. St. Osythe, taking advantage of his absence, fled with some of her maids, and took refuge with Bishop Acca of Dunwich and Bishop Bedwin of Elmham. From these two bishops she received the veil.

King Sighere, realising that she was bent on becoming a nun, gave her land at Chich, which was situated at the mouth of the river Colne. There in 673 St. Osythe founded a monastery. Chich is now called St. Osythe's.

St. Osythe is said to have been martyred by Danish pirates, and according to Butler in his lives of the Saints, they were led by Hinguar and Hubba in 870. That is certainly incorrect as she died about the year 675.

Who ever the pirates were, they cut off the saint's head, because she refused to worship their gods. The tale says she took up her head and walked about a third of a mile with it to the church door, and there she collapsed. On the spot where she suffered a fountain of clear water gushed forth. There is a fountain in a wood, known as the Nun's Wood, which in an Essex tradition is said to be the scene of her martyrdom.

For fear of the pirates, her parents took her body to Aylesbury. Forty six years later it was taken back to Chich and placed in the church of St. Peter and St. Paul, which she had built. The monastery and church were destroyed in the later Danish invasions. The present parish church is built on the site of the original church, and is dedicated to St. Peter and St. Paul and St. Osythe.

There are several local traditions; one is that one night in each year, probably October 7th, the saint visits the scene where she was killed, carrying her head in her hands; another relates that the inhabitants, when they raked out their fires at night before going to bed, made a cross in the ashes and called on God and St. Osythe to protect them from fire and water and all evil things.

There is also a tale told by the chronicler, Matthew Paris, about a man named Thurcillus, who lived in Tidstude in Essex; he was taken

75

into purgatory, then into hell and finally into paradise, and when he arrived at the most holy place of all in paradise, he saw St. Catherine, St. Margaret and St. Osythe.

St. Pandwyna. Died c.904, August 26th. A.C.

She was born in Scotland or Ireland, and was the daughter of a petty prince. Her father wished to arrange a marriage for her, but she was against it, as she wished to devote her life to the service of God in some religious order. She fled to Cambridge and took refuge with a kinswoman of hers, the Prioress of Ettisley. There she became a nun and lived a holy life, and her companions regarded her as a saint. When she died, she was buried near a well, which is said still to bear her name. The nunnery was eventually destroyed by the Danes. In the fourteenth century the saint's body was dug up and translated to the parish church.

St. Pega (Pee). Died c.719, January 8th. A.C.

Daughter of a Mercian nobleman named Penwahl, who had royal blood in his veins, being descended from Icles, great-great-great-grandfather of Penda, King of Mercia. Penwahl married a young girl of a Mercian noble family, named Tette. The couple had a son named Guthlac and a daughter named Pega.

Guthlac was about twenty six when he retired to a lonely spot called Croyland in the marshy fens of Lincolnshire. His sister became a recluse and retired to a place, now called Peakirk after her, which is only about five miles from where her brother dwelt. Although they lived so close to one another, they never saw each other. It was only when Guthlac was at the point of death, and attended by a brother monk, who acted as his servant, that he asked this servant to deliver a message to his sister:— "When the spirit has left this feeble body, go to my sister Pega and tell her that I have shunned her sight in this world in order that we may see each other in eternity before Our Father, in everlasting joy. Tell her also that she should place my body in the coffin and wrap it in the muslin which Ecgburg sent me . . ."*

The faithful servant waited until Guthlac died, then he immediately took his skiff and rowed hastily to where St. Pega lived. She was very distressed when she heard the news. The next day she set off with the brother, Guthlac's servant, to Croyland, and when they arrived at the island, she spent three days praising God for her brother's wonderful

76

life and commending his soul to Heaven. Then she assisted the brother to build a sepulchre for the saint's remains in the grounds of his oratory.

Twelve months later St. Pega decided to raise her brother and place him in another tomb. King Aethelbald of Mercia had had constructed a marvellous memorial vault for the saint. Before an assembly of the great men of the Church, they raised the coffin and removed the lid, and there they found his body lying in a perfect uncorrupted condition. They were all amazed and stood speechless, not daring to take a second look, but his sister, St. Pega, took his body in her arms and reverently rewrapped it in the muslin which the Abbess Ecgburg, the daughter of King Aldulf of East Anglia, had sent him. Pega knew that she was carrying out his wishes, and when she had done so, she placed his remains in the new burial tomb.

There was a man who was the head of a household in "provincia wissa" which may be the present town of Wisbech, who had lost his sight. He despaired of being cured, until someone suggested to him that if something that had been sanctified by St. Guthlac might touch his eyes, he might be cured. His friends took him in a boat to the island of Croyland where they sought St. Pega, who must have lived then in residence there. She was impressed with the man's great faith and took him to where the body of St. Guthlac lay. Taking a lump of salt which the saint had once consecrated, she scraped a bit into holy water, and slowly let it fall drop by drop into the eyes of the blind man. He was from then on fully cured of his blindness.

The above is a story of a devoted brother and sister who both gave their lives to the service of God.

St. Pega, at the end of her life made a pilgrimage to Rome, where she died. The Church at Peakirk in Northamptonshire is dedicated to her.

Life of St. Guthlac by Felix. Ed. C. W. Jones.

RECLUSES.

The name recluse was usually applied to those solitaries who were enclosed in their cells and gave up social contact with the world, apart from maintaining the necessities of life and receiving visitors for counsel, while those who were called hermits were freer to roam about from one remote place to another. Nearly all the female solitaries were recluses, and were sometimes called anchoresses.

The Reclusorium or Anchorhold was usually attached to a church and often situated in a churchyard. On the whole it was a quite comfortable dwelling and sometimes consisted of several rooms with a servant to wait on the recluse and to buy the necessary provisions.

Extreme austerity was discouraged, and Bishop Poore of Chichester and later Salisbury, who died in 1237, drew up a rule called "Ancren Riewle", by which the recluse should live. Their time was to be fully occupied with their prayers for a great part of the day, and the rest of the time with reading, writing, illuminating and needlework. Occasionally they were visited from outside by people asking for their prayers and advice. All contact with the outer world was made through a small window. Many of these women were left legacies in wills, and in the following list of female recluses I have added the amount of money that some of them received from different benefactors, on condition that the recluse would pray for the donor's soul. In many cases we have only the names and nothing else of the recluses, and in some, we only know that there was a recluse attached to a certain churchyard and we do not know the name.

This list is certainly not complete; there are bound to be many more women who lived this sort of life that we have never heard of.

Lucy de Newchurch — recluse in churchyard of St. Brendon, Bristol. Enclosed by order of Bishop William of Wykham in 1403.

Kathleen Audley — recluse at Ledbury. (See Life).

Isabella — recluse in churchyard of Holy Trinity, Lincoln, left in wills: 1374 — 12d, 1383 — 13s 4d, 1391 — 20s.

Matilda — recluse who later occupied the cell of the above in Lincoln, was left 15s 17d in will.

Dame Julian — recluse in churchyard of St. Julian's, Norwich. (See Life). Died c.1423.

Dames Agnes — recluse in churchyard of St. Julian's, Norwich in 1472.

Dame Elizabeth Scott — recluse in churchyard of St. Julian's, Norwich in 1481.

Lady Elizabeth — recluse in churchyard of St. Julian's, Lincoln in 1510.

Lady Joan — recluse in St. Edward's churchyard, Norwich; left legacy of 20s. and 40d to each of her servants.

Dame Anneys Kite — recluse in St. Edward's churchyard, Norwich in 1458.

Recluse (Name unknown) — in same cell as above, in 1516 left legacy by Margaret Norman.

Lady Emma — recluse under chapel of the Holy Cross in Monastery of the Carmelites in Norwich in 1442.

Anchoress of Nottingham (Name unknown) — in 1463 received 6s.5d from will of Sir Hugh Willoughby.

Ella — recluse at Massingham, Norfolk, niece of Walter de Suffield, Bishop of Norwich.

Isolda de Hungerford — recluse at St. Romauld, Shrewsbury in 14th c.

Emma Sprenghose — recluse at St. George's Chapel, Shrewsbury in 1310.

Three female recluses of York —

One in churchyard of St. Helens, in Fishergate.

One in churchyard of All Saints, North Street.

One in churchyard of St. Margaret's.

Each of them were left legacies from several wills: 10s in 1433, 5 marks in 1435, and another will in 1433, 2s each.

There were several other recluses in Yorkshire; one at Beston, one at Pontefract, and a Lady Agnes at Thorganby and Dame Margaret of Anderby near Richmond.

ROYAL NUNS.

The following list gives the names and parentage of those members of the Royal family since the time of William I, who became nuns.

William I — 1066–87, married Matilda, daughter of Baldwin V, Count of Flanders.

Cecilia — eldest daughter, became Abbess of the Benedictine Convent of the Holy Trinity at Caen, 1112. Died in 1126.

Adela — 5th daughter, married Stephen, Count of Blois and Chartres, who was killed at battle of Ascalon in 1102, and then she became nun in the Convent of Marsigny, and died in 1137. Her 3rd son was Stephen, King of England.

Henry I — 1100–1135, married Matilda (Edith), daughter of Malcolm III and Queen Margaret of Scotland.

Isabella — wife of William Atheling, son of Henry I, and who was drowned in the White Ship in 1119, and then Isabella became Abbess of Fontevrault and she died there in 1154. She was the daughter of Fulk, 5th Count of Anjou, and 1st King of Jerusalem.

Stephen — 1135–1154, married Matilda, Countess of Mortain and Boulogne, daughter of Eustace III, Count of Boulogne, and of his wife, Mary, daughter of Malcolm III of Scotland.

Mary — 2nd daughter, Abbess of Romsey till 1159. Married Matthew I of Alsace, Count of Mortain and Boulogne. This marriage was annulled on grounds of her vows of chastity in 1169. She then returned as a nun to the Convent of St. Austrebert at Montreuil.

Henry III — 1216–1236, Married Eleanor, 2nd daughter, and co-heiress of Raymond Berengar IV, Count of Provence.

Eleanor — after the king's death took the veil at Amesbury and died there a nun in 1291.

Isabel — great-granddaughter of above, became abbess of Amesbury about 1325.

Edward I — 1272–1307, married Eleanor, daughter of Ferdinand III of Castil.

Mary — 4th daughter, born 1279, became a nun at Amesbury and Fontevrault.

Edward III — 1327–1377, married Philippa, daughter of William, Count of Holland and Hainault.

John of Gaunt, 4th son of Edward III.

Joan, John of Gaunt's youngest daughter, married Ralph Neville 1st Earl of Westmorland, K.G.

Cecily — Joan and Ralph Neville's daughter, born 1415, married Richard, 3rd Duke of York, K.G., grandson of Edmund of Langley, 1st Duke of York (5th son of John of Gaunt); Richard and Cecily were therefore 1st cousins. Richard fell at the battle of Wakefield in 1460.

Cecily became a Benedictine nun, and died in 1495. Her third son was George, Duke of Clarence, whose daughter was Margaret, Countess of Salisbury, the last of the Plantagenets, and who was beheaded by Henry VIII.

Thomas of Woodstock, Duke of Gloucester, 6th son of Edward III married **Eleanor**, daughter and co-heiress of Humphrey de Bohun, Earl of Hereford, Essex, and Northampton. She became a nun at Barking after the death of her husband in 1397, and she died in 1399.

Isabel — their youngest daughter, became a nun.

Edward IV — 1461–83, married Elizabeth, widow of Sir Thomas Grey of Croby, and daughter of Sir Richard Woodville — their two sons murdered in the Tower.

Bridget — their youngest daughter born 1480, became a nun and then Prioress at Dartford in Kent, and died 1517.

James VI — of Scotland and I of England, married Anne, daughter of Frederick II, King of Denmark.

Elizabeth — their daughter, married Frederick V, Elector Palatine of the Rhine and King of Bohemia.

Elizabeth — their eldest daughter became Abbess of Hervorder. She died 1680.

Louise Hollandine — 2nd daughter, became Abbess of Maubisson, died 1709.

St. Sexburga. Died c.699, July 6th. A.C.

The eldest of the four saintly daughters of King Anna of East Anglia. She married King Ercombert, grandson of Ethelbert, the first Christian King of Kent, and she assisted her husband to get rid of the last pagan idols which were worshipped in Kent. Two of her daughters became saints — Ermenilda and Earcongotha.

St. Sexburga's husband died after twenty four years of married life, and for four years she acted for regent for her son, Egbert. In 668, she resigned the regency and took the veil, and was consecrated a nun by Archbishop Theodore, who had only that year arrived at Canterbury.

St. Sexburga founded a monastery at Minster on the Isle of Sheppey which must not be confused with that founded by her niece, Domneva, at Minster in Thanet, which is also in Kent. At Sheppey she ruled over seventy nuns, but resigned when she heard about her sister, Etheldreda, having founded the monastery at Ely, and leaving her daughter, Erminilda as Abbess of Sheppey, she joined her sister at Ely as a simple nun. The two sisters lived together in complete harmony, each serving God to the best of their abilities.

When St. Etheldreda died, St. Sexburga succeeded her as Abbess of Ely. She ruled the monastery for twenty years. It was during that time that St. Etheldreda's body was raised to a place of honour, and found to be uncorrupted. When St. Sexburga died she was buried near the tomb of her sister, and was succeeded as Abbess of Ely by her daughter Erminilda, who followed her from Sheppey.

St. Teath. 5th century? January 15th. A.C.

The titular saint of St. Teath in Cornwall. Nothing is known for certain who she was. She may have been one of the daughters of King

Brychan of Brecknock, but it has been suggested that she was the Abbess St. Ita, who died at the great age of ninety, who founded monasteries in Ireland, and is said to have churches and chapels dedicated to her in Devon and Cornwall. St. Teath's and St. Ita's feast days are both given as January 15th.

St. Sidwell, (Sativola). 7th century? August 1st. A.C.

There does not seem to be much known about this saint, although there are churches dedicated to her in Devon and Cornwall, one in Exeter and one at Laneast. She is said to have been of British origin and to be the sister of Paulus Aurelianus, who may have founded the church of St. Paul in Exeter.

St. Sidwell is supposed to have had three sisters, Jutwara, Eadwara and Wulvella. Jutwara may be St. Julitta who has a church dedicated to her at Lanteglos-by-Camelford in Cornwall, and Wulvella may be St. Wyllow of Lanteglos-by-Fowey in Cornwall.

There is a legend that St. Sidwell suffered martyrdom at Exeter, having had her head cut off by a scythe and then thrown into a well. At Laneast there is a holy well, which is said to be hers, and which is called Jordan, and the water was used for baptisms. Her sister, Wulvella is represented in one of the church windows at this place.

St. Tegla. June 1st. A.C.

She a Welsh saint, whose day is given as June 1st, but the century in which she lived is unknown.

She was the patron saint of the church and holy well at Llandegla in Denbighshire, and the holy well was used to cure epilepsy, which was known as Tegla's evil.

St. Tetta. died c.772, September 28th. A.C.

She was the Abbess of the double monastery of Wimborne in Dorset, and is said to have ruled over five hundred nuns. She was a very strict disciplinarian, and never allowed her nuns to have any communication with any of the men in the other part of the monastery. If it was necessary to address the men, or any one from outside the enclosure for the women, the Abbess spoke to them from a small window.

There was a prioress under St. Tetta, who was extremely unpopular with the nuns, and when she died, the nuns showed no reverence for the place where she was buried. Some of the young nuns trampled down the earth which was piled over her grave. The Abbess was horrified at their behaviour, and ordered them to fast for three days and to say prayers for the repose of the prioress's soul.

St. Tetta received letters from St. Boniface in Germany, requesting her to send over nuns who would assist him on his missionary work in Germany. He especially asked for his kinswoman, St. Lioba, who was a nun at Wimborne at that time. St. Tetta was a bit apprehensive about sending her nuns abroad, but she did comply with the request and it is to her credit that the training she gave them caused them to be a great success. Among the nuns who went to Germany from Wimborne and who both became abbesses, were St. Lioba and St. Thecla.

St. Thecla. Died c.790, October 15th. R.M.
She was a nun at Wimborne under St. Tetta, and was one of those who went to assist St. Boniface in Germany. St. Boniface made her the Abbess of Kitzingen.

St. Theneva (St. Enoch). 6th century, July 18th. A.C.
With her son St. Kentigern (Mungo), she became the patron saint of Glasgow. Her father's name is given in one account as Loth, the King of the Picts, but in another, as Llewddyn Lueddog of Dinas Eiddyn (Edinburgh); these are probably different names for the same person.

Most of the tales told of St. Theneva are said to be legendary, and it is uncertain whether there is any truth in them. One such tale says that her father wished her to marry Owen, the son of Urien Rheged, a British King of the region known as Cumbria. Theneva refused to marry him, and her father, in his rage drove her away from his door. She went and lived with a swineherd, who was a Christian, and he treated her with great reverence and honour, and where she may have learnt something of his religion.

She is then said to have become pregnant by a beardless youth. It is not stated who he was, but another account gives Eugenius III, King of the Scots, as her seducer. When her father discovered what had happened to her, he ordered his servants to have her stoned, and thrown from a rock on the top of a hill. Miraculously she was uninjured, and somehow managed to escape in a coracle, and accompanied by a "Shoal of fishes, she was wafted to Culrose", and there by the seashore she gave gave birth to St. Kentigern.

In the dim light of the dawn, a bishop, St. Servan, was saying Matins in his cell, when he thought he heard the voices of angels singing. Climbing down to the shore he found St. Theneva lulling her child to sleep. The sight so affected him that he cried out, "Mochocha, Mochocha — meaning "My dear, my dear".

He took the mother and child to his cell and baptised them both, and looked after them. From then on he called the child, Mungo, which means "Dearest", and to this day St. Kentigern is called in Glasgow, St. Mungo.

For the rest of her life, St. Theneva was honoured for the devout way in which she lived and for all the charity she showed to other people. She went to Glasgow, where she died and was buried. A Church in Glasgow, dedicated to her, called St. Theneukes Kirk, has gradually become known as St. Enoch's, which is a corruption of her name. The terminus of the railway line is also called St. Enoch's.

St. Veep (Wennape, Gwenafwy). 6th century, July 1st. A.C.

The village of St. Veep in Cornwall commemorates her name, and at one time the church there was dedicated to her, but for some obscure reason in the 14th century the dedication was changed to Saints Cryiacus and Julitta.

St Veep was a daughter of Caw, a king in North Britain, who was driven south by the Picts, and settled in Wales. He had a numerous family, which was known as the Third Holy Family in Britain. St. Veep had several brothers, including Gildas, one of our first historians. Another brother, Aedan, became the Bishop of Ferne in Ireland, and another was the famous poet, Aneirin or Aneurin, who was probably the author of "The Gododdin"; some authorities say Gildas and Aneurin were the same person.

St. Veep followed two of her brothers to Cornwall, and in the village which bears her name, a feast is held every year in her honour.

The Abbess Verca. 7th century.

Bede says she was a woman of a most noble character, who ruled over a convent situated at the mouth of the river Tyne, and a great friend of St. Cuthbert of Lindisfarne.

One day St. Cuthbert visited her convent, and she gave him a magnificent welcome, and after they had feasted, and he was taking a rest, he mentioned that he was thirsty. Asked whether he would like beer or wine, he asked for water, and when it was brought to him, he blessed it and drank from the cup, and gave it back to his attendant priest. The servant who had brought the water asked if he could drink from the cup out of which the Bishop had drank, and the priest allowed him to do so, and then he also drank from it, and passed it round to those assembled there. They were all astonished, saying that they had never tasted better wine.

In the 12th century Lawson Manuscript of the Life of St. Cuthbert by the Anonymous Monk of Lindisfarne, there is an illustration of this incident; St. Cuthbert is seen receiving a cup from a man in green, and to his right the Abbess Verca is seated. This is probably the only representation there is of her.

The Abbess gave St. Cuthbert a present of a linen cloth, and he said he would keep it for his burial, and would not wear it while *he was alive, "but for the love of that highly favoured woman, who sent it to me, The Abbess Verca, I have preserved it to wrap my corpse in."

*The life of St. Cuthbert by Bede, edited by Giles in 1843.

St. Walburga. Died 779, February 25th. R.M.

She was the daughter of St. Richard, a petty nobleman of Wessex, who went on a pilgrimage to Rome; but he died at Lucca on the way there. Walburga had two brothers, Saints Willibald and Winibald, who accompanied their uncle, St. Boniface, to Germany.

St. Walburga became a nun at Wimborne in Dorset under the care of the Abbess Tetta. When St. Boniface asked the Abbess to send his nuns to assist him in his missionary work, St. Walburga was one of the number chosen to go abroad.

After she had been in Germany for two years, St. Boniface made her the Abbess of Heidenham, which had been founded by her two brothers. In 750, when her brother Winibald died, she was given overall command of the monks as well as the nuns at Heidenham.

There is one tale about Walburga having cured a girl who had a ravenous appetite by giving her three ears of corn, and the saint is often represented in art with three ears of corn, or with a flask of oil on account of the fragrant oil which was said to be distilled from her relics.

St. Walburga died about 779, and in 870 her remains were translated to Eichstadt, where cures were ascribed to the rock on which her shrine was placed. Portions of her remains were distributed to a number of churches in Belgium, Germany and other countries in Europe, and were held in great veneration.

St. Werburga. Died c.699, February 3rd. A.C.
Her name will always be associated with the city of Chester, of which city she became the patron saint.

She was the daughter of King Wulfhere of Mercia and his wife St. Erminilda. Werburga was born at Stone in Staffordshire and was the youngest of four children. She was a devout child, and even when very young assisted her mother in reading the daily Offices of the Church.

She was considered very beautiful and had a number of admirers, who sought her hand in marriage. Many of these offered her gifts which she refused, taking no interest in any of them; her mind being set on service to God. One of her suitors was a knight of the King's court named Werbode, who was a man full of corruption with sinful ideas, imagined her refusal was due to the influence of her two brothers, who had become disciples of St. Chad, Bishop of Lichfield.

Then this knight decided to murder the brothers, but before he could carry out his evil design, he himself came to a wretched end.

Weburga's father had known of the man's murderous intentions, and when he heard of his miserable death, he became conscious of his own wickedness, and he was filled with remorse. He remembered all that he had promised his wife when they first married, and how they were going to stamp out idolatry and to encourage their people to live better lives. To atone for his past evil ways, he contributed towards founding the great Abbey of Peterborough, and also a Priory at Stone.

While he was in a repentant mood, Werburga seized the opportunity to tell her father that she wished to become a nun and devote her life to God. When she won his consent, she decided to go to Ely, which had gained a great reputation under the Abbess Etheldreda.

The king and his whole court escorted her to Ely with great state as became a royal princess, and she was received there at the entrance by a number of nuns, singing hymns and psalms of welcome. She remained there for some years until her uncle, Ethelred succeeded to the throne of Mercia.

King Ethelred put Werburga in charge of all the religious houses in his kingdom, and he assisted her to found new convents, and he endowed them well; two were built in Staffordshire, — Trentham and Henbury, and a third at Weedon in Northamptonshire. All these houses, under her supervision were free from any vice or evil living. Werburga is said to have been the most perfect pattern of what a holy nun should be. She attended all the usual Offices and recited the whole of the Psalter daily.

At the monastery in Weedon she spent a great deal of her time within its walls. There is a story that the good farmers of Weedon complained of the ravages committed upon their cornfields by flocks of wild geese. St. Werburga called the transgressors together and banished them for ever from her precincts, and it is said no wild geese have ever been known to molest the farmers since. There stood formerly on the south side of the churchyard a chapel dedicated to St. Werburga.

She lived to a great age in spite of the rigorous life she had led, and when she knew her end was drawing near, she visited all the houses under her care. Then she retired to Trentham, where she died. Her remains were taken to Hanbury and stayed there until 708, when they were transferred to a costly shrine; it is not definitely stated where.

In 875, at the time of the Danish invasions, the nuns removed the shrine to Chester, and later the Cathedral was erected over her remains. After the Reformation the shrine was made into the episcopal throne.

St. Werburga has nine churches dedicated to her in England.

St. Wilfrida. Died c.988. A.C.

There is a great deal of confusion about the day on which she should be commemorated, but it now seems that September 9th is generally accepted as the day.

Her name is also spelt in different ways:— Wilfrida, Wulftrude, Wulfhilda, Wilfreda, Wulfruda, and Walftrudis, in different Martyrologies.

The only real facts known about her are that she had a child by King Edgar, and that she was a nun at Wilton and later became Abbess. All the rest of the tales written about her are legendary.

According to one legend, St. Wilfrida's grandfather was called Nesting. He was given this name because he was found in an eagle's nest, and was adopted by a King of Wessex and brought up at his court.

Wilfrida, when she was quite young was put into the care of the nuns at Wilton to be educated. She was known as the most lovely maiden in England, and it was said that as soon as King Edgar saw her, he fell madly in love with her, and he was determined to have her, but she wished to remain in a convent, and so tried to avoid him.

King Edgar got in touch with a kinswoman of hers, named Wenfleda, and sought her assistance to get the maiden into his power. Wenfleda invited Wilfrida to her dwelling without telling her who else would be there. She had arranged a wedding feast at which the king and his nobles would seize the girl and force her to marry the king. Wilfrida being innocent of any plans to trap her, went to her cousin's house. When she was there she was locked in a room but managed to escape by letting herself down from a window. She fled to the Convent of Werwell, where the nuns took her in for the night, and the next day she returned to Wilton.

In one story it is said that King Edgar pursued her and overtook her at the church door at Wilton, where he seized her hand and besought her to marry him, but she left her hand in his, and, it is said, fled into the church without it. He was so overcome with horror that he left Wilfrida alone, but to make up for any distress he had caused her, he endowed the Abbey of Wilton with great possessions.

In another story the king carried her off from the abbey, and became the father of her child, St. Edith, and because he had violated a consecrated maiden, St. Dunstan forbade him to wear the crown for seven years.

St. Wilfrida received the veil at Wilton from Ethelwold, Bishop of Winchester in 963, a year after the birth of her daughter, Edith. She spent the rest of her life living a holy life, and became the Abbess of Wilton. She died about the year 988, three years after her daughter's death.

St. Winefride (Wenefrida). Died c.650, November 3rd. R.M.

At a place called Holywell in Flintshire the name of St. Winefride is intimately connected, and all because of the holy well from which it derives its name. Right down through the middle ages to the present day, pilgrimages have never ceased to take place there, in spite of the authorities doing their best to suppress them since the Reformation in the sixteenth century. People still come to wash in its waters and to be cured of their ailments. It is probably the most famous holy well in

Britain.

The tales of the origin on the well are full of legends, but there is some truth in the account of St. Winefride having lived close beside it. Her father was a native of Wales named Tenyth, and her uncle was St. Beuno, who founded several monasteries in Wales. Tenyth requested St. Beuno to instruct his daughter in the Christian religion, and she became a very willing pupil. His teaching decided her to devote her life to the service of God, and her parents, with great pleasure gave their consent to her becoming a nun.

St. Beuno had built himself a cell and church near St. Winefride's home. One Sunday, while her parents and the servants were attending the church, she received an unexpected and unwelcome visitor; a youth of royal blood named Caradog arrived, and attempted to ravage her. Winefride, to escape from him, ran into an inner room and out of the back door, and fled down to the church. Caradog pursued her and reached her just as she got to the church door.

There are two different accounts of what Caradog did then; one that he wounded her with his dagger in her throat, and her blood fell on the ground and on the spot the rock opened, and a fountain of water gushed forth. The other account says that with a sweep of his sword, Caradog cut off St. Winefride's head with a single blow. Her blood stained the stones at her feet, and her head rolled to the door of the church, and a stream of water flowed over the stones. Those inside the church, hearing a commotion rushed out, and St. Beuno, seeing what had happened, picked up the maiden's head and placed it on her body, and by his prayers, her head and body became united, leaving only a faint red line. St. Beuno cursed Caradog and the earth opened and swallowed him up.

The fountain of water flowed on over the blood stained stones and ever afterwards moss grew on the side of it, and which gave off a scent of frankincense. In gratitude, Winefride promised to send St. Bueno a cloak every year which she had woven herself; she would place the cloak on a stone in the well, and the stone would carry it down the stream into the river and then out to sea and away to wheresoever St. Beuno would be living.

About this time a council of abbots and bishops was held, at which it was decided that recluses should be brought together into communities and ruled over by one head in charge of them all, so that they should live under greater discipline. Eleven virgins were put

G

under the control of St. Winefride, and they took up their abode where St. Beuno had built his cell and where the fountain gushed forth. St. Winefride eventually went to Gwytherin, which was a double monastery under the direction of Abbot Elerius, and where she ended her days as the Abbess. Her relics were translated to Shrewsbury in the twelfth century.

The fountain bubbles up into a large basin nearly twenty nine feet in diameter, covered by a Gothic porch, which was erected by Henry VII and his mother, the Countess of Richmond. The water is very clear, and the red streaked stones can be seen at the bottom of the basin.

There are several churches dedicated to St. Winefrida in England and Wales.

St. Withburga. Died c.743. March 17th and July 8th. A.C.
She was the youngest of the four saintly daughters of King Anna of East Anglia. As a child she was brought up at Holkham in Norfolk, where after her death a church was dedicated in her honour.

When her father was killed by Penda, King of Mercia in 654, she sought refuge with a few companions at a small place called Dereham in Norfolk, and there she built a nunnery. She and her nuns had hardly any possessions and lived in great poverty, and the masons who built their dwelling, had only dry bread to eat.

Withburga prayed for help, and one day she found two does drinking at a nearby stream; it seemed an answer to her prayer, for every day the does returned, and the nuns were able to be plentifully supplied with milk.

Then a disaster very nearly occurred to the small community; some evil man tried to hunt down the does with his dogs, but fortunately for the nuns, the man had an appalling accident; he broke his neck jumping a high hedge while he was pursuing the animals, and so they were saved.

Withburga lived the rest of her life in this poor and humble condition, but she was greatly honoured by the people in the surrounding countryside. This veneration continued long after her death, and two centuries later the inhabitants of Dereham fought to keep her remains in the village, when the monks of Ely wished to take them to the Abbey of Ely to place them beside the remains of her sisters, Etheldreda and Sexburga. In the end the monks had their way, and her body was translated to Ely, but where she had rested at Dereham there is a well, which commemorates her name and is known as St. Withburga's Well. As her father died in 654, and she died about 743, which is eighty nine years later, she must have been a very great age at the time of her death.

St. Wulfhilda. Died 980, September 9th. A.C.
She belonged to a noble Saxon family, which must have been very well off as she built and endowed with her own money the Abbey of Horton on her estates in Dorset. She ruled it for a time and then went to Barking in Essex as abbess of the newly restored abbey there in 970. Exactly a hundred years before the Abbey at Barking had been wrecked by the Danes, and King Edgar, probably under the guidance of St. Dunstan, was responsible for rebuilding it.

After King Edgar's death, Wulfhilda had trouble with the queen, who was stepmother of the new king, and the queen drove her out of Barking. It is difficult to find the reason why she did this to the Abbess. The queen seems to have been involved with the murder of her stepson, and perhaps Wulfhilda disapproved of her conduct. During the next reign, when Ethelred came to the throne, Wulfhilda was restored to the position of Abbess of Barking, and she died there in 980.

APPENDIX TO PART I

Noble Families whose daughters became Nuns.

Balcarres, 1st Earl Alexander, 2nd Lord Lindsay — 2nd daughter, Anne, a nun.

Beaumont, 8th Baron, Thomas Stapleton — daughter, Monica, a nun. Cousin, Winifred, a nun, O.S.B. Cousin, Mary Elizabeth, a nun, O.S.B.

John de Botetourt, 2nd Baron. d.1385 — 2nd daughter, Matilda, Abbess of Polesworth, 3rd daughter, Agnes, a nun at Elstow.

Baroness Braye, d.1809–1879 — daughter, Francis Catherine Sarah, a nun.

John de Burgh, d.1286 grandson of Earl of Kent — Daughter, Marjoree, nun at Chicksands.

Camoys, 3rd Baron Thomas Stonor — 1st daughter, Charlotte, a nun, b.1822. 5th daughter, Agnes, Prioress at St. Mary's Rugby. 7th daughter, Caroline, a nun. 9th daughter, Eleanor Lucy, a nun.

Clifford of Chudleigh, Baron Hugh. b.1663 — Three unnamed daughters, who became nuns.

Reginald de Cobham, grandson of 1st Baron Cobham of Sterborough, Kent. cr.1342 — daughter, Anne, a nun at Barking.

Devon, 7th Earl, Baldwin de Redvers — eldest daughter, Margaret, nun at Lacock.

Dinan, 2nd Baron, Josce, d.1301 — great-granddaughters, Elene and Isabel, nuns.

Ferrers, 3rd Baron, William, 1330–72 — daughter, Elizabeth, nun in Convent of Minoresses, Aldgate Without, London.

FitzHugh, 4th Baron, d.1452 — 6th daughter, Lucy, nun at Dartford.

FitzHugh, 5th Baron, Sir Henry 1430–72 — 3rd daughter Joane, nun at Dartford.

De Genevill, Peter, 2nd Baron 1307 — daughters, Isabel and Beatrice, nuns at Aconbury.

Hungerford, 3rd Baron, beheaded 1463 — daughter, Frideswide, a nun at Syon.

Kent, 2nd Earl, Thomas Holland cr. 1360 — daughter, Bridget, a nun at Barking.

Lennox, 1st Duke, Esme Stewart, Lord of Aubigny, cr. Duke in 1581 — daughter, Gabriella, a nun at Glatteny in Berry in France.

Llandaff, Earl, Matthew, cr.1797 — daughter, Frances, a nun.

Llewelyn Griffith, Prince of North Wales. m. Eleanor, d. of Simon de Montfort — daughter, Princess Gwenllian, b.1281 nun at Sempringham.

de Manny, Sir Walter, K.B.1332 K.G.1347. M. Lady Margaret Plantagenet styled Duchess of Norfolk — sister, Mary a nun. Bastard daughters, Mallosel and Malplesant, nuns.

Lord Mohun of Dunster — daughter, Elizabeth, widow of William de Montacute, 2nd Earl of Salisbury, entered the Sisterhood of the Convent of St. Albans in 1408.

2nd Baron Montacute, cr.1300 — three daughters, Elizabeth, Prioress of Haliwell, Maud, Abbess of Barking, Isabel, nun at Barking.

3rd Baron Montacute, 1st Earl of Salisbury, crowned King of Isle of Man in 1343 — two daughters, Sibyl and Margaret were nuns.

2nd Viscount Montague, Anthony-Mary Browne, m. 1591 Jane d. of Thomas Sackville, Earl of Dorset, Lord High Treasurer of England — two daughters, Anne and Lucy, nuns abroad.

Baron Mortimer of Wigmore, d.1303 — two daughters, Joan and Elizabeth, nuns.

Lord John de Mowbray, 4th Baron. d.1368 — 3rd daughter, Anne, Abbess of Barking.

Earl of Northumberland, Thomas Percy. Beheaded 1572 — 4th daughter, Mary, Prioress of English Nunnery at Brussels.

Baron Norfolk, d.1374 — cousin, Catherine de Brews, who inherited his estates, then became a nun at Dartford.

Oxford, 12th Earl, John de Vere, beheaded in 1461 — daughter, Mary, nun at Barking.

Hastings Barons, cr.1264. Henry de Hastings, d.1250 — daughters, Margery and Hillaria became nuns.

Powis, 1st Earl and Marquess — daughter Lucy, a nun at Bruges.

Richmond, Earl. John de Dreux, m. the Lady Beatrixe Plantagenet d. of Henry III — youngest daughter, Alice, Abbess of Fontevrault.

7th Baron Ros, William, Lord Treasurer of England. d.1414 — eldest daughter Beatrice, a nun.

Salisbury, Earl, William Longespée, m. Ela, who in 1226 became Abbess of Lacock — daughter, Lora, a nun at Lacock.

Savage, 1st Viscount, Thomas, cr.1626 — 5th daughter, Catherine, a nun at Dunkirk.

Stafford, Earl, Sir William Howard. Beheaded 1630 — Descendants, Anne and Anastasia, nuns about 1720.

Suffolk, 3rd Earl. d.1415. Michael de la Pole — daughter, Katherine, Abbess of Barking.

Suffolk, 1st Duke. Nephew of above John de la Pole, m. the Lady Elizabeth Plantagenet sister of Edward IV — daughter, Anne, a nun at Syon.

Suffolk, 2nd Duke, Edmund de la Pole — daughter, Anne, nun at Minoresses, Without Aldgate, London.

de Ufford. Sir Robert, brother of 1st Earl of Suffolk cr.1360 — daughter, Sybil, a nun at Barking.

Simon de Wahull. d.1195. cr. Barons in 1297 — daughters, Mary and Cicely, nuns at Godstow.

de la Warr, 7th Baron, Sir Richard West, d.1475 — daughter, Margery, a nun at Syon.

Warwick, 4th Earl, Waleran de Newburgh, d.1205 — daughter, Gundred, a nun at Pinley.

Westmorland 1st Earl, cr.1398. Ralph de Nevil, 4th Baron — daughters, Margery, Abbess of Barking and Elizabeth and Jane, nuns.

Widdrington, 2nd Baron. d.1676 — daughters, Elizabeth and Dorothy, nuns.

Widdrington, 4th Baron, William, attainted for joining 1715 rebellion — daughter, Alathea, a nun.

Winchester, 1st Earl. 2nd son Robert de Quincy, m. Princess Helen d. of Llewelyn the Great and his wife illegitimate d.*of King John* — daughter, Anne, a nun.

William de Windsore. Castellans of Windsor Castle — daughter, Margaret, a nun at Ankerwyke near Staines.

PART TWO

A GAZETTEER OF MONASTIC HOUSES FOR WOMEN

Abingdon

The foundation of this monastery in Berkshire goes back to very early times. One tradition says that it was founded by Hearne, a nephew of Cissa, a prince of Wessex about the year 605. Dugdale says the original foundation was at Helvivton, near the present town of Abingdon, where the hermit Abed dwelt. Dugdale also says that Cissa was the sister of Hearne, and she became the first Abbess of the nunnery. She obtained some nails which were used at Our Lord's Crucifixion; she placed them in a cross, and dedicated the nunnery to Holy Cross and St. Helen.

During the reign of King Offa of Mercia in 779, the nuns were dispersed and monks took their place. It was destroyed by the Danes, and later restored, and became a great Benedictine abbey for monks only. The monks discovered among the ruins of the old nunnery, the Cross with the Nails. It became known as the Black Cross, possibly having gone black with age.

Aconbury

A nunnery of the Order of St. Augustine in Herefordshire, founded in the reign of King John by the Lady Margery Lacey. There were several other benefactors — Catherine Lacy, Margaret Clifford, Sibilla Eweas and William Breuse. No names of the prioresses are recorded, but the two daughters of Peter de Genevil, who succeeded his father as 2nd Baron in 1307, were nuns there; they were Isabel and Beatrice.

At the Dissolution the nunnery was valued at £67.13.2.

Alvingham

In this village in Lincolnshire, where now stand two churches side by side in a tree fringed churchyard, and almost hidden behind a watermill and farmhouse, stood a Gilbertine priory of the 12th century. The priory contained eighty nuns and forty canons; the canons supplying the services for the nuns.

The Church of St. Mary was the Priory Church, and mentioned in a Charter of 1150. It was given some years ago to the neighbouring village of North Cockerington as their parish church. The second church, dedicated to St. Adelwold or Ethelwold, Bishop of Lindisfarne (the only such dedication in England) was the church of the village of Alvingham. This church was restored in 1933, after having been closed for a hundred years.

Amesbury

Legend puts this foundation back into the dim past, maybe sometime in the 5th century.

An old French manuscript, according to Dugdale, states that there was a noble monastery at Amesbury of three hundred monks at the time of the first coming of the Saxons. An English Chronicle states that this monastery was destroyed by the Saxons and restored by Aurelianus Ambrosius, the leader of the British people, just before the time of Arthur; Arthur may have been his nephew. The monastery was again destroyed, this time when the Danes came in the reign of King Alfred.

About the year 980, the widow of King Edgar, Alfrida (Aelfthryth) refounded Amesbury and placed nuns there. Both Archbishop Dunstan and Bishop Ethelwold trusted and thought a great deal of this Queen, and placed nearly all the nunneries founded at that time into her care. It was not until the twelfth century that the rumour started that she had had a hand in the murder of her stepson, King Edward, in 978, and that she founded Amesbury for the expiating of her sin.

When a survey of all the monasteries was taken in 1066, and their annual incomes were assessed, Amesbury's was given as £50, which was considered as being small compared to some of the other houses.

In 1177, the immoral lives of the Abbess and her nuns shocked the King, Henry II, and he had them all dispersed, the nuns to go to other monasteries and the Abbess to go to wherever she wished with a pension of ten marks. The nunnery was then made a daughter cell of the Abbey of Fontevrault, and a prioress and twenty four nuns were brought over from France to replace the former inmates.

Amesbury then prospered and became one of the richest nunneries in England. Several of the Royal family took the veil there, including Mary, 6th daughter of Edward I, Eleanor daughter of the Duke of Bretagne, and Eleanor, widow of Henry III.

Isabel, 5th daughter of Henry Plantagenet, Earl of Lancaster, son of Edmund, surnamed Crouchback and 2nd son of Henry III, became Prioress of Amesbury c.1325.

Bishop Tanner, the historian, says that Amesbury at some time before the Dissolution of the Monasteries was given the status of an Abbey, and another historian, Aubrey, says that the last Abbess of Amesbury was 140 years old when she died.

During the reign of Henry VIII, before the king broke away from the Papacy, whether from greed or to please his king, Cardinal Wolsey often calumniated nuns of any monastery from which he wished to take their property. Amesbury was one of these monasteries and the Abbess there was the only one of all the houses who stood out against the Cardinal. She wrote to the King and the Pope stating that no proof of any improper conduct could be found against her nuns, and she demanded restitution, and Wolsey had to pay a fine to the nuns.

As much as they fought against circumstances, the fate of all these houses was doomed, and in the end Amesbury had to surrender the abbey. The nuns were more fortunate than some, they did get a pension. The names of the nuns and the account that they received have come down to us, so I give them in the following list: Agatha Sydnam – £6, Anne Newman – £5, Margaret Warde – £5, Elizabeth Alleyn – £5, Elizabeth Fetyplace – £5, Anne Buckley – £5, Elizabeth Elhurst – £5, Margaret Bambridge – £5, Alice Grifford – £6, Bridget Popley – £6, Johanna Anthyll – £4, Juhanna Price – £4, Margaret Acton – £4, Dorothy Goddard – £4, Katherine Allen – £4, Sibylla Anthyll – £4.

The nuns must have been very bewildered being cast out into the world with such small pensions. Perhaps they were luckier than some who were given nothing.

Ankerwick (Anderwyke)

A Benedictine nunnery in Buckinghamshire, founded by Gilbert and Richard Munchensi, probably not long after the Conquest. Dugdale says Henry I in 1111 confirmed the grants of a Charter. In the British Museum there is a deed of one of the Mother Superiors with a seal attached, dated c.1300. Murray's Handbook of Bucks gives Anderwyke House as part of what was once the nunnery founded in honour of St. Mary Magdalen. At the Dissolution it was given to the celebrated statesman, Sir Thomas Smith, Provost of Eton. There is an immense yew tree, measuring 28 feet in girth, beneath which, according to local tradition, Henry VIII made appointment with Anne Boleyn; it was most probably at the time when the priory was still standing. The only name of a nun recorded is that of Margaret, daughter of de Winsore, who was there about 1270.

The value of this nunnery at the Dissolution was given as £52.0.7.

Arden

A Benedictine priory in Yorkshire, founded by Peter de Hoton about 1150, and confirmed by Roger Mowbray, who was Lord of the Soil. According to Dugdale it was dedicated to St. Andrew. T. Langdale, writing in 1822, says, "Not a vestige of it now remains", but a chimney stack, east of the 1700 block of a house, is reputed to be part of the priory, and there is a spring in the wood behind called the Nun's Well. Lord Mexborough of Arden Hall has a painting said to be of the last Prioress. Lids of two stone coffins in the pavement of a yard were seen in 1859.

Armethwait (Armathwaite)

A Benedictine nunnery in Cumbria. It was situated on the river Eden about nine miles south of Carlisle. According to Dugdale it was founded by William I as a pure and perpetual alms for the souls of his progenitors and all Christians.

At the Dissolution of the monasteries this house was valued at £18.8.8.

Arthington

A priory of Cluniac nuns in Yorkshire, built by Pierce of Arthington, and augmented by his son Serlo. It was founded in the reign of Richard I. Nothing much is known about the priory, but at the dissolution it was valued at £11.8.4. It was surrendered by the last and only known Prioress, Elizabeth Hall, and nine nuns on November 26th, 1540. The Prioress was given a pension of £5 p.a.

A Tudor House was built on the site of the old priory dated 1585, and no doubt some remains are incorporated in this house, which still exists.

Barking (Berecingum)

This abbey was situated in the kingdom of the East Saxons, about seven miles to the east of London. It was built by Eorcenwold (Erkenwald) for his sister, Ethelburga. There is a tale told that while it was being built, one of the beams for the roof, was found to be too short, so Eorcenwold took one end and Ethelburga the other, and together they pulled it out to the proper length.

Eorcenwold was made Bishop of London in 675, and it was before then that he founded the Abbey of Barking, and placed his sister there as the first Abbess. To assist his sister he sent for Hildelith, who had been a nun at Chelles or Brie in France, and was very experienced in the rules and regulations of monastic discipline.

During that time the plague was ravaging the country, and it attacked that part of the monastery where the monks had their quarters, and very soon their small cemetery was practically full. The Abbess and the nuns were worried about what to do if the disease spread, and where to place the victims for their final rest.

One night the whole congregation went out to pray over the tombs of their brothers, and while they were singing praises to heaven, a great and bright light suddenly descended from above, and shone over them all and the graves of their brother monks. Then it lifted and moved away, spreading its rays over the buildings, until its rays settled on some ground to the south side of the monastery. This spare piece of land was gloriously illuminated for a while, and then its brightness was withdrawn, ascending upwards from whence it came, leaving the night in darkness again. The nuns in their amazement realised that this was the ground where eventually they would lie in peace.

Ethelburga died on October 11th in the year 676. She was buried in the abbey and became its patron saint. She was succeeded as Abbess by Hildelith. Eorcenwold, the bishop died in 686, according to one authority, and in 693 according to another. He was buried in the abbey near his sister.

It was the Abbess Hildelith who corresponded with St. Aldhelm of Malmesbury. Bede says she was extremely old when she died; the date of her death has been given as c.717.

From the death of Hildelith until the coming of the Danes we do not hear of any incident during those years, nor do we know the names of the abbesses. Then in 870 the Danes arrived and destroyed the abbey. It lay in ruins for a hundred years, until the succession of King Edgar to the throne of England in 970. The king restored the abbey, and placed St. Wulfhilda from Horton in Dorset, as abbess of the newly constructed building. From then on it was a community for nuns only.

We next hear of the abbey when the Domesday Book was being drawn up; it was valued at £162, which shows that it was not as wealthy at that time as some of the other abbeys, but it seems to have recovered and became quite flourishing.

It was decided to remove the body of St. Eoreenwald from Barking for interment in the Cathedral in London. This took place in the early 12th century. Queen Matilda, the wife of Henry I, who was on a pilgrimage to the image of "Our Lady of Berkynge", joined the procession.

To travel from Barking to London it was necessary to go along the old Roman road which went from London to Colchester. This crossed the river Lea by a ford near Stratford le Bow.

While the procession was crossing the ford, the waters rose in flood and many were drowned, and the queen herself got a wetting. She then decided to build a bridge, which from its shape was always known as Bow Bridge. It stood until the year 1835. The queen also gave to the Abbess of Barking, manors and a mill for the repair of the bridge.

The church of the monastery appears to have been quite a large size, with many shrines, chantries and chapels, and nearly all the abbesses seem to have been buried there. Dugdale has given a list of their names from the year 1173, which I give below:— some giving the date of their deaths, and the site of where they were buried:— Mary; Adelicia; Christiana de Vallonis; Mabilia de Boseham, who newly dedicated her Church, and was buried there under an arch; Matilda, or Maud, said to have been King John's daughter, and she was buried in the Chapel of Salutation; Matilda de Leveland; Isabella de Morton; Isabella de Basying, died June 8th, Matildis de Grey, was buried before the Altar of the Resurrection; Anne de Vere, was buried before St. Hildelith's Shrine; Alionora de Weston before St. Ethelburga's Shrine; Isabella de Weston before the Altar of the Salutation; Matildis de Monteacuto in the Choir near the Prioresses' stall; Sibilla de Felton, died October 14th, 1404, and she was buried near St. Hildelith's Shrine, and near her sister Mary, and father and mother, Sir Thomas and Joan de Felton; Margaret Swinford; Katherine de le Pole, who in 1440 petitioned Henry VI for a sum of money due to her for the maintenance of Owen Tudor's children by Queen Catherine, who had formerly been the wife of Henry V; Elizabeth Shouldam (Abbess at about the time of Edward IV); Elizabeth Lexham; Dorothy Barleighe, the last Abbess, who surrendered her Convent on November 14th, 1539 and had a pension of £133.6.8.

An interesting burial in Barking was the sister of St. Thomas à Beckett; she must have been a nun there.

At the Dissolution of the monasteries the value of Barking was given as £862.12.5, which shows that it must have become one of the richer houses. Only the Curfew Gatehouse and a few foundations remain.

Basedale (Baysdale)

A Cistercian priory of nuns in Yorkshire lying among the Cleveland Hills, three miles west of Westerdale, and about six miles south east of Stokesley. These nuns were originally at Nunthorpe, north of Stokesley but were removed from there to Basedale at the latter part of the reign of Henry II, and were given Basedale by the benefaction of Guido de Bovencourt.

Dugdale relates how Isabel, the Prioress and her nuns were obliged to pray for Robert Longchamp, Abbot of St. Mary's York, in payment of a grant for burial grounds for the nuns, and they were to pay half a pound of frankincense yearly to Gerald the owner of Stokesley for the ground.

The priory was dissolved in 1539.

A house was built on the site about 1812, but nothing appears to have been preserved of the old priory.

Bath

In former times there was a house for nuns on the site where now stands the glorious Abbey of Bath. Osric, a petty king of Wessex, in 676 erected this nunnery. He appointed as Abbess, Bertane, and gave her some property near the city to pay for the construction of the building, which was dedicated to the Blessed Virgin.

Bath soon afterwards must have passed into the control of Ethelred, King of Mercia, as he gave his approval to a nobleman named Ethelmod to grant some land to the nunnery. The Abbess's name at the time was Bernguidis; she was probably the second Abbess. We know nothing else about these two Abbesses except their names.

Eventually the nunnery was razed to the ground by the Danes. The nuns never returned, and later the site was taken over by secular canons. They were expelled at the time of St. Dunstan, and regular monks were put in their place, and the building of a forerunner of the present Abbey was started.

The Abbey of Bath was where the first Coronation of a King of England was held. King Edgar was crowned there in 973 in the presence of a great number of bishops, abbots and abbesses.

Berwick upon Tweed

The town of Berwick, situated between two nations, England and Scotland, which were often at war with each other, was the scene of so many battles for its possession, that one would have thought that in its long exciting history, it would think of nothing but its own protection, so that it could survive. Yet surprisingly enough the town in medieval times was almost full to overflowing with religious houses of several different Orders. Two of these houses were Cistercian Nunneries. It is known there were two because of references to both houses in some of the records.

David I, King of Scotland, 1124–1153, was very interested in the Cistercian Order, so much so that he went to France to see St. Bernard, who was responsible for the founding of a great number of the Cistercian monasteries. David, in 1141 founded a Cistercian nunnery in Berwick; and it is probable that he was responsible for both of them.

Ridpath in his History of the Borders, says "He also erected a convent of Cistercian nuns in the neighbourhood of Berwick upon Tweed; on which four less considerable nunneries did afterwards depend, as cells. These were the nunneries of St. Bothans and Trefontan, situated among the hills of Lammermuir in the Mers, a few miles north of Dunse, and of Elbottle and Gulan in the County of East Lothian, on the side of the Firth of Forth."

This nunnery in Berwick is mentioned by Matthew of Westminster, and is thought to be St. Leonard's Nunnery situated near Halidon Hill, which was in the region of what is now called Castle Terrace.

The other Cistercian nunnery was said to be within the bounds of the town of Berwick. Its exact location is not known, but from local hearsay it may have been near Tweed Street with a view over the river.

We next hear of the houses in 1296 in the Ragmans Rolls, when Edward I came to Berwick to receive homage from the townspeople, and the two Prioresses are both said to have sworn fealty to him on the same day, and one is mentioned by name as Agnes de Berinham. The two of them are again mentioned in the Scottish Exchequer Rolls of 1331.

In 1333, during the reign of David Bruce, the son of Robert the Bruce, Edward III of England again invaded Scotland, and there was fought the battle of Hallydown Hill (Halidon Hill), in which the

English king was victorious, and Berwick surrendered to him.

Edward ordered a public thanksgiving, and he made a donation of £20 a year to the Cistercian nuns of St. Leonard's, near which the battle had been fought, to recompense them for the damage done to their nunnery, and he ordered that their church and buildings were to be repaired and rebuilt at his expense.

J. Scott writing in 1888, says that payments were made at the same time to both houses. He mentions a connection between the two, as they both belonged to the same Order, and one could have been a cell of the other.

Neither of the houses lasted for long; it is not surprising considering the troubled times that Berwick went through. When Robert III succeeded to the throne of Scotland in 1390, he suppressed the Cistercian nunnery in Berwick, with the consent of the Bishop of St. Andrews, and gave their whole property to the Premonstratensian canons at Dryburgh Abbey. There is some confusion about which house was suppressed, but J. Scott says "because the numbers had shrunk to only two nuns, quite possibly if one was a cell of the other that both were suppressed at the same time. Neither survived into the 15th century."

Beverley

A monastery situated in the southern part of the kingdom of Northumbria, in which St. John of Beverley spent the last years of his life after he had retired from the position as Bishop of York in 717. He may have been the founder of the monastery. Bede calls the place "Inderauude", that is, "In the wood of the Men of Deira".

In this monastery, St. John built a cell for nuns, and at the south end of the church, an oratory, especially for the nuns as a place of worship. He dedicated it to St. Martin.

In the 9th century the monastery was destroyed by the Danes, and in the next century King Athelstan restored the buildings and refounded it for men only; there was no mention of any nuns.

Bishopsgate London

The Benedictine priory of St. Helens for nuns was founded by William Fitzwilliam, a goldsmith, about 1210. It was built with the consent of the Dean and Chapter of St. Paul's. When each prioress was elected, she had to be presented to the Chapter and swear fealty to them.

The Dean and Chapter wrote a constitution for the nuns, part of which I quote from Dugdale:- "Also we enjoyne yow, that alle daunding and revelyng be utterlely forborne among yow, except Christmas, and other honest tymys of recreacyone, among yowre selfe used in absence of seculers in alle wise." This was dated MCCCCXXXIX–1439.

The church of the nuns of St. Helens Priory is still standing. Before the suppression of the monasteries in the sixteenth century, the choir was screened from the nave, and the nuns entered from a door in the north wall, which was later blocked up.

The nun's refectory was only pulled down in 1779.

Blackburg (Blackburgh)

The Benedictine nunnery of St. Catherine in Norfolk was given land by the family of Robert de Scales and his wife Muriel. Robert died about 1265, and after his death, his son, grandson and great grandson, who were all named Robert, became benefactors to the nunnery.

Dugdale says that at one time there were monks at Blackburg, and that the first Robert de Scales had a son named William, who was a canon at Blackburg. The date when the nuns took over is not given.

The last Abbess was named Elizabeth Dawney, and it was she who surrendered the nunnery at the Dissolution in the 16th century.

Sir Henry Spelman, whose dates are given as 1561–1641, wrote about the purchasers of the nunnery after the Dissolution. He said that all were involved in lengthy lawsuits and lost a lot of money, and many of them came to a sticky end. Sir Henry, himself was involved but managed in the end to survive as "hereby he first discerned the infelicity of meddling with consecrated places".

Blithbury

A priory for nuns, situated in the parish of Mavesyn Ridware in Staffordshire, founded during the episcopate of Roger de Clinton, who was Bishop of Lichfield from 1129–1148.

Dugdale says that Hugh Malveysin gave Blithbury to the nuns there for the service of God and St. Giles, which grant was confirmed by Hugh de Ridware and his son William, who also gave land. The grant gave them the right for as much timber as was necessary for the repair of their house, and Bishop Roger de Clinton excused the nuns from all synodal and episcopal dues and also granted an indulgence of

H

twenty one days to all the benefactors.

Burke, Extinct and Dormant mentions other benefactors:- "Edric of Eadright de Wulsellegh, temp. of William Rufus, had issue Reinner, who held Wolseley, Staffs, under Nigel de Stafford, granted lands at Galley, near Penkridge, to the nuns at Blithbury 1158-65."

About 1189, the lands and woods at Galley passed to the nunnery at Brewood, with which Blithbury was closely associated, and about 1170 the nuns of the two houses made an agreement with William de Ridware about holding land jointly at Ridware. It appeared that when they sold or made any deal about any land the two nunneries always consulted with one another. In 1275, we have the names of the two Prioresses — Mabel, Prioress of Brewood and Alice, Prioress of Blithbury. In that year Mabel with the consent of Alice disposed of land in Pipe Ridware to Robert de Pipe, and both Prioresses sealed the grant.

It appears that eventually Blithbury became merged with the Nunnery of Brewood; the exact date is not certain, but probably before the end of the 14th century.

During the 18th century a farmhouse had been built on the site of Blithbury Priory, and the ruins were dismantled, part of the old chapel being identified.

Bretford

An early 12th century nunnery in Warwickshire. It is said that Geoffrey de Clinton gave the land to build it. He was Lord Chamberlain to Henry I. Very little is known about the nunnery and it was evidently of not much importance.

Brewood (Whiteladies)

An Augustinian priory of nuns close to the village of Brewood (pronounced Brood) in Shropshire dedicated to St. Leonard. Founded in the 12th century. The la Zouch family were benefactors and Elizabeth of that name became prioress in 1314. It was a small house of about six nuns. There are ruins of a late Norman church and cloister.

Brewood (Blackladies)

A priory of Benedictine nuns in Warwickshire. It may have been founded by Roger de Clinton Bishop of Lichfield from 1129-1148.

One of the first donors was Ralph Bassett of Drayton, who in the 12th century gave the nuns· half a virgate at Hardwick, with common pasture and woods free from all secular services.

There was a very close relationship between the priory at Brewood and the nuns at Blithbury, and there is a deed which confirms that they shared portions of land around Rideware and Galley which had been given by William Rideware about 1170. Galley eventually passed to Brewood before 1189. Then Henry II seized Galley, and King John gave them the manor of Broom instead in 1200. In 1204 Brewood and Blithbury were among the nunneries which received a gift of two marks each from the king.

Brewood had many other donors and they felt they needed some protector to manage their affairs, and they petitioned the Pope. Pope Gregory IX (1227-41) took the priory under his own protection. He recognised the right of the nuns to elect their own Prioress. They were allowed to receive outsiders for burial in the priory grave yard, and they were allowed to admit into the priory free, women who wished to withdraw from the world, and those women could not leave without permission from the Prioress.

In Henry III's reign the nuns were given several more grants of land but in spite of these gifts they were considered poor, and at one time they had to pawn their chalice, in order to pay their debts. Then in 1241 the king came to their rescue with a gift of one mark in order that they might redeem the chalice. Another time they were accused of the theft of a stag; the animal had been drowned in the priory fishpond, and the nuns had divided it with John Gifford of Chillington. Gifford was imprisoned and fined but the king pardoned the nuns because they were so poor. In 1291 the mill of the Priory only brought them in 16 shillings a year. In that year the Pope granted an indulgence of one year and forty days to all who should visit the priory on the Feasts of the Virgin Mary and the anniversary of the dedication of the church, hoping it is presumed that they would benefit the priory.

In the 14th century the Priory of Blithbury is said to have become merged with that of Brewood.

In 1323 the bishop found a great deal of laxity in the running of the priory; Anabel de Hervill, the Cellaress was dismissed from her post, and a new set of rules were drawn up. An unusual appointment was made for a Benedictine priory, a Franciscan friar was given the post of the nun's confessor. For a while the priory was without a Prioress;

there seems to have been a difficulty in finding a suitable person, but one was appointed in 1442.

The following is a list of known Prioresses:—

Isabel — 1258

Mabel — 1272

Emma — 1301

Alice de Sinnerton — 1324, resigned 1373

Heloise of Leicester — 1324-1373; she probably ruled jointly with the one above.

Parnell — 1395-1412

Margaret Chiltern — 1442

Elizabeth Bottery — 1452

Margaret Cawardyn — 1485

Isabel Lawnder — 1521; she surrendered the priory in 1538.

It was valued at £20.13.0. and sold to Thomas Gifford of Stretton, and no part of the monastic buildings has survived.

Brodholme

A small nunnery in the parish of Thorney in Nottinghamshire. It was of the Order of the Premonstratensians; this Order was brought to England in 1140 and first settled at Newhouse in Lincolnshire, founded by Peter Gousla for canons.

According to Bishop Tanner, Agnes de Camville, the wife of Peter Gousla, placed a prioress and nuns at Brodholme towards the end of the reign of King Stephen, who died in 1154. She dedicated the nunnery to the Blessed Virgin Mary. Her daughter Sarah is said to have been one of its greatest benefactresses, having added to and confirmed the original grant. The nunnery's possessions were rated at £60.

Dugdale gives the names of the first donor to Brodholme as Ralph de Aubigny, and he does not mention Agnes de Camville or her family.

There is in an old manuscript, which is in the British Museum, a tale that suggests that the morals at the nunnery were not always that which they should be. I quote the passage, leaving out the Latin sections, which describe the incident:— "I find under the year XXIV of the King Edward III, that William Fox, Parson of Lee near Gainsborough, John Fox, and Thomas de Lingestine, Friars minors of the convent in Lincoln, were indited before Gilbert d'Umfravill and other Justices .... for that they came to Bradholme, a nunnery in the county of Nottingham, the XVIII of the Kalands of February, and then ...... violently took, and forcibly carried away thence, against the peace of their Sovereign Lord the King, a certain nun by name Margaret de Everingham, a sister of the said house (stripping her of her religious habits, and putting upon her a green gown or robe of the secular fashion) and also divers goods to the value of XL.S."

Broomhall (Broomhall)

A small priory of Benedictine nuns in Berkshire, built in the 13th century. The de Lacy family were donors and gave land to this priory.

Bruisyard (Bruseyard)

A nunnery of Poor Clares or Minoresses in Suffolk. Founded in 1357. Leland says it was founded by the Duke of Clarence, who was Lionel Plantagenet, 3rd son of Edward III, and who married Elizabeth de Burgh, daughter of William de Burgh and his wife, Maud, sister of Henry Plantegenet, Duke of Lancaster.

Dugdale gives an account of Maud, who married as her second husband, Sir Ralph de Ufford, viceroy of Ireland, and how she was indirectly responsible for the origin of the nunnery at Bruisyard.

Her husband, Ufford was very unpopular in Ireland, and when he died, she took his body and all her treasures to England, and travelled disguised as a poor sorrowing woman. She buried him beside her first husband, William de Burgh, Earl of Ulster, and founded a chantry with five chaplains, to pray for their souls, near the nuns at Campsey (Campass) in Suffolk.

The priests of the chantry found themselves distracted by the nearness of the nuns at Campsey and they had trouble in performing their duties in a proper manner, so the whole chantry was removed to Bruisyard in Suffolk.

William, Bishop of Norwich took over the governing of the place, and eventually formed the monastery of the Order of Poor Clares; the nuns being endowed with all the revenues originally belonging to the said chantry.

There are traces of the nunnery in the grounds of the old moated Manor House.

Bullington (Bolington)

A Gilbertine priory in Lincolnshire, situated about a mile from the village in wooded country and surrounded by a moat.

The founder was Simon de Kyme, who married Roese, daughter of Robert Dapifer, steward to Gilbert de Gant, Earl of Lincoln. Stephen was on the throne at the time (1135-1154), and the Master of the Order, St. Gilbert was still alive. Simon's son Philip de Kyme, founded the Priory of Kyme about 1180; he also granted twenty acres of land to the nuns and canons of Bullington for supporting the charge of their garments.

The priory was very richly endowed by many of the great landowners, who gave their gifts so that the nuns would say special prayers for their souls. Among the rich endowments they were given were seven Lincolnshire churches.

The number of nuns at Bullington was one hundred, and the canons numbered fifty. At the Dissolution the house was valued at £158.7.11.

All that remains at the present day is the moated site, and a few stones, which have been built into the walls of some of the farm houses. On the road to Stainfield is an eight foot high pillar made up of the last remaining stones of this once famous priory.

Bungay

A Benedictine nunnery in Suffolk, founded before 1167. Much of the land and the great castle belonged to Hugh Bigod in the reign of King Stephen; it is possible he founded the nunnery or donated the land. Dugdale gives the name of Roger de Granvil who granted some of the lands to the nunnery.

The ancient church of Holy Trinity contains the grave of Margaret Dallinger, a prioress in the 15th century.

At the Dissolution the nunnery was valued at £62.2.1.

Burnham

A Benedictine abbey about 1 mile from the village of Burnham in Buckinghamshire, founded in 1265 by Richard, Earl of Cornwall, known as the King of the Romans. He was the second son of King John and brother to Henry III, and he died in 1272. Dugdale says he was the brother of Edward III, but this is a mistake as the dates of King Edward III and the Earl are about a hundred years apart.

Burnham was a mitred abbey, which meant that the Abbess was a Peeress of the Realm, but being a woman she would not then take her seat in Parliament.

The names of the first four Abbesses are known:— Margery de Eston, 1265; Maud de Dorkcester, 1273; Margery de Louth, Temp. Edward III; Joan Turner, whose date is not given. Then there is a gap in the list until we come to the last two Abbesses, Margaret Gibson and Alice Baldwin, who surrendered the Abbey at the Dissolution of the monasteries. The Instrument of Surrender is dated September 1539, and signed by the Abbess and nine nuns. They were given pensions; the Abbess £13.6.8. and the nuns from £4 to £2. The Abbey was valued at £51.8.4.

There are very few remains of the abbey to be seen.

Cambridge

A Benedictine convent of nuns. It is difficult to give the exact date when it was founded. It was dedicated to St. Radegundis. I quote the following from Dugdale:- "The nuns of St. Radegundis at Cambridge held a place at Greencroft, where they dwelt, and where their church was founded, containing ten acres of land, which they had of the Gift of Malcolm, King of Scotland as a perpetual alms, to build their said church". It is not stated whether this was Malcolm I or II; Malcolm I reigned from 924-954, and Malcolm II from 1008-1034. The above quotation appears to show that the nuns were already established but had no church, and the King gave land to build the church.

William the Goldsmith was another donor to the convent, but their possessions always seemed to be small.

The following is a list of prioresses whose names we know:- Dera, c.1260; Amicia Chamberlayne, 1277; Helena, 1292; Mabilia Martyn, 1333; Margaret Claril or Clavyle, 1369; Eva Wasteneys, 1358; Alicia Pilet 1377; Isabella Sudbury, 1401; Margery Harling, 1408; Agnes Gaytlow, 1415; Joan Lancaster, 1467; Joan II de Cambridge, 1483; and Joan de Fulborne, the last prioress, who succeeded 1487, and ruled the priory until it was suppressed during the reign of Henry VII.

Dugdale says that the convent was suppressed by Henry VII and converted into a college, to consist of a Master, 6 Fellows, and some Grammar Scholars, "as appears by License of Henry VII for Suppressing the Nunnery, and erecting the College"; he goes on to say: "the cause of the suppression is said to be the ill lives of the nuns,

111

occasioned by the nearness of the University of Cambridge; and the revenues of the house being wasted and all things gone to decay".

Campsey (Campass, Campsey Ash)

A nunnery of Poor Clares or Minoresses near Ufford in Suffolk. Teoband de Valvines made a donation of land at Campsey to his sisters, Joanna and Agnes for them to build a nunnery, and this was confirmed by King John, so it must have been built before 1216.

In the reign of Edward III, Maud, Countess of Ulster, and sister of Henry Plantagenet, Duke of Lancaster, founded a chantry of five chaplains, near the priory of the nuns, to pray for the souls of her two husbands, William de Burgh and secondly, Sir Ralph de Ufford. The nearness of the priests in the chantry to the nuns in the priory caused trouble, and so William, Bishop of Norwich had the chantry removed to Bruseyard and the nuns were left in peace.

The name of the last Prioress at the Dissolution of the Monasteries was Elizabeth Buttry.

Canonlegh (Cononsleigh)

A convent of the Order of St. Augustine in Devon.

First founded for regular canons by Walter Clavely, but afterwards the Lady Maud Clare (Nee St. Liz), Countess of Clare and Hertford, placed nuns in the convent. Her husband was Steward to Henry I.

Canterbury

A Benedictine nunnery without the gates of Canterbury in Kent, dedicated to St. Sepulchre. Dugdale gives Anselm as the founder. He was Archbishop of Canterbury from 1093–1109. William Calvell, a citizen of Canterbury was one of the chief benefactors to the nuns. The nunnery remained under the patronage of the Archbishops, but we only know the name of one of the Prioresses, Phillipa Johanna (Jones); she was the last one and is said to lie buried in the north aisle of St. George's Church, which in her will she calls The Chapel of the Blessed Mary. There are no remains of the priory to be seen.

Canyngton (Cannington)

A Benedictine priory of nuns, situated a little more than three miles from Bridgwater in Somerset. It was founded in 1138 by Robert de

Curci or Curcy, who was chief butler to the Empress Maud.

To the north of the present parish church there are signs of some ancient buildings, which are the remains of the priory, and according to Leland the nun's church was "hard adnexid to the est of the Paroche Church." The priory and the present parish church were both dedicated to the Blessed Virgin Mary.

There is a legend that the "Fair Rosamond", mistress of Henry II, had some connection with the priory, but there does not seem to be much truth in it.

Carrow

A Benedictine nunnery at Norwich, to which King Stephen gave much land. The exact date of foundation is not given, but it was probably sometime early in the twelfth century. The great mystic, Julian of Norwich, most probably came under the guidance of the Benedictine Community at Carrow, as the church of St. Julian, where she had her cell belonged to Carrow.

At the Dissolution of the monasteries the nunnery was valued at £64.16.6.

Castor (Dormuncaster)

A nunnery in Northamptonshire near Peterborough. It was founded by Kyneburga, daughter of King Penda of Mercia, sometime after she had contributed with her brother King Wulfhere, in the establishment of the great Abbey of Medeshamstedi (Peterborough). This was about the middle of the 7th century. Kyneburga became the first Abbess of Castor and was joined by her sisters, Kyneswide and Eadburga, and also by a kinswoman of theirs named Tibba.

The three sister's relics were transferred to Peterborough. There is no further record of what happened to the nunnery, but the present church at Castor is dedicated to St. Kyneburga, and the base of a Saxon cross can be seen. The old nunnery was probably destroyed by the Danes.

Catesby

A Benedictine priory for nuns in Northamptonshire. It was founded at the time of Richard I, or possibly a short time before, as Pope Gregory VIII, who was only on the Papal throne for one year — 1187, took these nuns under his protection. The priory was enriched with the donations of many benefactors, including John de Vallibus, who gave land.

The priory prospered, and it was probably due to the unusual institution in a nunnery of an officer, entitled the Warden, or Master of the House. He was nominated by the convent with the approval of the Bishop. He administered the revenues and kept the accounts, and seems to have filled a position of special honour and dignity.

Edmund Rich, Archbishop of Canterbury, 1233 — 1240, sent his sisters to be nuns there, and his sister, Alice became the Prioress. She died about 1270.

After the year 1370, the Bishop's registers of the priory contain no record of the Warden, so possibly he was found to be too much of a luxury. But the nuns always maintained their reputation for hospitality and also for their piety.

At the Dissolution when Henry VIII's Commissioners came, they reported to Cromwell that they had not found such "Dyscrete Enterteyment' at any other religious House and their charity to the poor was without rival in the county: "We founde the House in verry perfett order, the Prioress a sure, wyse, discrete, and verry relygious woman, with IX nunnys under her obedyencye, as we have time paste seen, or belyke shall see." They submitted, therefore, that if any house was to be spared, a more deserving one was not to be found. Needless to say no attention whatever was paid to this plea.

At Catesby in the modern church, built 1861, the only remains of the old Priory church are three canopied arches containing sedilia and a piscina.

Chateridge (Chateris)

A Benedictine monastery for nuns in the Fens of Cambridgeshire founded by Edward, Abbot of Ramsey, sometime before 975. King Edgar gave the manor of Chateridge to the Abbot, who built the monastery and sufficiently endowed it so that the nuns were able to prosper under his direction. Then the Abbot was murdered by the Danes in 1016, and the nuns suffered without his care and leadership.

It was not until the reign of Henry I, that Hervey, who became the first Bishop of Ely in 1109, took pity on the nuns in Chateridge and had them annexed to his See. The Bull of Pope Alexander III in 1142 and that of Pope Innocent IV in 1242, both confirmed all gifts and privileges belonging to the said monastery and enjoined the nuns to follow the Rule of St. Benedict for ever.

The nunnery was burnt down by accident in the year 1302.

Chesthunt (Cheshunt)

A Benedictine nunnery. Originally it was a house for canons founded in 1183 but Henry III removed the canons and replaced them with nuns and gave them all the former lands in Hertfordshire. We have the name of only one prioress, Margaret Hill, who was probably the last; in 1553 she was given a pension of £5 per annum.

Before the nunnery was dissolved the monks of the Abbey of Waltham seem to have been misbehaving themselves with the nuns of Cheshunt. There is one tale which John Timbs relates in his book on the Abbeys, which I will quote:— "Fuller relates that Sir Henry Colt, of Nether Hall, who was a great favourite with Henry VIII, for his merry conceits, went late one night to Waltham Abbey, where, being duly informed by his spies that some of the monks were indulging in female converse at Cheshunt Nunnery, he determined to intercept their return. With this intent, he had a buckstall pitched in the narrowest part of the meadow, or marsh, which they had to cross on their way home; and the monks getting into it in the dark, were enclosed (or trapped) by his servants. The next morning Sir Henry presented them to the King, who heartily laughing, declared that he had often seen sweeter, but never fatter venison." What punishment was doled out to the nuns is not recorded, but the nunnery was soon dissolved. It was valued at £14.10s p.a. according to Dugdale but Speed says £27.6.8.

Chester

A priory dedicated to St. Mary dates from c.1140, founded by Ranulf, Earl of Chester. There are records of benefactions but practically nothing remains of the buildings. The site is now occupied by the County Police H.Q.

Chich

A nunnery situated at the mouth of the Colne in Essex. The place is now called St. Osyth. It was founded by St. Osyth about the year 673.

The land for the nunnery was given to St. Osyth by Seghere, King of East Saxons, to whom at one time she had been betrothed. The nunnery probably followed the Rule of St. Benedict, as St. Osyth had been brought up under a monastery of that Order. About 675 some Danish pirates arrived at the mouth of the river Colne and attacked the nunnery and murdered St. Osyth, and the nunnery was destroyed at that time. The church of the nunnery was dedicated to St. Peter and St. Paul and the present church stands on the same site.

In the reign of Henry I, a house of regular canons was built on the site of the old nunnery and dedicated to St. Peter, St. Paul and St. Osyth, which surrendered to King Henry VIII in 1539.

Chickesands (Churchsands)

A Gilbertine priory in Bedfordshire. It may have been one of the religious houses which Geoffrey de Mandeville, or his grandson Geoffrey, founded. Geoffrey, the grandson was created 1st Earl of Essex by King Stephen in 1140, but the Earl defected to the Empress Maud, and the King took away all his lands and castles. In revenge he ravaged and plundered some of the abbeys and was eventually excommunicated.

He married Rohesia, daughter of Alberic de Vere, Earl of Oxford, and she left him, probably when he was excommunicated and went to Chicksands, where she became Prioress.

When the Earl was mortally wounded he repented of his sins and his body was found by some Knights Templars, and they took him and placed him in a leaden coffin and hung the coffin on a crooked tree near the old Temple in London. With the help of the prior of Walden and the Earl's wife, he obtained absolution from Pope Alexander III.

His wife, the Prioress of Chicksands, then tried to get hold of his body to bury him at Chicksands, and she sent some knights to seize his coffin, but her son forestalled her and had his body buried at Walden.

We have no records of the names of any of the Prioresses who followed Rohesia, but eventually the priory prospered. Dugdale gives the number of nuns there as one hundred and twenty, and at the dissolution of the monasteries in Henry VIII's reign the value of the priory is given as £212.3.5 per annum.

The priory was taken over as a private residence, and in 1576 the family of Osbern purchased it and a great deal of the former priory remains.

Clerkenwell

The name is derived from Clerks' Well, "en" being plural in

Anglo-Saxon. Situated at Finsbury, London, was a Benedictine nunnery founded about 1100 by Jordan Briset. At the same time or according to Dugdale slightly later, he founded the adjacent priory for the Hospitallers of St. John of Jerusalem.

The deed concerning the founding of the nunnery, I quote from Dugdale:— "Jordanus, the son of Radulphus, the son of Brian, gave to God, to St. Mary and All Saints, and to Robert, his Chaplain, in Alms for himself and his wife, 14 Acres of land in the Field by the Clerk's Well, free from all Incumbrances, so as that the Knights Hospitallers might claim nothing of them . . . . He . . . . gave all this to the said Robert to the end that he should there build a Place to serve God". In another deed, the donor says that he gave as above that it should be bestowed on grey monks or nuns. The deed also states that Lucy de Muntency, the founder's daughter, confirms all her father's grants. From this it appears that she married Baron Muntency (Munchensi), and that is probably the reason why he is given as being the founder. He would be one of the donors who gave many gifts to the nunnery.

A document of Richard I's time, says that the lands belonging to the nunnery were more extensive than those of the priory of the Hospitallers.

This is the only nunnery in England the names of whose Prioresses have been preserved complete; there were twenty-four of them, as follows:— Christina, Ermegard, Hawisia, Eleonor, Alesia, Cecily, Margery Whatvile, Isabel, Alice Oxeney, Amice Marsey, Dyonisia Bray, Margery Bray, Joan Lewkenor, Joan Fulham, Katharine Braybroke, Lucy Atwood, Joan Viene, Margaret Blackwell, Isabel Wentworth, Margaret Bull, Agnes Clifford, Catherine Green, Isabel Hussey, Isabel Sackville, the last Prioress, who surrendered the priory in 1539, and she died in 1570, and was buried before the high altar of the Church of Clerkenwell.

After the Dissolution the nuns' hall was used as a workshop as late as 1773. Later the priory became known as Newcastle House. At the end of the 19th century, a few fragments of the old building were discovered, and in 1974, a great deal more was found.

Coldingham

One of the great double monasteries of the seventh century. They housed both monks and nuns, but died out during the Danish invasions, and never seem to have been revived, with the exception of the Gilbertines.

Bede calls Coldingham Coludi Urba. It was situated on a cliff, high above the sea, and the promontory where the monastery was built is now called St. Abb's Head. It was probably once the site of a Roman hill fort, protected by a bank and a deep ditch across the promontory on the landward side.

It was here that St Ebba sought shelter when she was fleeing from her suitor, and was miraculously saved by the rising of the tide which cut her off from the mainland. This happened when Oswy, St. Ebba's brother, was king of Northumbria, and St. Finan was Bishop of Lindisfarne. St. Finan succeeded St. Aidan in 651, and he died about 660, so the monastery of Coldingham must have been built between those dates.

St. Finan consecrated Ebba a nun, and she became Abbess of Coldingham. It is uncertain whether she actually founded the monastery, but if she did, she must have taken over part of the buildings of the old fort, and greatly extended them.

Saints, kings and queens visited Coldingham; the former Queen of Northumbria, Etheldreda, took the veil there, and was consecrated by St. Wilfred. She remained there as a nun before she went south and founded the Abbey of Ely.

St. Cuthbert stayed there, being a friend of the Abbess, often giving her help and advice. It was while he was at Coldingham that Bede tells the story of a monk spying on him when one night the saint was standing in the cold sea, praying and singing psalms, and then coming out of the water, two otters came and dried his feet, and warming them with their fur.

It was at Coldingham that the Abbess Ebba rebuked king Ecgfrith for his hardness and bad conduct to St. Wilfrid, and his behaviour, she told him, was the cause of the queen's illness.

The Abbess was a saintly woman, but she was a bad organiser and had not much control over her charges. Although the men and women were housed in separate compartments, unbeknown to the Abbess, they met in each others cells, where the nuns would weave fine cloth and dress themselves up in gay colours, and feasting and drinking would take place, and these monks and nuns would completely forget their vows of poverty, obedience and chastity. Among all the double monasteries at that time, Coldingham was the only one about which

118

there was a breath of scandal.

It was one of the monks, a man named Adamnan, who first informed the Abbess of the behaviour of these men and women in the monastery over which she was supposed to rule. Adamnan had been an inmate of Coldingham for many years. At one time he confessed to one of the priests about a great sin which he had committed. The priest told him that as penance he was only to have food and drink for about two days in the week. He was to continue this until the priest returned from a visit to Ireland. Unfortunately the priest never returned from Ireland; he died there. So Adamnan continued with his penance for the rest of his life, and he became greatly venerated.

One day, when he and another monk had been on an errand away from the monastery, on their return journey, as they approached the dwelling, he stopped and burst into tears, and his companion asked him what was troubling him, he replied, "All these buildings which you now see, both communal and private, will shortly be burnt to ashes".* The other monk went and told the Abbess, and when she questioned Adamnan, he told also of a vision he had had one night. He had seen a stranger standing beside him, who related to him how he had visited all the cells in the monastery and found only one at prayer, and that one was Adamnan. He then said that the vengeance of heaven would fall on the place. The Abbess was greatly disturbed, but Adamnan told her not to worry as it would not happen in her lifetime.

Now that the Abbess knew what was happening in the cells, she endeavoured to improve the conduct of the nuns, but when she died in 683, the inmates of the monastery returned to their bad ways and committed even worse crimes, and then the punishment came and the monastery was burnt to the ground and left in ruins. This is said to have happened soon after St. Ebba's death. At some time the monastery of Coldingham was rebuilt, and the occupants were nuns only. I do not think it is known when it happened. Bede talks about it being left in ruins, so it must have been rebuilt sometime after his death, which was in 735. All we know is that at the time of the Danish invasions in the ninth century there was a nunnery at Coldingham. The name of the Abbess was Ebba, and she must not be confused with the first Abbess of the same name, who lived two hundred years earlier.

As far as I can ascertain the history of the destruction of the Abbey of Coldingham, while Ebba was Abbess in 870, by the savage Danes, is only told in the Chronicle of Matthew of Westminster, and not mentioned by any of the other old Chroniclers. Matthew wrote in the fourteenth century.

As the Danes ravaged the north eastern coast in the year 870, and drew near to Coldingham, the Abbess dreaded the effects of their brutality and the result to herself and her nuns. She called all the nuns together and told them of her plans to preserve their chastity, they all agreed they would follow her example. Thereupon she drew forth a knife and cut off her nose and upper lip, and her nuns immediately did likewise, and so disfigured themselves, that when the Danes arrived and saw the horrible sight that the nuns presented, in their fury, they set fire to the whole place, and the Abbess and her nuns perished in the flames.

The ruins of the priory which are seen at Coldingham belong to a later date than the old abbey and was of a priory of Benedictine monks which was founded by King Edgar of Scotland, and was built about 1098, part of which has been restored and is now used as the parish church. But on the high cliffs overlooking the sea there are some ruins which are almost certainly part of the buildings where the nuns lived.

*Bede's *Ecclesiastical History* IV,25.

Coldstream

The priory of Coldstream for nuns of the Cistercian Order situated in the ancient parish of Lennel where the Leet joins the Tweed in Berwickshire. It was dedicated to the Blessed Virgin, and was founded by Gospatrick, 3rd Earl of Dunbar, and his wife Derder about the year 1165.

The foundation charter grants to the sisters of Wotehou (probably the original name of the site) half the Church of Linnel, also a portion of land at Birgham on the Tweed. The ruined remains of the church are still visible.

The Countess in another charter gave sixty to a hundred acres of the Hirsel with the church.

There were many witnesses to these charters and they were confirmed by Richard, Bishop of St. Andrew's, who was consecrated in 1165. Earl Gospatrick died in 1166.

His son, Waldeve succeeded his father as 4th Earl of Dunbar. He confirmed all his father's grants to the nuns of Coldstream, and as well bestowed on them the lands of Whitechester. He died in 1182. Waldeve was succeeded by his son Patrick, who granted to the nuns several more portions of land. He was a great benefactor of the Church, and bestowed gifts on Kelso, Melrose and Dryburgh. He married Ada, illegitimate daughter of William the Lion.

His son Patrick succeeded him in 1232, and was known as the 2nd Patrick, Earl of Dunbar, adding the name of March for the first time. Both he and his sister Ada gave a great deal to the Priory of Coldstream. Ada married her cousin William, who assumed the name of Home. He also became a patron of the priory.

The 2nd Patrick married the daughter of Walter, the High Steward. They had a son known as the 3rd Patrick who became the Earl in 1248.

During his lifetime in 1263, King Alexander III of Scotland took the nuns of Coldstream under his protection.

The nuns suffered during the struggles between the two nations, and when Edward I of England came to Coldstream in 1290 and again in 1296, their property was severely damaged, but Edward was generous enough to pay them compensation.

The rest of the family of the Earls of Dunbar and March continued to be benefactors to the Priory of Coldstream until the last Earl, who succeeded in 1309, the 5th of the name of Patrick, gave to the nuns the land of Putanyshalwe and that was the last donation that the family provided.

Several of the great landowners continued to patronise the priory. The nuns must have been well thought of, even among the humble folk, as there is a list existing giving the names of donors; they include a boatman of Berwick, and a daughter of a glassmaker of Alnwick and others who were not of the great ones of the land.

When Edward III invaded Scotland in 1333, he granted protection to the Prioress and sisters of Coldstream.

In 1434 the Prioress requested of Pope Eugenius IV that a transcript should be made of all their charters and other muniments, the reason given that they were suffering from age and through fear of an English invasion they might be destroyed and liable to be burnt. The request was granted and so they have been preserved to this day.

In 1472, James III of Scotland confirmed a charter granted at Perth of land by his father James II.

In 1490, James IV gave land to the priory, and mentions the name of the Prioress Margaret Hoppringill, and in 1509 the Prioress and nuns were give a royal letter giving them leave to traffic with the English in times of war or peace.

The next Prioress was a sister or cousin of the previous one, her name was Isabella Hoppringill. She was at first a great supporter of the Scots, and at the battle of Flodden, which was fought not far from Coldstream in 1513, she did her best to see that those who had been killed had a decent burial.

Later she became attached to the English cause. She was in a very difficult position, situated between the two nations. Isabella became friends with the widowed Queen Margaret, sister of Henry VIII. The Queen sought protection for the nuns, and she wrote to Lord Dacre, the English minister. In a letter in which he replied to the Queen he wrote, "The said Priores of Caldstreme hath a protection of the Kingis grace"; the king being Henry VIII; and an edict by Henry for the protection of the Prioress, Isabella, and her convent was issued on 1st July 1515.

Isabella appears to have acted as a spy for the English, and she even reported on the Queen's movements and the regent's as well. About the year 1523, she found herself in a fix, and wavered about what was her best policy when she heard that the regent with a large force was crossing the border into England, but the Earl of Surrey threatened the burning of her house, if she did not continue her alliance with the English, and Queen Margaret had to intercede again on her behalf.

Prioress Isabella Hoppringill died on 26th January 1537, and she was succeeded by Janet Hoppringill; the election was confirmed by the Archbishop of St. Andrew's. She was the last Prioress, as the priory was burned to the ground in 1545 by the Earl of Hertford. What happened to the eleven nuns who were occupying the building at the time is not known. They may have perished or they may have been given pensions. The site of the priory was valued at £201.

A large orchard is shown which belonged to the priory but no buildings are visible.

The bell of the priory was taken by the English to Durham Cathedral. The chartulary of the priory is preserved in the British Museum.

Coquet Island

A small island situated at the mouth of the river Coquet in

Northumberland. There was a monastery there about the year 684, and it is not certain whether there were nuns there as well as monks, but it was the place where the Abbess Aelfflaed and her nuns met St. Cuthbert, while he was a hermit on the Farne Islands and she was Abbess of Whitby. It may have been under her supervision.

It was on this island that Aelfflaed obtained from St. Cuthbert a very reluctant promise that if he felt he could render the state better service as a bishop, he would not refuse the honour.

The early buildings were probably destroyed during the Danish invasions, but sometime later there were cells on the island belonging to Benedictine monks, who came under the control of the monastery of Tynemouth. There is no mention of any nuns there. Tomlinson in his guide to Northumberland says there was a hermitage on the island at some distant period, "for buried at Tynemouth, lies Henry the hermit of Coquet Isle." From this it appears that occasionally only one monk was living there.

Tomlinson also says that the remains of the cells are incorporated with the keeper's house, and on the ruins of the old tower a lighthouse was built.

Coupland

A nunnery in Cumbria, built by St. Bees (Bega) soon after she landed from Ireland about the year 650. It was probably situated where the town of St. Bees now stands. In 1120, Henry I turned it into a Benedictine priory for monks, and the present parish church, which was restored in 1855–58, was part of the priory.

Coventry

The name according to the Encyclopaedia Britannica is derived from Conventre or convent town from a Benedictine priory founded in 1043 by Earl Leofric and his wife Godiva.

After the Norman conquest Coventry was given to the Earl of Chester. Nearby Robert de Marmyon owned the castle of Tamworth, and was also given the Abbey of Polesworth. Dugdale says that Marmyon's son Robert had a great enmity to the Earl of Chester, and entered the Priory of Coventry in 1143 and expelled the monks and nuns. He does not say whether this was the original priory founded by Earl Leofric, but it most likely was, and must have been a double priory, which was unusual after the Danish invasions.

Marmyon then proceeded to turn the priory into a fortification digging deep ditches in the surrounding fields. Unfortunately for him he fell into one of these ditches and broke his thigh, and a common soldier seizing him, cut off his head.

Crabhouse

An Augustinian nunnery in Norfolk founded for Lena de Lynne, an anchoress. Little is known of its history but there are records of benefactions and improvements and a serious fire in 1426 caused by a careless woman. Prioress Margery Stutfield surrendered the priory at the Dissolution. The site is now occupied by a house called Crabb's Abbey.

Cressewell

Dugdale mentions that both Henry III and Edward III confirmed grants to the nuns at Cressewell in Herefordshire, but there is very great confusion whether there were ever any nuns there; there was a priory of the Order of Grandimont at which there seems to have been only monks. The de Lacy gave the land for the priory and he may have given land for a nunnery as well, probably some time in the 13th century.

Dartford

A nunnery in Kent on the river Darent, a tributary of the Thames. There is a legend of there having been a very early nunnery of noble women at Dartford. It was said to have been founded by King Ethelbert, and if this is true, it must have been the earliest Saxon nunnery built in England. The legend goes on to say that it was burnt by the Danes, and among those murdered was the daughter of a Saxon King named Editha. There is a ballad about a Saxon named Offa, who vowed to revenge her murder by the Danes; the last verse is as follows:-

Revenge. Revenge. my soul inspires —
To loved Editha's manes,
I vow, till fleeting breath expires,
Fell vengeance on the Danes.*

The poet Pope also mentions the Darent — "Silent Darent, stained with Danish blood."

The nunnery, of which the present ruins can be seen, was founded in 1371 by Edward III for Augustine nuns, but in the reign of Richard II the nuns appear to have been under the direction of the Order of Preachers — the Dominicans.

Edward IV's daughter Bridget was a nun there and became the Prioress; she died in 1517.

At the Dissolution the buildings were made into a royal palace.

*J. Timbs — *Abbeys, Castles and Ancient Halls.*

Davington

A nunnery in Kent founded in 1153.

Donors of land to the nunnery were the son of FitzHamon and also Gervasse Resevil. Henry III in 1255 confirmed these gifts of land. Evidently the nuns there were very poor as they petitioned Edward III, who reigned from 1327 to 1377, that by reason of their great poverty they were unable to pay the common aids, as other religious houses did. The nave and north aisle of the conventical church is now the parish church.

Denney

A nunnery of minoresses in Cambridgeshire.

In the eleventh century there was a monastery of monks at this place. Burke, Extinct and Dormant, states that Conan, Duke of Brittany and Earl of Richmond confirmed the grant to these monks made by his Chamberlain. Dugdale says that this Chamberlain, Robert, gave the cell of Denney to the monks of Ely in 1169. He also says that Mary de St. Paul, Countess of Pembroke gave the Manor of Denney to the nuns of St. Clare (Minoresses). Mary de St. Paul married Aymer de Valence, 2nd Earl of Pembroke. She was the daughter of Guy de Chastillon, Comte de St. Paul, and great granddaughter of Henry III, and she founded by grant from her cousin, Edward III, the college of Mary de Valence, now called Pembroke College.

This Mary de Valence, Countess of Pembroke, was reported on the same day to have been maid, wife, and widow, her husband being killed in 1323 on their wedding day. It was then that she started to give away her possessions to the church and the poor, and among other pious works she is said to have founded the nunnery of Denney, to which she brought some nuns from Waterbecham about the year 1341. It is not stated what happened to the original monastery of monks.

At the Dissolution in the sixteenth century the nunnery of Denney was valued at £172.8.3.

Dereham

A nunnery in Norfolk, founded about the year 654 by St. Withburga, the youngest of the four daughters of King Anna of East Anglia. After her father's death, St. Withburga retired to this place with a few other women, but they were so very poor that they could hardly pay the masons to build the nunnery for them.

Withburga remained as Abbess for a great number of years, and she and her nuns were greatly venerated in the surrounding district.

The nunnery was probably destroyed about the year 870 during the Danish invasions.

There is still shown a holy well which is called St. Withburga's Well.

Easeburne (Easebourne)

A nunnery near Midhurst in Sussex. During the 13th, 14th and 15th centuries the land around this nunnery belonged to the Bohun family. Dugdale says that a John de Bohun founded the nunnery, but he gives no dates. It may have been founded about the year 1284, when the first John in the family is mentioned in Burke Ex. and D. In 1432, there was another John de Bohun, who had a daughter named Mary, who married Sir David Owen of Easeburn, natural son of Owen Tudor, grandfather of Henry VII. This Sir David Owen is most probably the Sir David Owen, whom Dugdale mentions as being a donor or later founder. There is no further information of the nunnery, except that it belonged to the Benedictine Order.

Ebchester (Ebbcastre)

A nunnery on the river Derwent in County Durham. It was founded in the 7th century by St. Ebba, sister of King Oswy of Northumbria. The King gave her the land. The nunnery was built where there had been a Roman fort, hence the name Ebchester; Chester being derived from the Latin word Castra, meaning camp or fort. The remains of the fort are being excavated at the present day. Ebba most probably used some of the Roman buildings and stones for her nunnery, which was later destroyed by the Danes.

Eccles

A Cistercian nunnery in Berwickshire, a few miles west of Coldstream. Said to be founded by Gospatrick, 3rd Earl of Dunbar, and his wife Derder, about the year 1156. It suffered greatly in the 16th century and was burned to the ground by the English in 1545. The land was given to Sir George Home in 1609.

Ellerton

A priory in Yorkshire. There are varying accounts as to which Order it belonged to, Cistercian or Gilbertine. Different writers give the names of different founders. Dugdale says it was of the Order of Gilbertines, and that William FitzPeter was the founder. The Victoria County History, and the historians Whellan and Pevsner, all say it belonged to the Cistercian Order. The V.C.H. mentions that it was founded by Warnerius, Steward to the Earl of Richmond, or by his son, Whynerus, in the reign of Henry II.

Another account by J. E. Morris, in his guide to East Yorkshire published in 1906, gives William FitzPeter as having founded the priory before 1212, and the charter for this foundation was witnessed by Geoffrey, Archbishop of York 1191–1215, and that it was of the Gilbertine Order. Morris also says that it was for canons and does not mention nuns, but Gilbertine priories were usually for nuns as well as canons; the canons looked after the nuns and took the services.

Dugdale gives the names of many benefactors to the priory during its existence.

The church was restored in the early years of the Gothic revival during the last century, but a west tower and lower parts of the enclosing walls of the body of the old priory still remain, and a few grave slabs and loose fragments of masonry of the 13th century can be seen.

Elstow

An abbey of Benedictine nuns about a mile and a half south of Bedford. There are the remains of an old Saxon cemetery, which probably had its own parish church on which the medieval abbey was built. The name Elstow is said to be a derivation of Aellen's Stow meaning the place or homestead of a Saxon named Aellen, who settled at this site at some stage of the early Saxons' migration to England.

The abbey was founded for nuns by Judith, a niece of the

Conqueror, who married Waltheof, son of Siward, Earl of Northumberland. Waltheof, while he was in favour with William I, was made Earl of Northumberland, Huntingdon and Northampton, but later was accused of treason and beheaded in 1076. His widow, Judith, who may have been responsible for betraying him to William, as an atonement, founded the Abbey of Elstow about the year 1078. It was dedicated to St. Mary and St. Helen. Dugdale called Elstow, Helenstow; it may have been because the abbey was dedicated to St. Helen.

The Countess Judith also endowed the abbey with the villages of Elstow, Wilshamstead and part of Maulden. There is a Charter of Henry I, dated 1126 confirming the gifts of many benefactors to the abbey, and among the names is the Countess Maud, daughter of Judith, and wife of Simon de St. Liz. From the thirteenth century it was considered a royal foundation, and it became one of the richest religious houses in the country.

The majority of the nuns who entered this abbey appear to have belonged to noble families. The first Abbess was named Cecily, and from her time onwards, the nuns were engaged in a great number of lawsuits, and in some cases these seem to have even been carried before parliament. Records of these lawsuits have been kept; an account of the abbey's disputes have been written out in "Chronicles of the Abbey of Elstow" by Wigram.

It appears that some of the Abbesses were rather aggressive; one named Mabel, who ruled from 1213–1222, had at least a fighting spirit, when as Matthew Paris, the Chronicler records, she seized the sword from the hand of the statue of St. Paul in the abbey church and called on him to avenge the destruction and burning down of St. Paul's Church in Bedford in 1216, by Faweskes de Breaute, who occupied Bedford Castle at that time.

The abbey came under the jurisdiction of the Bishop of Lincoln, and he made several visits to correct abuses of which the nuns seemed to have been accused, such as entertaining too many visitors from the Court and becoming too worldly and adorning themselves in gay clothes. They had forgotten the Rules of the religious life, although no actual cases of immorality were proved against them.

The abbey was surrendered in 1539, and the Abbess, Elizabeth Boyvill, was given a pension of £50p.a., and twenty three nuns were given smaller amounts. The abbey itself was valued at £234.8.7 and was the eighth wealthiest nunnery at the time of the Dissolution. Henry VIII proposed that the church should be made into a Cathedral for Bedford, but nothing came of the suggestion. The conventual buildings were given to Sir Humphrey Radcliff, and in 1616 the Hillersdons built a mansion using part of the abbey material; this now is in ruins.

But a great deal of the old abbey church remains, and is used as the parish church, and in 1628, in the font, which is still used, the infant John Bunyan was baptised.

Eltisley

A nunnery in Cambridgeshire. When it was built I think is unknown, but it is connected with the names of two saints, Pandwyna and Gwendraeth, both of which are Celtic names. Pandwyna is said to have died about 904, and a kinswoman of hers was Prioress there. The nunnery was destroyed by the Danes.

Ely

In 673, St. Etheldreda, a daughter of King Anna of East Anglia, founded a double monastery for men and women at Ely. According to Dugdale there had been a former monastery there, built by St. Augustine in 607. This was done with the approval of Ethelbert, King of Kent, who appointed ministers to perform the Divine Offices. King Penda of Mercia came with his army and drove them away and left the place a desert.

Penda was killed c.656, so the place must have remained desolate for some time, until St. Etheldred arrived from Northumbria and founded a monastery of both sexes; she, herself becoming the first Abbess. She was soon joined by her sister, Sexburga, the wife of Ercombert, King of Kent.

Etheldreda died in 679 and was succeeded by Sexburga, who ruled as Abbess for twenty years, and it was during that time that St. Etheldreda's body was raised to a place of honour in the church, and was found to be uncorrupted.

When St. Sexburga died in 699, she was succeeded by her daughter, Erminilda, the former wife of King Wulfhere of Mercia.

It is interesting to note that the first three Abbesses of Ely had all been queens before they had entered monasteries. The abbey continued peacefully being governed by its abbesses for one hundred and ninety seven years, until in 870 the Danes came and burnt the place down, and all the nuns were destroyed.

Eight of the clergy soon returned and repaired the church, and placed monks there, but no nuns. It flourished under ten abbots, until in 1018 the abbey was converted into the See of a Bishopric.

Esteholt (Esholt)

A small priory of Cistercian nuns in Yorkshire founded by Simon de Ward about the middle of the 12th Century. It was a cell to the Sinningthwait nunnery. It was dedicated to St. Mary and St. Leonard. A Bull of Pope Alexander III, dated 1172 took this nunnery under his protection, authorising them to protect any that should fly to them for Sanctuary, and enjoining the nuns for ever to continue in the Cistercian Order, confirming all their possessions and enjoining all persons not to commit rapine or violence upon their lands.

In the early seventeenth century Sir W. Calverley built on the site of the old priory a large house called Esholt Priory or Hall. In this house a few pointed arches in some of the offices alone remain to attest a religious origin.

It was valued at the Dissolution at £13-0-4, (Dugdale) and £19-0-8 (Speed).

Eton

There was a nunnery at Eton in Buckinghamshire, founded by Robert Bossec, Earl of Mellent, whose father came over with William the Conquerer, and was made Earl of Leicester. Robert's wife Amicia became a nun at Eton when her husband died in 1187. Henry V suppressed many of the alien nunneries including Eton, and in 1440 Henry VI used the revenues from these religious houses to found Eton College.

Evesham

A Benedictine monastery in Worcestershire, founded in the early eighth century by Egwin 3rd Bishop of Worcester. The name Evesham was derived from the name of a swineherd of Egwin's, who was called Eoves and who had an interview with the Blessed Virgin on the spot where the monastery was built.

The monastery became a mitred abbey, and housed sixty seven

monks and five nuns. The Bishop gave up his bishopric in 714 and became the first Abbot. William of Malmesbury says there had formerly been a church at this place built by the Britons before the Saxons arrived.

Farewell

A Benedictine nunnery in Staffordshire about $2\frac{1}{2}$ miles north west of Lichfield. Roger de Clinton, Bishop of Lichfield from 1129-1148, at the request of three anchorites, Roger, Geoffrey and Robert, who were brother monks at Farewell, and with the consent of the Chapter of the Cathedral of Lichfield, gave to the nuns and women devoted to the service of God, the Church of St. Mary of Farewell, and as Dugdale says with all its appurtenances and all that lies between Brook of Chistaley and Blacksille, with many other particulars mentioned in his two Grants.

King Henry I was also a benefactor to the nunnery, he gave the nuns three caruscates (one caruscate was as much as could be ploughed with one plough in a year) at Farewell, and one at Pipe and one at Hamerwich besides 40 acres of the Waste of Canod.

Geoffrey Peche gave the nuns his land at Marhale as a dowry of his daughter Sara as she became a nun at Farewell.

There is some confusion about Farewell sending nuns to found a nunnery at Langley in Leicestershire in 1150. Langley is said to have been founded in the century before, so the statement that Farewell founded Langley cannot be correct; Farewell must have sent her surplus number of nuns there. In 1209 the Prioress of Farewell claimed she had the right to preside over the elections of a new Prioress at Langley, and the Pope had to appoint arbitrators in 1246 in the matter. Farewell had to abandon her claim.

In 1331 an Episcopal visitation drew up fresh rules for the nuns:— The nuns were to be addressed in French; nuns not to wear girdles and burses of silk but to wear their habits; no secular women over twelve years to be admitted to the convent unless they were going to be nuns.

There were several other new rules, and the next bishop drew up a few more; one which must have been very hard on the nuns was that no fires were allowed except in the Infirmary.

The nunnery was suppressed by Cardinal Wolsey in 1530.

Flamstead

A Benedictine nunnery near Harpenden in Hertfordshire. A charter of Henry III states that Agatha, wife of William Gatesden granted lands to this nunnery, as also did Isabel, daughter of Bernard, son of Nicholas. The house was under endowed and the nuns suffered extreme poverty. Little else is known of them. The site is now a private residence called Beechwood Park.

Flixton

A nunnery of the Order of St. Augustine. It was founded by Margery wife of Bartholomew Creke. No date given, but Dugdale gives a list of Prioresses as follows:— Emma de Behalm, 1301; Margery de Stanham; Isabella de Weltham, 1345; Margery Hewell, 1376; Catherine Herward, 1394; Elizabeth Moore; Catherine Pilley, 1414; Maud Pitcher, 1432; Marione Dalingho, died 1446; Cecilia Creike, 1446; Helen: Margary Artis 1466; Isabella, 1503; Alice Wright 1520; Elizabeth Wright, 1532.

Elizabeth Wright was the last Prioress, for then the nunnery was suppressed and the revenues taken to endow colleges by Cardinal Wolsey.

Folkstone

A nunnery in Kent founded by King Eadbald for his daughter Eanswida in 630. Her grandfather Ethelbert was the first Christian King of Kent, who received St. Augustine, when he first set foot on English soil. The nunnery was one of the first to be built among the Anglo-Saxons. Eanswida, who became the Abbess dedicated the Church to St. Peter, and it was built on a cliff overlooking the sea.

Baring-Gould says that the nunnery became a great agricultural establishment and a literary school. It even had its own water supply which was carried in a canal from a mile away from a spring which the Abbess had discovered by striking her crozier on the ground and from which spot water had gushed forth.

The Danes came and damaged the buildings and left them in ruins.

Then in 1095, Nigell de Mundeville, Lord of Folkstone, built a house for Benedictine monks on the same site of the original nunnery. As the sea had gradually been encroaching on the land, within a year the whole edifice was washed away into the waves. In 1137, William de Overanche built a new church and monastery further inland, and it was dedicated to St. Mary and St. Eanswida. St. Eanswida's relics had been saved from the old nunnery, and they were translated into the new church.

The monastery was dissolved by Henry VIII, but the church still stands.

Foss

A Benedictine nunnery in Lincolnshire. Henry III in 1236 gave land to the nuns for which they had to pay him 20 shillings yearly. Dugdale then says King John discharged them from their usual payments of two marks a year to the Exchequer. There seems to be some confusion here as John reigned before Henry III, so it makes it difficult to say when the nunnery was founded.

Foulkeholme

On the site of a farm known as Nunhouse, there was a Benedictine priory of nuns lying at the foothills of the Hambleton range in Yorkshire. The priory existed during the 13th and 14th centuries, and was dedicated to St. Stephen. The farmhouse was built in the 18th century, but there does not appear to be any trace of the walls of the ancient priory. Some dressed stones have been dug up near the house, and an old fishpond can be seen a few hundred yards away.

Gloucester

The site where Gloucester Cathedral now stands has long been connected with Christianity. King Wulfhere is said to have given some land to lay the foundations of a nunnery. He died in 675, and it was his brother Ethelred who succeeded him on the throne of Mercia, and who in 681 granted charters to Osric to found the nunnery. Osric was his kinsman, and the brother of Kyneburga, as some authorities say, but there was an Osric who was the son of Kynrburga and Alhfrith of Northumbria and I think that he must be the Osric mentioned and not the brother of Kyneburga.

The nunnery was dedicated to St. Peter, and St. Kyneburga became the first Abbess; this must have been before she went to Castor near Peterborough. The second Abbess was Eadburga, who is given as the wife of Wulfhere, but I think she was his sister. The third and last Abbess was Evah, who ruled the nunnery for thirty years until about 765. Then the Danes came and destroyed the buildings.

After about fifty years King Bernulph of Mercia repaired the buildings and gave them to secular canons. In the reign of Canute in 1014, Wulfstan, Bishop of Worcester, replaced the canons by monks, and in 1072 Serlo, the first Abbot, built a new church.

Another authority says it was Aldred, who in 1058 built the Benedictine monastery. He was Bishop of Worcester. No further nuns were placed there.

The present Cathedral Church was the monastic Church of St. Peter, and during the reign of Henry VIII it was dedicated anew to the Holy and Invisible Trinity. The only connection with the old nunnery is in the north ambulatory — an effigy of its founder, King Osric of Mercia, whose remains were said to be translated to this spot.

Godstow

A Benedictine nunnery in Oxfordshire, founded in 1138 by the Prioress Editha, a lady of Winchester. She dedicated it in honour of St. Mary and St. John the Baptist, and it was consecrated by Alexander, Bishop of Lincoln, in the presence of King Stephen and his Queen. The donors of this nunnery, which included archbishops, bishops and nobles were released a year's penance and other indulgences by the Pope's Legate.

When Bishop Hugh of Lincoln visited the nuns in 1191 he saw a tomb in the middle of the choir of the chapel. It was covered with silks and surrounded with lamps and wax candles. Asking whose tomb it was, he was told that it was the Fair Rosamund's, who had been mistress of Henry II, and that for the sake of her kingly lover, she had done much good to the church. "Take her away," the Bishop answered, "for she was a strumpet, and bury her without the Church, among the rest, lest the Christian religion be vilified, and that other women may avoid unlawful and adulterous embraces."

The Fair Rosamund was the daughter of Walter de Clifford. By Henry II she was the mother of William Longespée, Earl of Salisbury.

Dugdale gives a list of the prioresses of Godstow as follows:— Editha, the Founder; Juliana, during the reigns of Henry II and John; Felicia de Bede, 1216; Flandrina, 1239; Emma Bluet, 1250; Isolda de Derham, 1270; Roysia Oxney, 1270, who built the Church of All Saints, of High Wycombe in 1273; Mabilla Wafre, 1286; Alice de Gorges, 1297 and 1305; Matilda de Upton, c.1307; Margaret Dine, alias Tracy, 1318 and 1329; Matilda Beauchamp, 1337; Agnes

Stretelegh, 1373; Margaret Mountney, 1403 and again 1408; Elizabeth, 1412; Agnes de Witham, 1425; Alice de Huntley, 1464; Katherine Felf, 1480 and 1493; Isabel Brainters or Braynton, 1495 to 1516; Margaret Teuxsbury, 1520 to 1533; Catherine Bukley, alias Bulkeley, who was the last Abbess, and by ill usage was driven to surrender the nunnery, to avoid being turned out by force.

Godstow was very highly thought of and many prominent people tried to save the nunnery from being dissolved. One Scottish historian, Bishop Gilbert Burnet, who after having raked together all the dirt he could to throw at the monasteries, could not but clear these virtuous ladies. He says, "Tho' the Visitors interceded earnestly for one Nunnery in Oxfordshire; Godstow, where there was great strictness of life, and to which most of the young gentlewomen of the country were sent to be bred, so that all the gentry of the country desired the King would spare the House; yet all was ineffectual." The Abbess herself wrote to Thomas Cromwell. But in the end the nunnery was dissolved. John Timbs, in his book on the Abbeys and Castles writing in the last century, says there were remains of the north, south and east walls of the nunnery still standing in his day, and there was a small building, which he identified with the Chapter-House.

Gokewell (Goykewell)

A Cistercian nunnery situated in a wooded hamlet near Broughton in Lincolnshire. The Cistercians always chose isolated spots in which to build their houses. Dugdale gives the name of the founder as William de Alta Ripa. The date of the foundation is not given but it was probably the 12th or early 13th century. It did last until the Dissolution of the monasteries, otherwise nothing much is known about it, and it has long since vanished.

Grace Dieu

An Augustinian nunnery in Leicestershire, founded by Roesia Verdun (or Verdon) in the thirteenth century. She married Theobald de Botiller, who was of the family of Butler, who became Earls of Ormunde of Ireland. Roesia retained her maiden name as she was a great heiress. She died in 1248.

Dugdale says, "This House stood low in a valley, upon a little brook, in a solitary place, compassed about with a high strong wall, within which the nuns had made a garden in resemblance to that upon Mount Olivet, Gethesemane, whither Christ with Peter, James and John, went up to pray."

The name of the last Prioress was Agnes, who surrendered the Convent in October 27th 1539.

Greenfield

A Cistercian nunnery in Lincolnshire, founded by Eudore Greinley and Radulphus de Aby, who according to Dugdale were father and son, and Hugh, Bishop of Lincoln from 1140–1200, confirmed their grants. It is also stated that the Chapel of Our Lady for the nunnery was founded by Adam de Welles during the reign of Richard I, (1189–1199).

Adam De Welles's descendant, John de Welles, who was 4th baron, in 1349 purchased a rent from the monks of Bardney of £10 p.a. to be given to the Abbess and nuns of Greenfield, so that they should celebrate masses, matins, placebo, dirge and commendation everyday in the Chapel of Our Lady, for the health of the souls of his Lordship's ancestors.

Grendale (Handale)

A Benedictine priory in the Parish of Loftus in Yorkshire. It was founded in 1133 by William de Percy and dedicated to the Virgin Mary, and endowed with lands at Grendale, Dunsley and Staxton.

Dugdale says that Engeram de Bovington gave some lands to the nunnery, which Avica, Prioress of the nunnery let to Ralph, Prior of Giseburn at a yearly rent of four quarters of corn.

At the Dissolution of the monasteries there were only eight nuns, and the nunnery was valued at £13.19.

According to Graves, little remains of the building, except the west end of the chapel, and some of the old walls can be seen incorporated in a farmhouse erected on the site, but the Victoria County History in 1923 says, "There are now no remains."

Grimsby

A Benedictine nunnery in Grimsby in Lincolnshire. Dugdale gives no date, but that it was founded by a Bishop of London. There was a nunnery dedicated to St. Leonard, which was closely connected with the Church of St. James, which has in a chapel, an effigy of a knight in armour, representing Sir Thomas Haslerton, which was taken from St. Leonard's Nunnery at the Dissolution. Sir Thomas had helped to rebuild this nunnery after a fire. Dugdale says that the Benedictine nunnery had at one time been accidentally burnt, and the nuns lost all their books, writings and everything they possessed. So it is logical to assume that the nunnery that Sir Thomas Haslerton was interested in is the same one that Dugdale mentions.

It came under the patronage of Henry IV and by a charter all their possessions were confirmed to them.

Guyzance (Gysyns)

A nunnery lying in a green haugh by the north bank of the river Coquet in Northumberland. Gilbert Tyson, Lord of Alnwick at the time of the Norman Conquest, gave to his second son, Richard, the land at Guyzance. Richard founded a nunnery there, and the church was dedicated to St. Wilfrid.

Eustace FitzJohn, who had married Beatrice de Vercy, great granddaughter of Gilbert Tyson, built in 1147 the Premonstratensian abbey of white canons at Alnwick, and annexed the nunnery at Guyzance to the abbey, so that the nuns should be under the protection of the canons. In the Lincoln Taxation in 1291 the nunnery was valued £70.0.4.

In 1198, William de Hilton became the Overlord of Guyzance, through marriage with Benéta, great granddaughter of Richard Tyson. There were many lawsuits between the nuns and the owners of the land. Alexander de Hilton, son of William, at last acknowledged the right of the Abbot of Alnwick and the nuns to their land at Guyzance, and confirmed all grants made to them in former times.

In the fifteenth century the land passed from the Hiltons to the Percies.

It is uncertain at what date the nunnery was dissolved, but sometime before 1534 the nunnery was converted into a parochial curacy, and John Lilburn, who had been a monk at Alnwick was put in possession of the chapel and lands. In 1567, a survey shows that the inhabitants in the surrounding cottages were using the chapel as their parish church, and the land that had belonged to the nunnery was divided up into tenancies.

Up to the middle of the eighteenth century the chapel was used for marriages and occasional services, until the roof fell in, and no repairs were done, so it now stands there in a ruinous state, only a new wall has been put round it for protection. It is even now sometimes known by another name: Brainshaugh instead of Guyzance.

A great deal of the old walls are standing, and there it remains, open to the sky, in a green field surrounded on three sides by the lovely river Coquet. The chancel is still used as the burial place for the Tate family, and the last one was interred there in 1966.

Gwytherin

A monastery in Denbighshire. I cannot find the date of its foundation but St. Winifride died there when she was abbess in 650. On the site there are traces of inscribed stones to be seen, which seem to belong to the Romano-British period.

Hackness

A cell to Whitby Abbey in Yorkshire, founded by St. Hilda just before her death in 680. It was about thirteen miles from the abbey and possibly intended as a place of retreat and rest for the nuns. Bede described a vision that one of the nuns had at the time of the saint's death, and when messengers came the next morning to tell the nuns at Hackness the news, they said that they had already been informed by this heavenly vision. Frigyth was the nun in charge at the time. The original cell was destroyed by the Danes, and in 1088 Serlo de Percy, Prior of Whitby, built a cell there for monks, and it was dedicated to St. Mary. Crockford gives the dedication of the present church at Hackness as St. Mary, also St. Hilda.

Near the site of the nuns' old cell now stands Hackness Hall, and the presumed site of the cell is now occupied by a large fishpond with no other visible remains, but Colgrave in his introduction to the book by the Anonymous Monk of Whitby, says, "There is also still to be seen a remarkable cross in the church at Hackness, . . . The cross probably dates from the eighth century . . .", from which statement it can be presumed the cross was there in the nuns' time, before the Danes came.

Haddington

A Cistercian nunnery founded in 1159 by Ada, Countess of Northumberland and Huntingdon, widow of Henry, son of David I of Scotland. The Prioresses swore fealty to Edward I of England in 1291 and 1296. It suffered much from the English, being burnt down in 1335 and again in 1544. In 1461 there were 24 nuns, and at one time it was said to be one of the largest of the Scottish nunneries. It lasted until the property was given to John Maitland in 1621. It was situated near what is now known as Nungate in Haddington. The seal of the nunnery is in the British Museum, and the inscription on it reads, "Santa Marie de Hadentyne".

Hampole

A priory situated 6¼ miles from Doncaster in Yorkshire, built about 1170 by William de Clairfait and his wife, Avicia, for fourteen to fifteen Cistercian nuns. It was dedicated to the Blessed Virgin Mary. Their grandson Ralph Tilly confirmed all their donations. They were also confirmed by Roger, Archbishop of York from 1154-1191. The Priory "stood in a pleasant vale near to the high road from Wakefield to Doncaster. At present there is an old hall, which seems to have been part of the Priory or built out of its ruins."

Richard Rolle, the great English mystic, had a hermitage attached to the priory, and it is due to the care that the nuns took to collect and preserve all his writings and the legends about him that we know so much of his life. He made one of the first attempts to translate the Bible into English. He died in 1349, and the nuns buried him in the church of their priory.

Hanbury

A nunnery in Staffordshire founded by St. Werburga, daughter of King Wulfhere of Mercia. The nunnery was endowed by her uncle, King Ethelred after he came to the throne in 675. In 699, St. Werburga died at Trentham, and at her own wish her body was conveyed to Hanbury, where she was buried.

In 708, a costly shrine was built at Hanbury and her body was transferred to it.

The nuns at Hanbury remained undisturbed for the next one hundred and seventy years, until in 875 the Danes came and almost certainly left the nunnery in ruins, but not before the nuns with the shrine of St. Werburga had escaped to Chester.

Harreld (Harewold)

In this village in Bedfordshire on the site of where there is now a farmhouse there was an ancient priory. According to H.W. Macklin in the guide book to Bedfordshire, this priory was founded by Sampson le Fort in 1150 and was first occupied by Austin canons and then later by a prioress and twelve nuns.

Dugdale says that King Malcolm of Scotland confirmed the possessions of the nuns that they were given in the days of his grandfather David I who reigned from 1124-1153. The priory was also given land in Stevington where they had a hospital, which was pulled down in 1873, this with the church at Stevington was given them in the reign of Henry II. Henry IV also confirmed the nuns at Harrold's possessions at Chakiston, which I think may be identified with Chellington or Carlton, which are both only about a mile away from the village of Harrold.

Hartlepool (Heruteu) The island of the Hart

A double monastery for monks and nuns, founded about 640 by Heiu who was the first woman to take the habit and vows of a nun in the north of England among the Anglo-Saxons. She was ordained by St. Aidan the first Bishop of Lindisfarne, and he made her the Abbess to rule over the monastery.

Sometime before St. Aidan's death, Heiu retired, and St. Hilda was appointed as the second Abbess. Bede says that St. Aidan greatly admired St. Hilda, and often visited her at Hartlepool and instructed her in the ways of a religious life. King Oswy placed his daughter under the care of St. Hilda when the child Aelfflaed was only one year old. One of the monks who studied at Hartlepool before going on to Whitby, was Oftfor, who later became Bishop of the Hwice.

The Abbess Hilda had charge of the monastery until about the year 657, when St. Finan gave her the management of the monastery of Whitby.

The monastery of Hartlepool was destroyed by the Danes about 800. In 1833 memorial name slabs were discovered, carved with crosses with the names of the dead, and they included both men and women, all dating from the seventh century.

Haverholm

A priory of the Order of St. Gilbert in Lincolnshire, founded by Alexander, Bishop of Lincoln in 1139. At first there were living there some rheumatic monks, whom the Bishop moved out, and he gave the priory to St. Gilbert, who moved in with his nuns and canons. The nuns followed the Gilbertine Rule, and the canons were of the Augustinian Order. St. Gilbert is said to have lived at Haverholm from about 1164; he would then have been over eighty years of age. At that time there were a hundred nuns and fifty canons.

Hedingham
A Benedictine nunnery, built in the eleventh century by Albericus de Vere's father, the first Earl of Oxford, who also built the great castle at Hedingham. Albericus confirmed the grants of land which his father had given to the nuns. The nunnery was dedicated to Holy Cross. Lucy, the Earl's wife became the first Prioress. Nearby there was a hospital for the relief of poor and disabled persons, and the chaplains to the hospital took an oath to the Prioress that they would be just to the parish.

Henwood
At one time known as Estwell, a priory in Warwickshire. No name of the founder is given, but a list of Prioresses gives the date of the second as succeeding in 1310, so the priory was probably built in the late 13th century. It was of the Order of St. Benedict, and in 1404 was a small nunnery with only twelve nuns. The name of one of the donors was Kavelbern de Langedon, who gave land and privileges to the nuns.

The list of Prioresses is as follows:— Catherine Bovdin, no date given; Margaret le Corzon, 1310; Millisanda de Fokerham, 1339; Johanna de Fokerham, 1349; Johanna de Pickford; Alionora de Stoke, 1392; Joesia Middlemore, 1400; Jocusa Middlemore, 1438; Alice Waringe, 1460; Elizabeth Pultney, 1498; Alice Hugford, 1535; Johanna Hugford, who ruled the priory from 1536 until she surrendered it in 1537, when she received a pension of £3.6.8.. Some of the prioresses, except the last, each held the office for quite a number of years, and in some instances appeared to have been related to each other.

At the Dissolution the priory was valued at £21.2.0.

Heyninges
A Gilbertine priory in the village of Knaith in Lincolnshire, founded in the 12th century. Reyner de Evermer and Odo de Sancta Cruce were donors of land. The priory was dissolved in 1539. The value of

the land and buildings was £49.5.2.. Nothing remains of them, but the village church still contains fragments of the old priory church.

Hitchin

In this small town in Hertfordshire, the Biggin Alms Houses, situated close to the church, still preserve some of the fabric of the Gilbertine nunnery which was founded in the reign of Edward III.

Holland Brigg

A Gilbertine priory in Lincolnshire. It is not certain whether there were nuns there as well as canons. It was situated near a bridge over a canal which is known as the Forty Foot Drain. A rich man of Lincoln named Godwin gave the land on condition that the priory repaired the bridge, and the money left over they could keep for their own maintenance.

The place is now known as the New Bridge.

Holystone (Halistane)

A Benedictine priory in Northumberland near the river Coquet about five and a half miles west of Rothbury. The history of Holystone goes back to Saxon times; it was here that St. Paulinus is said to have baptized many of the Northumbrians in the waters of the well, which can still be seen standing surrounded by trees with a cross in the centre.

The priory was founded by one of the Umfraville family of Harbottle Castle, who were given the lordship of Redesdale by William I in 1075. Alice de Alneto gave the nuns one toft and croft in Etherston; and Roger Bertram, Baron of Mitford, gave them the whole waste of Baldwins-wood, and the liberty of grinding their corn at any of his mills in the parish of Mitford, and pasture on the common of Newton and Throphill. These grants were confirmed to them by Henry III in 1255. In 1296, Marjorie, the Prioress did homage to Edward I at Berwick, and signed the Ragman's Roll. H.V. Morton says that the seal is still preserved on a fragment of Homage.

The nuns were also given the livings of the churches of Harbottle, Corsenside and Holystone. Richard Kelloe, Bishop of Durham signed the deed for these, dated 1311. He did this at the request of Lord Richard Umfraville, who took Holy Orders and became their chaplain and vicar.

As well as all these gifts the nuns had a hospital at Alwinton, and four houses at Newcastle-upon-Tyne. According to Mackenzie in his History of Northumberland, dated 1855, in the Lincoln taxation of 1291 the property of the priory was rated at £24, but in the book "Beauties of Northumberland" it is said they were rated at £40.

At the Dissolution, Dugdale says their annual revenues were valued at £11.5.6d, and Speed gives them as £15.10.8d.

There are very few remains of the priory left, except a few fragments in the Mill House and other buildings in the village, Morton mentions a few stones near the church and a field called the Nun's Close, and St Mungo's Well on the Holystone burn.

Holywell (Haliwell)

A priory of Benedictine nuns situated among green fields where now stands the parish of Shoreditch to the east of London. In Dugdale's Monasticon it was said to have been founded by a Bishop of London and "it was commonly called Holywell because of a certain sweet, wholesome and clear fountain or well in the compass thereof", and it was dedicated to St. John the Baptist. It had a great number of benefactors, and Richard I confirmed their grants. Stephen Gravesend, Bishop of London in 1318 gave a great deal to this priory.

John Timbs writing in the last century, says that Holywell Priory was founded in 1100, and stood upon the site of New Inn-yard and was bounded on one side by the present High street, Shoreditch. He also says there exists upon the spot a very old wall, nearly 100 feet long, which is considered to be all that remains of the priory church.

During the reign of Henry VII, Sir Thomas Lovel K.G. built for the priory a large chapel in which, when he died in 1524, he was buried. The windows of the chapel were of stained glass, and in them were the following words:-

Al the nunnes in Holywel
Pray for the soul of Sir Thomas Lovel

The last Prioress, Sibylla Newigate surrendered the priory in 1538. John Timbs mentions that under the floor of the "Old King John" public house part of the chapel remains and the stone doorway into the porter's lodge of the priory still exists.

Horton

A Benedictine monastery in Dorset. It is said to have been founded by the father of King Edgar's queen, who was Ordgar, Ealdorman of Devonshire, and who also founded Tavistock Abbey. Baring-Gould says that St. Wulfhilda founded the monastery and became the first Abbess. It is possible that Ordgar gave the land to Wulfhilda about the year 961 to build the monastery. Later on King Edgar made her Abbess of Barking, but she still governed the nuns at Horton.

At some time Horton became a cell of Sherborne, this may have been soon after Wulfhilda's death. I can find no further account of the monastery, but part of it was used to build a manor house, which was restored in 1920, and given to the church by Lord Shaftesbury for use as a vicarage.

Huntingdon

A Benedictine nunnery dedicated to St. James. Dugdale says the site of the nunnery was "Huntingdon without". There does not appear to have been a nunnery in Huntingdon itself nor a church dedicated to St. James, but a mile from the market-place there now stands Hinchingbrooke House, which was built on the site of a Benedictine nunnery; this is mentioned in the guide book by Herbert Macklin. He says that nuns were removed from the nunnery of Eltisley during the reign of William I to Hinchingbrooke, and there is a bridge over the river Alconbury called the Nuns Bridge. This seems to be the nunnery to which Dugdale is referring. He gives the names of two Prioresses:— Sister Emma, who was succeeded by Helen Wills. Dugdale also mentions that one of the patronesses of the nunnery was Lady Dervorgal; it is possible she was the Lady Devorgilla, the wife of Sir John de Baliol.

At the Dissolution of the monasteries, the property of the nuns was given to Sir Richard Cromwell by Henry VIII.

Hutton Lowcross

A small Cistercian nunnery built by Ralph de Neville by permission of Adam de Brus of Skelton, Yorkshire, who died about 1167.

The house was removed to Nunthorpe within a few years, but did not remain there for long, and the nuns eventually went to Basdale, sometime before 1211. There are only slight remains of any ecclesiastical buildings having been there, and these are thought to be fragments of a leper hospital dedicated to St. Leonard, which had been close to the nunnery.

Icklington

A Benedictine nunnery in Suffolk, built by the de Veres, Earls of Oxford, in the 11th century. They also built Castle Hedingham. There are two old churches in this village; the oldest one, St. James may have been the nun's church.

At the Dissolution the nunnery was valued at £71.9.10.

Iona

This is the island made famous by the great St. Columba. A Benedictine nunnery was founded on the island in 1203 by Reginald, son and heir of the great Somerled, Lord of the Isles, "in honour of God and St. Columkill". The deed of confirmation of the foundation still exists in the Vatican. The first Abbess was Reginald's sister Beatrice. Later the nuns were changed to the Augustine Order.

The ruins of the nunnery lie about a quarter of a mile south of the abbey. They are grouped round what was the cloister garth, with parts of the church still standing on the north side. Other parts of the nunnery can be seen on the east and south sides of the cloisters. The roof of the church only fell down at the end of the last century.

Ritchie, in his book on Iona, says that in 1923 the nunnery was repaired and a garden in the cloister was planted by her family in memory of Mrs. R. J. Spencer.

The last Prioress was Anna who died in 1543, and her effigy is now in St. Ronan's Chapel, which is close to the nunnery.

The nunnery was said to be the burial place of all the ladies of that part of Scotland.

Ivingho

A Benedictine nunnery in Buckinghamshire, dedicated to St. Margaret. It was said to have been founded by Henry of Blois, who was brother of King Stephen and Bishop of Winchester from 1129. Dugdale mentions that Edward I granted lands to the nuns in 1280.

A list of the names of a few of the Prioresses has been preserved as follows:— Matilda de Hocclive, who died in 1296, and was succeeded that year by Isolda de Beaucham. Sidilla de Hamsted is the next name given, who retired or died in 1340. Then there is a gap until Elenor Crosse, who died in 1469, and who was succeeded by Elenor Symms. The last Prioress at the time of the Dissolution was Margaret Hardwick.

Nothing remains now of the nunnery but some mounds covered with turf.

Keldholme

A Cistercian nunnery in Yorkshire, founded c.1190 by Robert, son of Nicholas de Stuteville. It was dedicated to St. Mary and St. Lawrence. King John confirmed all the donations in 1201.

A list of the known Prioresses is as follows:— Marca de Ross; Joan de Pykering, 1310; Isabella Whyteby; Elizabeth; Elizabeth de Kirkby Moorside, 1336; Margaret Chamberlin; Joan Bradley, 1468; Margaret Ripon; Joan Baddenby, 1505; Maud Felton, 1521; Mary Marshall, 1527.

At the Dissolution there were only one Prioress and eight or nine nuns, and the house was valued at £29.6.1. On the site was erected an oil and flax mill. In 1813, on clearing away part of the foundations there were discovered several tombstones and stone coffins, and the present owner says they may still be seen, and there is an old wall believed to be part of the nunnery buildings.

Kilburn

A small nunnery in what is now part of London. The following account is taken from Dugdale's Monasticon:— In the reign of Henry I, Herbert, Abbot of Westminster, Osbet the Prior and all the monastery, with the consent of Gilbert, Bishop of London, gave to three holy maids, Emma, Gumild and Christina, the Hermitage of Cuneburn (Kilburn), which had been built by Godwin, with all the land belonging to that place, upon the same condition, and the same liberties as King Ethelred gave Hampstead to the Church of Westminster. Westminster monks were to choose an ancient person of their number to be Chaplain to the nuns. The Abbot Herbert also gave the Manor of Knightsbridge.

There arose a controversy between the bishop and abbot about the jurisdiction over the nuns. This was made up in 1231, and the bishop might visit the nuns, preach and hear confessions.

After that the history of the nunnery is obscure though there are records of its properties.

It was valued at the Dissolution at £74.7.11.

Kington

A Benedictine nunnery in Wiltshire, known as Kington St. Margaret. The exact date of the nunnery is not known, nor who was the founder, but it was built before Robert Burnell was made Bishop of Bath and Wells (1274–1292), as he confirmed to the nuns the grants of land and the church, which they had been already given.

There were a number of donors to the nunnery.

Kirkless (Kirklees)

A Cistercian nunnery in the parish of Dewsbury in the West Riding of Yorkshire. It was founded by Reiner the Fleming in the reign of Henry II. Earl Warren, who died in 1240, confirmed the granting of the charter to the nuns. It was situated in a warm and fertile piece of land, raised just high enough above a deep brook to the south of the nunnery so that it was protected against flooding.

The Nunnery was a small community, and at the Dissolution there were only about seven nuns. The last Prioress was Joan Kyppes, who surrendered the house in 1539, and it was valued at £19.8.2.

During excavations quite a deal of the buildings of the priory and the church have been discovered. In some parts only the outline is showing. A cloister court about forty foot square is distinctly seen, and north of this was the body of the church with transepts and choir. There are two railed-in tombs, one covered with a slab on which is a cross and is said to be the grave of one of the prioresses named Elizabeth Stainton. There is a gate-house, which is half timbered, on a stone foundation with mullioned windows, which may be part of the original nunnery, and so may be parts of the farm house which is still standing.

Tradition says that Robin Hood shot an arrow from one of the windows to indicate the position of his grave, after he had asked one of the nuns to cut his veins so that he should bleed to death.

Lacock

An abbey in Wiltshire, founded by Ela, Countess of Salisbury, in 1229 after the death of her husband, who was William Longespée, the natural son of Henry II and Fair Rosamund.

The nuns at Lacock were of the Order of St. Augustine. It is said that Ela was directed by visions to build the abbey in remembrance of her husband. In 1238, she took the veil and became the Abbess, and five years before her death, she retired. She died in 1261, about the age of 74. The historian Aubrey says she was about 100 when she died and had become quite senile.

The following is the list of nuns who became abbesses and succeeded the Countess:— Beatrix; Alice; Juliana, 1288; Wymarca; Agnes, 1299; Margery of Gloucester at the time of Edward IV; Jahanna Temys 1517 and she continued as Abbess until she surrendered the Abbey at the Dissolution in 1539, and she received a pension of £40 p.a.

The church was destroyed, but the epitaph of the founder was preserved, and the cloisters and the nun's cells and most of the walls are still standing, together with the Chapter House, and an interesting old relic, the Nun's Boiler, from the kitchen, which can contain sixty seven gallons.

The house was valued at £168.9.2. It was sold in 1544 and made into a private dwelling house, and brought by the Sherington family, and one of this family married a Talbot, and the Talbots have owned the abbey ever since.

Lambley

A Benedictine nunnery in Northumberland, which stood on the banks of the Tyne about three and a half miles south of Haltwhistle. King John confirmed all the grants given to this nunnery in 1201 by Adam de Tindale and his wife Helewise (Heloise), which included land and rights of pastures on both sides of the Tyne and the Chapel of Sandiburnesele. Helias, nephew of Adam also granted the nuns land and a house in Newcastle. The place was wasted and burnt by the Scots in 1296, and the nuns suffered. At the Dissolution there were only six nuns, and the yearly income of the nunnery was £5.15.8.

Langley

A Benedictine nunnery near Breedon in Leicestershire. Eudo, who came over with William the Conqueror is said to have founded this nunnery in the 11th century. He was the ancestor of Robert de Tattersale, who owned the land. The nuns claimed the right to have no interference from Robert de Tattersale, and also the right to choose their Prioress. When there was a vacancy a lad was placed to guard the door, to stop anyone from outside from entering. For his trouble the lad was given his food.

In 1150 the nunnery of Farewell in Staffordshire seems to have had some connection with the nunnery of Langley. The Prioress of Farewell claimed the right to interfere in the organisation of the other nunnery, and in 1209 wished to have a word in electing the Prioress of Langley, but Langley appealed to the Pope, and by 1249 Farewell had to give up any claims to Langley.

After the Dissolution it is recorded that a nun of the late convent was given a pension of £20 to look after the place. Perhaps she was the only one left; her name was Isabel Seaton.

Leominster

A nunnery in Herefordshire built in the 7th century by King Merwald, one of the sons of King Penda. The Welsh called this place Llanieny; meaning the "Place of Nuns". There is a legend that King Merwald, while he sat at supper, gave a piece of bread to a lion that came tamely towards him, and because of that incident he called the place where he built the nunnery, Leominster.

The nunnery was destroyed by the Danes, but sometime during the 9th or 10th centuries it must have been restored, as after the murder of King Edward, and his body was exhumed from Wareham, it was taken to Shaftesbury, but a portion of it was given to the nuns of Leominster.

In the year 1121, the nunnery was in a decaying condition. Henry I gave the land to the monks of Reading, where he built a new Abbey.

Lingebrook

A Benedictine nunnery in Herefordshire. The date of the foundation is unknown, but Adam Eager is said to have given land to the nuns at a place called Brokheswodepower, on condition that they always prayed for him on the anniversary of his death. He gave this land in the reign of Edward III (1327-1377).

Little Gidding

At Little Gidding in Huntingdonshire in the year 1625 a venture was started which was unique in the history of the Church of England. Since the reformation and the Dissolution of the monasteries in the 16th century anyone in Britain wishing to live a life according to a Rule of a Religious Order, had to go abroad. For nearly a hundred years no monastic houses existed in England. The conception of such a place was generally frowned upon, until Nicholas Ferrar with the assistance of his mother, Mary Ferrar, gathered her large family of sons, daughters and grandchildren together to lead a life of devotion and sanctity.

Mrs Ferrar bought a large manor house in a village which was practically depopulated, with a church nearby which had been badly neglected.

Nicholas was ordained a deacon and he and the rest of the family vowed to live an existence as a religious community in accordance with the principles of the Anglican Church. They first repaired the church and made the house into a habitable home. The entire household consisted of about thirty persons, men, women, and children, and they all helped.

Nicholas became their chaplain, and laid down a Rule of daily devotions. On weekdays they all went to the church three times a day, starting with Matins at six in the morning, and they also said their private prayers in their own rooms. The vicar in the next parish came over every Sunday and Nicholas assisted him in the service in church.

The poor in the neighbourhood were encouraged to visit them and the Ferrars did all they could to help those in need. They received a great number of visitors, including the Bishop of the Diocese, who gave all the support that he was able to the Community. Even the king, Charles I, came to Little Gidding, and to the end the family were loyal to him.

But the puritanism of the times was against them, and often the house was called scathingly the "Protestant Nunnery".

When Mary Ferrar died in 1634 and Nicholas in 1637, the household began to get smaller. John Ferrar took over the leadership and found great difficulties as the Civil war was approaching. The king paid a last visit when fleeing from his enemies, and the Prince of Wales in 1646 came as a fugitive to seek shelter. Because of this information was laid against John Ferrar and he was named a traitor and he had to depart and hide away from Little Gidding.

Then the soldiers of Cromwell entered and plundered the house and stripped the church of all its furnishings. John died in 1657, but by that time the rest of the family were scattered, and this unique and great experiment came to an end, and was not repeated for more than two hundred years.

When the Community was first formed the household consisted of

Nicholas, the Founder, his mother, Mary Ferrar, his elder brother, John with his wife and their three children, his sister Susanna, who married John Collet, and eleven of their children. Also a cousin, Ralph Woodnoth, a son of Arthur Woodnoth, a friend of George Herbert. With three schoolmasters and the servants, there were thirty persons living in the Manor House.

Little Mareis

A Benedictine nunnery in Yorkshire, called Yedingham Priory and also De Parvo Marisco. It was founded by Roger de Clare before 1168 for eight or nine nuns, and he gave all the land round about. Henry II confirmed the grant. The nunnery was dedicated to the Blessed Virgin Mary.

It appears to have been the duty of the convent to maintain wolf dogs (for hunting?), as the following supplies of bread were delivered daily: to the Prioress and nuns 62 loaves, to nine brethren 12 loaves apiece weekly, to Brother James 14 loaves, to three priests and other officers accordingly; and "Canibus in singulis manneriis trigente movem panes de pani duriori".

At the Dissolution the house was valued at £21.16.8., and the Prioress and five nuns received pensions. All that can be seen now is a long wall of a shed, which lies south of Abbey Farm; this was the south wall of the aisleless church. It has a moulded storey course and a doorway near its west end, and a second doorway only showing on the inner side. Both of these doorways are presumed to have led into the cloisters.

Livenestre

A Benedictine nunnery in Sussex, which was a cell to Almeneschy in France. Pope Alexander in 1178 gave these nuns many privileges, including exemption from paying tithes. The Statute of Carlisle in 1285 forbad any alien abbots or clergy from laying hands on any house in these islands. In Parliament in Richard II's reign it was ordained that no French alien should enjoy any benefice in the kingdom and English persons were put in their place. This affected the nunnery at Livenestre.

London

A nunnery of Minoresses or Poor Clares, situated Without Aldgate in the Parish of St. Botolph. Edmund Crouchback Earl of Leicester and Lancaster, brother of Edward I, had been invested with the crown of Sicily by the Pope, and not finding it very profitable, he returned to England and built his House of Savoy in 1293, and at the same time he built this nunnery to the east of London. His wife, Blanche, who was Queen of Navarre, is said to have brought the nuns for the nunnery from abroad.

The nunnery was called "The House of Grace of St. Mary". The Pope gave it many privileges, and it owned the Church of Hertingdon.

One of the nuns there was Margaret, whose husband had been Steward to Edward I, and had been executed for treason. When she became a widow, she went to the nunnery and was given two shillings a day for her maintenance.

In the year 1515, there was a plague in the City of London, and it spread to the nunnery, and twenty seven of the nuns died of the disease, as well as lay-people, who were servants in the house. The last Prioress was Dame Elizabeth Savage, who surrendered the nunnery in 1539. It was valued at £318.8.5.

According to J. Timbs the nunnery was not suppressed until after 1544, as Bishop Clerke was buried in the church of the "Sorores Minores" in that year. It was he who presented to the Pope, Henry VIII's book against Luther, and gained for the king the title of "Defender of The Faith". On the site of the nunnery was built the Church of Holy Trinity and some of the walls belonged to the original nunnery.

Lyminge

A double monastery of monks and nuns in Kent, whose remains of great antiquity can still be seen. After King Edwin of Northumbria was killed in 633, his widow, Ethelburga, daughter of King Ethelbert of Kent, escaped with her chaplain, Paulinus, and her children back to her home, which was in Kent. Her brother Eadbald, who was then the King of Kent, gave her land at Lyminge to build a monastery, and Ethelburga became the first Abbess. Her chaplain, Paulinus remained at Lyminge until he became Bishop of Rochester.

Ethelburga died in 647, and we are not given the name of her successor, and only the name of one other of the Abbess — Saethryth, who ruled the monastery in 804. But we know of several donors — Romanus gave land, and the Romney Marsh is supposed to commemorate his name; the Earl Oswulf gave marshland, and the Reeve known as Abba, gave ewes and cows before 835. Cuthbert, who was Archbishop of Canterbury from 740-760, was at one time at Lyminge.

Malling
A nunnery of the Benedictine Order in Kent. In 1090, Gundulphus, Bishop of Rochester placed nuns there. Formerly the land had been granted to Bishop Burhrick by King Edmund in the tenth century, and there was it seems, a religious house there in honour of St. Andrew.

Bishop Gundulphus either added to the old building or built a fresh house for the nuns. It consisted of two quadrangles with cloisters and a large hall. The Bishop also built them a beautiful church.

In 1090, when the nuns went there, the place was very isolated with no inhabitants living anywhere in the vicinity, and the village was really non-existent and was called Millinges Parva, but very soon the nunnery attracted many people and a large village grew up. The name of the first Abbess was Avicia, but I can find no other names recorded. Part of the nunnery was destroyed by fire in 1091, but it was rebuilt.

There is a tradition at Malling that the murderers of St. Thomas à Becket called at Malling after the murder. There is an account in the "Memorials of Canterbury" by Dean Stanley, which J. Timbs has given, and which I will now quote:—

"On entering the house they threw off their arms and trappings on the dining-table, which stood in the hall, and after supper gathered round the blazing hearth. Suddenly the table started back and threw its burden to the ground. The attendants, roused by the crash, rushed in with lights, and replaced the arms. But a second and still louder crash was heard, and the various articles were thrown still further off. Soldiers and servants with torches scrambled in vain under the solid table to find the cause of its convulsions, till one of the conscience-stricken knights suggested that it was indignantly refusing to bear the sacrilegious burthen of their arms — the earliest and most memorable instrance of a rapping, leaping, and moving table."

Quite a great deal of the nunnery remains, and parts have been built in to dwelling houses, and a residence, now known as Malling Abbey was built in 1738 on the lands of the nunnery.

L

Malton

A Gilbertine priory in Yorkshire about a mile north east of the present town of Malton. It was founded in 1150 by Eustace Fitzjohn, whose wife was the daughter of Ivo de Vesci, and their son, who took the name of Vesci, gave to the priory the Hermitage at Spaldingham.

Although the Gilbertine houses usually consisted of nuns and canons, this priory at Malton seems to have been the exception, as there is the record of there being eighty five canons but no mention of any nuns. At the Dissolution it was valued at £197.8.2.

There are considerable remains to be seen at the present day.

Markyate (Margate)

A Benedictine nunnery in Hertfordshire, whose nuns came under the direction of the Abbot of the great Abbey of St. Alban's.

Geoffrey, 16th Abbot, in 1145, built a nunnery for the holy maid Christina and twelve other nuns who resorted to her. The Abbot called it the "Holy Trinity in the Bossa, or in the Wood". He made Christina the first Prioress; she had been instructed by the Hermit Roger, and her nunnery became famous for its learning, for the writing of poetry and all manner of beautiful embroidery.

The nunnery was burnt down while Abbot Geoffrey was still alive, but he soon rebuilt a second one.

The last Abbess before the Dissolution was Joan Zouch.

Marham

A Cistercian nunnery in Norfolk, founded in 1252. Elizabeth D'Aubigni, Countess gave the Manor of Marham to build this nunnery.

Marlow

A small Benedictine nunnery, founded about 1220, by Geoffrey, Lord Spencer. In the church belonging to the nunnery is the tomb of the builder of the chancel, Nicholas de Ledwyck, who added it to the church in 1430.

The following list of Prioresses has survived:— Matildis de Anvers, 1230; Cecilia, 1232; Christiana de Witteners, 1258; Felicia de Kenebel, 1264, who resigned after a year's government; Gunnora 1265; Agnes de London, 1270; Agnes de Clivdon, 1299 and who resigned; Juliana de Hampden 1299; Roesia de Weston, 1305. Then there is a gap in the list until Joan, elected 1403; Elenor Kirby, 1492; Elenor Bernard, 1516; and then the last Prioress, Margaret Vernon, who was appointed 1534, but the Nunnery was then annexed to Bisham Abbey in Berks, and very soon all the abbeys were dissolved.

Marrick (Marrig)

A Benedictine nunnery in Swaledale in Yorkshire founded in the 12th century by Roger de Aske. It lies close to the remains of a disused dam which was used for the nuns' water-mill.

The nunnery was, Dugdale says dedicated to the Blessed Virgin Mary, but according to a manuscript in the Bodleian Library, to St. Andrew.

The nave of this priory church was used for divine service until 1811, when it was pulled down and rebuilt of the old materials, but it seems to have been disused for some years now.

Parts of the original east and south walls of the old nunnery, lying about forty two feet east of the present church, and the western tower, are still standing.

In the east wall, there is part of a large pointed window of about the 14th century. It lacks the head and tracery. Under this is a strong and chamfered plinth. In the south wall is a 14th century window with two lights and fragments of tracery. Under this window a sedilia can be seen.

Some sort of youth organization has been occupying the adjoining farmhouse, and has been using the church on which at least some restoration work has been carried out.

A steep flight of stone steps connects the church with the village.

The last Prioress Christabel Cowper surrendered the nunnery in 1539; it was valued then at £48.18.2.

Marsey

A Gilbertine priory in Lincolnshire. Dugdale says that Elizabeth Chauncy and her predecessors gave the land, otherwise he gives no further information.

Melsonby

Five miles from Richmond in Yorkshire opposite the rectory of Melsonby are some slight remains of a religious house; which is thought to have been a Benedictine nunnery founded by Roger d'Aske, late in the reign of King Stephen or early Henry II.

Marton

An Augustinian priory near Easingwold in Yorkshire, founded in the 12th century, originally for monks and nuns, but shortly after its foundation, the nuns moved out, prior to 1167, to Moxby Priory, or, as it was once called, Molesby.

Minster in Sheppey

A monastery on the Isle of Sheppey in Kent. Founded by Sexburga, the eldest daughter of King Anna of East Anglia. Her husband, King Ercombert of Kent died in the plague in 664, and for four years, the Queen acted as Regent for her son Egbert. In 668 she took the veil from the hands of Archbishop Theodore of Canterbury, and her son Egbert gave her the Isle of Sheppey where she built the monastery.

Sexburga became the Abbess and she ruled over seventy-seven nuns with a staff of monastic chaplains. But when her sister Etheldreda founded the monastery of Ely, Sexburga left Kent, and appointed her daughter Ermenilda, the widow of King Wulfhere of Mercia, to succeed her as Abbess of Sheppey.

After a time Ermenilda followed her mother to Ely. We are not told the name of the abbess who succeeded her. The next we hear of the monastery is from the Anglo-Saxon Chronicle in the year 835 — "In this year the heathen devastated Sheppey"; the heathen being the Danes.

After the Conquest, William, Archbishop of Canterbury, rebuilt the monastery and nuns occupied the new building. This William must have been William de Corbeuil, who was Archbishop from 1123-1136.

Minster in Thanet

One of the very early monasteries built in Kent. It lies in the Isle of Thanet. King Egbert of Kent gave the land to his cousin Domneva, who was wife to King Merwold of Mercia. Her two brothers had been murdered by a man named Thumor, and King Egbert felt partly responsible. To compensate, he promised to give Domneva whatever she should ask. She requested that the king should give her as much land that her tame deer could run over in one course. The deer started and crossed to the Isle of Thanet and encircled a tract of land of about ten thousand acres, which the king, keeping his word, gave her, and there she built a nunnery in memory of her brothers.

156

The nunnery was consecrated by Archbishop Theodore in the year 680, and dedicated to the Blessed Virgin Mary, and Domneva became the first Abbess, having filled it with seventy nuns. Her daughter Mildred who had been educated in France, came back to England, and joined her mother at Thanet, and when Domneva died about 690, St. Mildred succeeded her as Abbess.

St. Mildred was held in very great honour, and after her death the Minster Abbey became known as St. Mildred's Abbey. The date of her death is uncertain; it has been given as 700 or 725. The first date is more likely to be the correct one, as she was succeeded as abbess by Eadburg, to whom St. Boniface wrote in 717, and she was then presumed to be ruling the monastery.

Under St. Eadburga the standard of education at the monastery became very high, and she and her nuns often communicated with St. Boniface in Germany, and sent him gifts of books and vestments.

St. Eadburga built a new church for the community, which must have been raised to the status of an abbey, as the nun in charge was always known as the Abbess. The new church was dedicated to St. Peter and St. Paul, and was consecrated by Cuthbert, who was Archbishop of Canterbury from 740-758.

St. Eadburga died in 751, so she must have ruled as Abbess for over fifty years. She was succeeded by Sigeburga. From then on life for the nuns became one of fear and harassment. Being right on the east coast, it was one of the first places ravaged by the pirate Danes, and they were being continually plundered. Still they managed to survive for some years, till disaster finally overtook the Abbey. The exact date is not certain, but 1011 is usually given when Swein, the Dane, is said to have burnt the whole place down to the ground, together with all the nuns.

But the body of St. Mildred was preserved by a miracle and the monks of Canterbury secretly at night time took the body to Canterbury.

Moxby (Molesby)

A priory in Yorkshire. The nuns there originally came from Marton Priory, which was one of the Augustinian Order, and founded by Bertram de Bulmer, so the Moxby Priory was of the same Order presumably, and had the same Founder. The nuns moved there before 1167, and Henry II confirmed "the gift of Molesby to the nuns

157

serving God there" it was dedicated to St. John. It stood in a low fruitful valley near the Foss river, where the nuns had a mill.

It is said to have flourished until the Dissolution, and then valued at £32.6.2.. Only three names of the Prioresses are mentioned — Euphomia in 1310, Elizabeth de Nevil about 1350, and the last Prioress, Philippa Jenison, with nine nuns surrendered the House.

Very little traces of the priory can be seen now only some foundations and lower brick courses, and on the site a farm house has been built, and part of a moat is still showing.

About a mile away there is a wood called St. John's Wood, where there is a spring called St. John's Well, which formerly had a domelike building over it. The water is supposed to have medicinal properties. There are remains of a causeway running from the Priory to this well.

Newstede (Newstead)
A small Gilbertine priory on the banks of the river Ancholme in Lincolnshire. Peter, son of Henry Bilingey gave the land during Henry II's reign.

On the site of the priory there is now a farm house, in which there is a large room with round arched vaulting, and was said to be the refectory built in the 12th century. There is also another room with a 15th century window.

Northampton
A Cluniac priory of St. Mary de Pratis, sometimes called de la Pre. This priory was one of the three great religious foundations that Simon de St. Liz started to build in the year 1084.

Simon was a friend of William I, and the King wished him to marry his niece Judith, who was the widow of Waltheof (son of Siward, Earl of Northumbria), but she refused. Then Simon married Maud, the daughter of Judith and Waltheof, and William gave him the Earldoms of Huntingdon and Northampton.

Simon de St. Liz built the great castle of Northampton, and inside the walls of the town, he built the Augustinian Abbey of St. James; just outside the walls, the Cluniac Priory of St. Andrews, and across the river Nene, the Priory of Delapre or St. Mary de Pratis. The meaning of de Pratis or de la Pre is "in the meadow". The nuns were some of the very few of the Order of Cluniacs in England.

In the year 1329, Edward III confirmed all donations to this priory. At the Dissolution it was valued at £119 p.a.

North Berwick

A Cistercian nunnery in the County of East Lothian. It was founded by Duncan, Earl of Fife (1136-1154). His son Earl Duncan, his successor, mentions in a charter that his father made a donation of land to the nuns. Other authorities mention Malcolm, Earl of Fife (1203-30) as being the founder, but, according to Easson in the "Medieval Religious Houses, Scotland", he only confirmed the possessions of the nunnery.

The nunnery frequently suffered from hostile action between the nations of the English and the Scots, but it survived until after 1544, when there were twenty nuns and the Prioress.

In 1587, it was said to be in ruins, and the property of the nunnery was given by James VI to Alexander Home.

The hospitals of North Berwick and Ardross were attached to this nunnery.

Nun-Appleton

A Cistercian priory about nine miles from York. The land was given by Adkeliza de Sancto Quintino and her son Robert. Their grant was confirmed by Thomas, Archbishop of Canterbury from 1162-1170.

Some very curious injunctions were laid on the Prioress and nuns in 1489; in the following I quote a few of them from Dugdale:— "First and principally, we command and injoyne, that the Divine Service, and the rules of your religion, be observed and kept accordingly to your Order that ye be professed.

Item. That the Cloyster-doores be shett and spary in Winter at seven, and in Summer at eight of the clocke at night, and the keys nightly to be delivered to your Prioress, and then after the said houres suffer no person to come in or forth without a cause reasonable.

Item. That none of your sisters use the Alehouse, nor the watersyde where the couse of strangers daily resorte.

Item. That none of your sisters bring in, receive or take any Lay-man religious or secular, into the the chambre or any secret place, day or night, nor with thaim in such private places to commune, etc or drinke, with lycense of your Prioress."

From these injuctions, (there were six more of them) it seems that the nuns in the priory needed reprimanding for their behaviour.

At the Dissolution the house was valued at £73.9.10.. On the site of the priory, Thomas Lord Fairfax built a mansion, and it is said that no trace of any ruins remain.

Nunburnholme

A Benedictine nunnery in Yorkshire. Dugdale says it was founded by the ancestors of Roger de Morlay, who lived during the reign of Henry III (1216-1272). But one of the Prioresses was fined in 1206, so it must have been founded before that date.

At the Dissolution it was valued at £10.3.3.. The site can still be traced. Some interesting remains of a cross, Saxon or Danish, were found in the wall of the south porch.

Nun Cotham (Nun Cotum)

A Cistercian nunnery near Brocklesby Park in Lincolnshire, founded by Alan de Marcels in the 12th century. Pope Alexander III (1159-1181) confirmed all donations given to the nunnery, and granted the nuns the liberty to bury the dead, except any that had been excommunicated. Hugh, Bishop of Lincoln from 1181, established the Constitution of the House, ordaining that it should be composed of thirty nuns, ten lay sisters and twelve lay brothers to do the work for the nuns that had to be done outside the nunnery. There was also a Master Chaplain with two others to assist him for the services of the church.

The Constitution also decreed that no one should own any property, but all in common; that all men and women and any stranger calling at the nunnery, should have the same bread and drink, unless something more dainty be provided for the sick; that no nun should talk with anyone from outside alone; that no nun should go out to visit a friend or kindred without leave, and that neither man or woman should be admitted by compact for money, or any temporal consideration.

Nun Eaton

A Benedictine nunnery in Warwickshire, founded in the 12th century by Robert, Earl of Leicester. It was a cell of the Monastery of Font-Ebraud (Fontevrault) in France, and which the nuns of Nun Eaton considered their Mother House, and from which they took all their orders.

Nunkelling (Nunkeeling or Nunkilling)

A Benedictine nunnery in Yorkshire. It was founded in the 12th century. Sometime between 1149 and 1154, Agnes de Arches donated the land. Some authorities say she was the widow of Herbert St. Quintin, but Burke (Extinct and Dormant) says she was the wife of de Falkeberge (Fauconberg).

The nunnery was dedicated to St. Mary Magdalene and St. Helen. At the Dissolution there were only nine nuns and the Prioress and they surrendered in 1539, and the house was valued at £35.15.5.

The present parish church was originally part of the nunnery. It retains some of the round pillars of the old building, and the original font. The nunnery chapel was only 46 by 20 feet, and was at the west end of the church. There are recumbent figures of Sir Andrew Fauconberg and his wife. He was probably a descendant of the original founder. There is also the remains of a shaft of an ancient cross against the wall of a nearby cottage.

Nun Monkton
A Benedictine nunnery situated at the junction of the rivers Nidd and Ouse in Yorkshire. It was endowed by William de Arches and his wife Ivetta, and the grants were confirmed by Henry Murdac, Archbishop of York, who died in 1153. It was dedicated to the Blessed Virgin. The nuns were given some lands at Beningborough, so at first they seemed to have been quite well off. The Nunnery was valued at £75.12.4. at the Dissolution.

The nave of the priory is still used as the parish church, only the east end is new. The west end has a very beautiful doorway, and the nave has a remarkable shape. It is well worth a visit.

A large house now stands on the actual site of the domestic building of the nunnery; some of the walls are very ancient. It is called the Nun Monkton Priory.

Nunnington
There is said to have been a nunnery at this place in Yorkshire, and that it stood on the present site of the Old Hall. Tradition said in 1619 that it had been suppressed 400 years before, because of the incontinency of the nuns.

Oldbury
A nunnery in the north of Warwickshire. It was given to the nuns of Polesworth, by Walter de Hastings, when they were turned out of the Abbey of Polesworth. To explain how this happened I will quote from Dugdale:—

"At the period of the Norman Conquest, Robert de Marmyon, having been granted by King William the castle of Tamworth, in Warwickshire with the adjacent lands, expelled the nuns from Polesworth to a place called Oldbury, 4 miles distant. After which, within a year, as it is said, making a costly entertainment for some friends, amongst whom was Sir Walter de Somerville, Lord of Whichover, his sworn brother, it happened as he lay in his bed, St. Edith appeared to him in the habit of a veiled nun, with a crozier in her hand, and told him that if he did not restore the Abbey of Polesworth (which lay within the territories of his Castle of Tamworth) unto her successors he should have an evil death, and go to hell; and that he might be the more sensible of this her admonition, she smote him on the side with the point of her crozier, and so vanished away. Moreover, by this stroke being much wounded, he cried out loudly that his friends in the house arose; and finding him extremely tormented with the pain of his wound, advised him to confess himself to a priest, and vow to restore the nuns to their former possessions. Furthermore, having done so, his pain ceased, and in accomplishment of his vow (accompanied by Sir Walter de Somerville and others), he forthwith rode to Oldbury, and craving pardon of the nuns for the injury done, brought them back to Polesworth".

The Prioress at the time was Osanna, and Marmyon presented her with a Charter giving her back the Abbey at Polesworth and it appears that they had Oldbury as well.

Ormesby (Now known as North Ormesby)
A Gilbertine priory in Lincolnshire, situated in the Lincolnshire Wolds higher up the valley than where the village now stands.

It was founded in the 12th century by Gilbert, son of Robert of Ormesby, with the consent of his Lord, William, Earl of Albemore.

The priory consisted of one hundred nuns and fifty canons.

All that remains to mark the site of this house is a big pond near a farm. It may have been the fish pond of the priory. There is a lifesize figure in a field nearby, known as the White Lady; it is carved out of stone, and said to be placed there to mark the spot where a woman was killed while hunting, but there is a possibility that it was meant to commemorate one of the Prioresses or nuns.

Oxford
The account of the foundation of a nunnery at Oxford by St.

Frideswide is full of legends, but there may be some truth in it. The saint, while being pursued by a suitor, fled for shelter to the nunnery, which her father is said to have had built for her at Oxford. It was dedicated to St. Mary, and she became the first Abbess. She also built a chapel in the wood of Thornbury, where at one time she had hidden, and which later became a place of pilgrimage.

St. Frideswide died about 735. During the Danish invasions her nunnery was burnt to the ground, and afterwards a house of secular priests was established there. In 1111, Roger, Bishop of Salisbury, founded a monastery of regular canons on the site of St. Frideswide's church.

In 1525, Cardinal Wolsey built the College called Christ Church where once the nunnery had stood, and in 1546, Henry VIII made it into the Cathedral of Oxford.

St. Frideswide's remains are said to be interred there, and she is called the patron saint of Oxford.

Pinley

A little Benedictine nunnery in Warwickshire, founded by Roger de Pilardinton. Grants were confirmed by Simon, Bishop of Worcester from 1125, and by his successor Alured. The Archbishop of Canterbury granted indulgences to any donors in 1195.

Only the names of six Prioresses are given:- Lucia de Sapy, 1269; Helewysia de Langelegh, 1321; Matilda le Bret; Amicia de Hinton, 1358; Alicia Myntyns, 1426; and the last Prioress, Margaret Wigston, who surrendered the Priory at the Dissolution in 1536, and she obtained a pension of 4 shillings p.a., and the rest of the convent were given nothing.

Polesworth

A Benedictine monastery in Warwickshire, founded by King Egbert for his daughter Edith. King Egbert reigned from 802-839. He had his daughter instructed in the Rule of St. Benedict by St. Modwena. She was the daughter of an Irish King of Cunocke. Legend says that she cured the King's son from leprosy, and the king, being grateful, sent for her to come to England, promising her that he would give her land to build an abbey. This account of the connection of St. Modwena and St. Edith is from Dugdale, but other authorities state quite a different tale, saying that Edith was the sister of King Athelstan. All that is certain is that she became the first Abbess of Polesworth.

The Abbey seems to have prospered until the time of William the Conqueror, when William gave the Abbey and all the land to Sir Robert Marmyon. Sir Robert turned out the nuns, and they went to Oldbury which was given to them by Walter de Hastings.

Eventually Sir Robert regretted his conduct, being influenced by a vision of St. Edith, which I have related in the account of the Nunnery of Oldbury. He was so terrified by this vision, that he restored the nuns to their Abbey of Polesworth.

The name of the Abbess when they first returned was Osanna, and she ruled the Abbey during the reign of Henry I.

The following is a list of Abbesses who succeeded her;- Muriel, at the time of King John; Margery de Apelby, 1236; Sarah de Mancestre, 1269; Albreda de Camvilla, 1276; Catherine de Apelby, 1293; Erneburga de Hardzrshull, 1302; Matilda de Pipe 1321; Lettice de Hexstall, 1347; Agnes de Somervile, 1348; Matilda Bottourt 1361; Catherine de Wyrlegh 1400; Benedicta Prede 1413; Margaret Ruskyn, 1465; Elizabeth Bradfield, 1500; Anne Fitz-Herbert, 1505; Alice Fitz-Herbert, 1509, who was the last Abbess who surrendered the Abbey in 1539. She received a pension of £26.13.4., and fourteen of her nuns also were given pensions.

Little remains of the Abbey, except a 14th century Gatehouse, and the Nave of the Church. In the Gatehouse there is a sculptured effigy of an abbess, probably the only one still to be seen from the old abbeys of England.

Pollesho (Polsloc)

A Benedictine nunnery in Devon said to have been founded by D. Bruar (Brewer) Brother of William Bruar, Bishop of Exeter from 1224-1245, and who was uncle to King John, but this has been disproved. There is a history of pleading poverty and accusations of high-living and 'wandering' by the nuns! Very little remains but there are indications of a rare two-storied cloister.

Pulton

A Gilbertine priory in Wiltshire. The land was given by Thomas St. Maur Kt. in 1348.

Redingfield

A Benedictine nunnery in Suffolk, founded in 1120. Manasses, Comes Gisnensis and his wife Emma donated the land. The church and a farm, built on the site, stand in a lonely field, and to quote from Arthur Mee, "Eight hundred years ago a company of nuns knelt in prayer". The stones of the old nunnery have been used in the building of the church and the farm.

Reading

There is said to have been an ancient nunnery at Reading in Berkshire, which was founded by Elfreda, the wife of King Edgar, in penance for the murder of her stepson, Edward, so it would have been built soon after 978. It was burnt by the Danes in 1006.

In the year 1121, King Henry I built a Benedictine monastery for monks on the site of the old nunnery. In it he is said to have placed the hand of St. James.

Repton (Repindon)

There was a monastery here in Derbyshire in the 7th century. It was the burial place of some of the Mercian kings. St. Guthlac was a monk there for about two years, and while he was there, the Abbess Aelfthryth ruled the monastery; which shows that it must have been a double monastery for monks and nuns at that time.

It must have been destroyed by the Danes, as in 1172, it was refounded out of the ruins by Maud, daughter of Robert Earl of Gloucester, and wife to Ranulphus, Earl of Chester, and she placed there Augustine Canons.

The church dedicated to St. Wystan was built during the 14th century but it incorporates remains of a Saxon church.

Rosedale

A nunnery in Yorkshire. Dugdale says it belonged to the Benedictine Order but Pevsner says Cistercian. It was founded by Robert de Stuteville about the year 1190, and dedicated to St. Lawrence and St. Mary.

At the Dissolution there was only a prioress and eight or nine nuns, so it was only a fairly small nunnery.

All that remains now are the south west angle of the south transept of the church with two buttresses, and a spiral staircase to the north east. In 1822, Langdale says "Of the Nunnery that remains is the square of the Cloister, which is almost entire; the buildings having been converted into dwelling houses." There is a lithograph of 1855, which shows more substantial remains than can now be seen, but the village was ruined in the latter half of the last century by iron-mining and smelting operations.

Rothwell
About four miles from Kettering in Northamptonshire there are some old buildings called the nunnery; they stand on the site of what was once a priory of Austin nuns, founded by Robert Clare, Earl of Gloucester at the end of the 13th century. It was dedicated to St. John the Baptist.

Rowney
A Benedictine nunnery in Hertfordshire, built about 1150. It was founded by Conan le Petit, Earl of Richmond and Duke of Brittany. He was a great benefactor to the church and made numerous grants. He died in 1171. He married Margaret, sister of William the Lion, King of Scotland 1165-1214.

In the reign of Henry VI, Anne Selby, the Prioress of Rowney, finding that the revenues were not enough to keep her and her nuns, surrendered the nunnery to John Fray, who converted it into a chantry for one priest.

Rumsey (Romsey)
The town of Rumsey was very ancient and was called by the Romans *Insula*, as it stood on an island in the river Test in Hampshire. During the reign of Edward the Elder, 899-925, the king built an Abbey there, and his grandson King Edgar placed nuns in the building. St. Merwenna was made Abbess there in 967, and St. Elfleda was put in her charge by the king, and was consecrated a nun by Bishop Ethelwold of Winchester.

St. Merwenna died in 993, and was succeeded as Abbess by a nun named Elwina, who only ruled the Abbey for three years, dying in 996, and then St. Elfleda was summoned to take her place. It is said that she spent a great deal of money on charities for the poor, rather more than the Abbey could afford. She died in 1030.

Christina, the sister of the Atheling and Margaret, Queen of

Scotland, was a nun there, and the Scottish Queen put her two daughters, Edith (Maud) and Mary, into her charge at Rumsey.

St. Anselm, Archbishop of Canterbury took an interest in the nuns of Rumsey, and once rebuked them for venerating an individual who was by no means a saint. The nuns are also mentioned by William of Malmesbury as being very proficient in literary matters. He also says that St. Merwenna and St. Elfleda were buried in the Abbey.

During the reign of King Stephen, the Abbey was plundered by Geoffrey de Mandeville, Ist Earl of Essex, who was first on the side of Stephen, and then deserted the king and went over to the Empress Maud's party. Stephen took the Earl prisoner and deprived him of his lands. Out of revenge, when he escaped from prison, Geoffrey plundered several of the abbeys, including Rumsey.

The Church today at Rumsey is known as the Abbey Church of St. Mary and St. Ethelfleda (Elfleda), and was completed about 1282.

At the time of the suppression there were only twenty five nuns and the Abbess left in the Abbey, and of the conventual buildings they were nearly all destroyed. There is a carved full length crucifix with the Hand of God extending from above, probably of 12th century workmanship. It stands against the west wall of the south transept near the nun's entrance to the church.

Saint Albans

A monastic institution situated on the outskirts of St. Albans in Hertfordshire known as the Hospital of St. Mary de Prato (de le Pre-). It was run by Benedictine nuns for leprous nuns and came under the control of the Abbey of St. Alban's; it was founded by Warren de Cambridge about the year 1199.

Just before the general Dissolution of the monasteries, Cardinal Wolsey procured a Bull from Pope Clement VII (1523-1534) for the suppression of this nunnery, alleging misbehaviour of the nuns, (a course he took to close those religious houses he was willing to convert to his own use).

In the churchyard which was attached to the nunnery, gravestones could still be seen as late as 1827, and part of the building itself which was incorporated into some cottages known as "Three Chinnies" were only pulled down as late as 1849.

Sanford (*alias* Littlemore)

A Benedictine nunnery which was situated a few miles south of Oxford, dedicated to St. Nicholas. The exact date of its foundation is not given, but it was probably built during the 13th century, as at that time, there were a number of donors, who gave much land. According to Dugdale, "Roger Thoery gave to this Nunnery 20 acres of land above Moderul; Roger Sanford, the third part of the Island at Keniton, between Keniton and Sanford, and by another Deed the lands at Begey; Thomas Bussel, in 1254, gave one Rood of land at Sanford; Geoffrey Vancy gave them some land at Lewartone, and calls them the Nuns of St. Mary, St. Nicholas and St. Edmund at Sanford; William Vancy granted to them, by the name of St. Nicholas of Littlemore, all his pasture of the Down of Lewartone; Geoffrey, son of William confirmed the same; finally, Geoffrey Tapping gave all his land at Lewartone".

"Robert, Abbot of Abingdon confirmed to these Nuns of St. Nicholas at Sanford, all the tithes of Reyworth in Berks being the gift of Thomas Sanford. Roger de Quincy, Earl of Winchester in the early 13th century remitted to the Nuns the Duty of appearing every three weeks at his Court at Chinnore, and the Bull of the 2nd year of Pope Innocent IV (1245) granted an Indulence of ten days of enjoined Penance to all as should for three years, from the date thereof, contribute towards building of the Church of these Nuns".

Near the church at Sanford there are remains of what may have been this nunnery, but there is hardly anything to be seen.

Sandleford

A priory once stood here near Newbury in Berkshire. According to Bishop Tanner it was founded by Geoffrey, Earl of Perth and his wife Maud in the reign of King John for Canons of St. Augustine, and dedicated to St. John the Baptist, but Dugdale says it was a nunnery, and that a grant of Edward I's gave free warren in all the lands of this nunnery. He also says that Sayer of St. Andrews gave it a revenue of five shillings a year in his town of Littlemore.

The priory has been destroyed and a house called Sandleford Priory stands on the site.

Sempringham

A famous priory in Lincolnshire belonging to the Gilbertines, the one monastic Order which had originated in England. It happened that while St. Gilbert was the priest in charge of the parish of St. Andrew's in Sempringham, seven women came to seek his advice, as they wished to lead a life devoted to the service of God. St. Gilbert built them a small dwelling against the north wall of the church, and they became the nucleus of his Order. This was about the year 1131.

Very soon the number of women wishing to join the Order increased, and a larger house had to be built. Gilbert de Gaunt gave land on which to build the larger Priory in 1135. It was situated close to the church, and it became the Mother House of the Order. The Order consisted of nuns and lay sisters, canons and lay brothers. At Sempringham before St. Gilbert's death, there were 120 women and 60 men, and when he died at the great age of 106, there were 11 houses belonging to the Order, with 1500 women and 700 men. The Prior of Sempringham was given a seat in Parliament, which was usually only given to mitred Abbots of the greater Abbeys.

When St. Gilbert drew up the Rule, he made provision for all contingencies of misbehaviour, and how they should be dealt with. He composed it so that the nuns had a real voice in the settlement of their own affairs. Dugdale gives an account of the visitations for inspection of all the houses at least once a year. He gives a list of the rules drawn up separately for the four branches of the Order. There were thirty five rules for the Penitent Nuns; a few are mentioned here:-

"1. All the men of the Order carefully to serve the nuns, and care to be taken that their houses be, in all respects, neater and better furnished than those of the men.

2. All the wool from the lambs of every monastery to be delivered to the nuns, and after supplying their own wants, that to spare to be given to the poor, the nuns to have in their keeping all the gold, silver, cloaks and other like things.

3. Three particular nuns to be appointed by the rest to keep the Common Seal, gold, silver, etc.

6. The windows at which any thing is delivered in or out, to be with wheels to turn, so that the sisters may not see the men, nor the men the sisters . . . . . The window where the nuns talk to their kindred, to be the length of a finger square, ...

10. None to go into the Nunnery while the nuns are at their Hours, or in the refectory, or in the dormitory; but in the case of

absolute necessity, several to go in and out all together; excepting in case of fire, robbery or danger of death.

There were also rules for the canons; rules for sick nuns and sisters, and rules concerning the Office of the Dead. Some may seem strange to us with our ideas of hygiene at the present day, such as the rule that none to bathe unless for health or great necessity, and when done in such cases, not to be naked, but covered with linen. The Rule was to be read four times a year in each house.

Yearly a Great Chapter was held at the Mother House in Sempringham, at which all the Priors and two Prioresses of the other houses attended.

At the Dissolution the Priory was valued at £317.4.1., and the site was given to Lord Clinton, Earl of Lincoln, who pulled down all the buildings and built himself a mansion. In 1938 the foundations of the Priory were excavated. The church belonging to it was discovered to be 325 feet long; the nun's section being 35 feet long, with St. Gilbert's shrine beside the wall between the canons and nuns chancels. Close by is the old church of St. Andrew, where St. Gilbert first built the small dwelling for the first seven women.

Sewardsley

A Benedictine nunnery in Northamptonshire, built in the 14th century. Robert de Pinkeny, who was in Edward III's service in 1382, gave the land.

Shaftesbury

A Benedictine abbey for nuns in Dorset, founded by King Alfred the Great for his daughter Elfgive, who was sometimes called Aethelgiva. According to a grant dated 878, he endowed it well with lands. The town of Shaftesbury was of very great antiquity, and stood on a steep hill; Geoffrey of Monmouth says it was called by the Britons, Palladour or Mount Paladour.

The Abbey was dedicated to St. Mary the Virgin, and Elfgiva became the first Abbess. It was destroyed by the Danes, but was magnificently restored by subsequent kings, who greatly favoured the Abbey. The martyred King Edward was brought there after his assassination and miracles took place at his shrine, many pilgrims came to pay him homage, and greatly added to the wealth of the Abbey. In 1035 King Cnut died there while on a visit.

Archbishop Anselm took an interest in the nuns of Shaftesbury and called them his spiritual daughters, including one whose name is given as Eulalia. Education of these nuns seems to have been extremely high and there were several poets among them, including the half sister of Henry II, Marie de France.

Shaftesbury became of such importance that the Abbess was entitled to a seat in Parliament, she having the rank of a peeress.

The following is a list of some of the Abbesses after the Abbey was restored:- Herleva, whose date is given as 966; Cecilia, at the time of Henry I; Emma; Laurentia, 1295; Margeria Auchier, 1314; Alice Gibbs, 1493; Margeria Twyneham, 1505; Eliz. Thelford, 1523; and the last Abbess, Elizabeth Zouche, 1529.

At the time of the Norman Conquest the annual income of Shaftesbury was £234, next to Wilton, the richest Abbey in the country. At the Dissolution of the monasteries the last Abbess was given a pension of £133 p.a. She surrendered the Abbey in 1539, and her 38 nuns were also allowed pensions.

There was a saying that "If the Abbess of Shaftesbury might wed the Abbot of Glastonbury, their heir would have more land than the King of England". This mighty Abbey was razed to the ground; Dugdale says there was nothing left standing, but excavations which started in the last century revealed a great deal of the foundations, and they show that the Abbey church was almost the size of Salisbury Cathedral.

Shouldham

A Gilbertine priory in Norfolk, which, according to Burke Ex. & D. was founded by Roger de Newburgh, 2nd Earl of Warwick, who died in 1153, and was "memorable for pious foundations among which was the Nunnery of Shouldham." So it must have been founded during the lifetime of St. Gilbert, who died in 1189.

Dugdale says that Geoffrey, son of Peter, Earl of Essex, was the founder, and that he translated the body of his wife, who had been buried at Chicksands, to Shouldham. Geoffrey was probably a donor of land to the Priory, and not the founder.

The Earls of Warwick were always patrons of Shouldham, as many of their daughters became nuns there, including Roger's great-great-granddaughters Anne and Amy. Thomas Beauchamp, 3rd Earl, 1313–1369, sent his daughter Margaret, as a nun, and his eldest son, Guy's three daughters, Kathleen, Elizabeth and Margaret also went there. Lastly, the 4th Earl Thomas, sent his two daughters Margaret and Katherine. The Priory appears to have become a family concern of the Earls of Warwick.

Sixhills (Sixil)

A Gilbertine priory in Lincolnshire founded in the reign of King Stephen. The name of the founder or donor of the land is given as de Grille. Edward I is said to have sent Lady Christina Seton, the sister of Robert the Bruce, to this priory, after her husband was hanged as a traitor. The King also sent the daughter of Davydd, the last native prince of North Wales. There she lived as a nun for a great number of years.

The normal number of nuns at Sixhills was 120 and 55 canons. At the Dissolution the priory was valued at £135.0.9. The site is now a farmhouse, and there are still to be seen some sculptured heads from the old building.

Sopewell (Sopwell)

A Benedictine nunnery situated about half a mile south east of St. Albans in Hertfordshire. Legend says that it got its name from two holy women sopping their crusts in a neighbouring well. They had built themselves a poor habitation of branches of trees. They lived a most austere and religious life, living on bread and water. They became famous and many women joined them. In 1140, Geoffry, Abbot of St. Albans, built them a nunnery and bestowed on them more possessions so that they might live in better conditions. He gave them a churchyard where only the nuns were to be buried. He also stipulated that only virgins were to be admitted and their number was not to exceed thirteen.

Other donors granted them land, and their patrons included Henry de Albini and Richard de Tany.

After the foundation had been existing for about two hundred years, Michael, Abbot of St. Albans, in 1338 decreed that certain rules were to be more strictly observed. Dugdale gives a list of these rules which I quote as follows:

1. Commemoration of St. Albans should be kept.
2. Only three nuns to sit in Chapter.
3. That silence should be observed in Church, Cloister, Refectory,

and Dormitory.

4. That the little bell be rung for nuns to rise, and none to go out before it rings.

5. That the garden door be not opened till the Hour of Prime, and in summer the garden and parlour doors not to be opened till the Hour of None, and to be always shut when the bells ring for Curfew (Couvreseu).

6. None to talk in the parlour with her cowl on and face covered with her veil.

7. Taylors and other workmen to have a place outside and not to enter and to be persons of good repute.

8. Those that are under penance not to be excluded from the duties of the Church.

9. The sick to be kept in the Infirmary.

10. No nun to be out of the Dormitory nor a guest within it.

11. All the nuns to be present at the Mass of Our Lady.

There are still fragments of some walls of the ruins to be seen. At the Dissolutution the nunnery was valued at £40.7.1.

Southwark

There was a very ancient nunnery called St. Mary Overie. It occupied the site where now stands Southwark Cathedral. This Cathedral, in the course of its history, has had three different names: St. Mary Overie; St. Saviour; thirdly Southwark Cathedral. The first name was a dedication to the Virgin, and the second part of the name, Overie, meaning "of the ferry". The nunnery is said to have been founded long before the Norman Conquest, by a maiden named Mary.

Mary was the daughter of the ferryman who ferried a boat across the River Thames, as then there was no bridge. She helped her father row passengers across the river. His name is said to have been John Overs, and he charged an exorbitant price, and in time amassed a great deal of money. He became very mean and unpopular. One night he was killed quite accidentally by his servants, who, imagining him to be the devil, attacked him.

Mary was very beautiful and had many suitors but in her distress rejected them, and with the money she inherited from her father, she built the Church of St. Mary Overie, and founded a nunnery, to which she retired as a nun.

This nunnery was dissolved in 852, and St. Swithun, Bishop of

Winchester established a College of priests there. Some say that these priests built the first wooden bridge across the Thames, and it is probably the bridge about which the ballad, "London bridge is falling down", is written.

In 1107, William Giffard, Bishop of Winchester made this ancient site of the nunnery into a priory for canons of St. Augustine. Dugdale mentions two knights, William Panlane, and William Domcius, who both gave an endowment to the priory.

The priory was dissolved in Henry VIII's reign and the last Prior received a pension of £100 p.a.

Mary Overs is said to be buried in the choir of the church.

In 1937 a new Constitution was set up under the title of the "Cathedral and Collegiate Church of St. Saviour and St. Mary Overie, Southwark", the incumbent becoming Provost and head of the Chapter.

Stainfield (Steinsfield)

A Benedictine nunnery in Lincolnshire, founded by Henry Percy in 1054. Dugdale gives two founders — Henry Percy and William Perry; probably Perry was the donor of some land to the nunnery.

What relation Henry Percy was to the first Lord William Percy, who came over with the Conqueror in 1066, is uncertain; he may have been his father. Lord William had a grandson, William, who owned the land round Stainfield. He had two daughters. One of them named Agnes married Josceline of Louvain, brother of Adeliza, wife of Henry I. Josceline adopted the name of Percy, and on his father in law's death, inherited the Nunnery of Stainfield.

The nunnery survived until the Dissolution.

Stamford

A Benedictine monastery in Lincolnshire.

William, Bishop of Peterborough in the reign of Henry II built a monastery for nuns in honour of God and St. Michael, and established there forty women, who were always to be under the control of the Abbot of Peterborough. In 1355, Thomas de Holland annexed the Nunnery of Wothorpe to Stamford, as the nunnery at Wothorpe was so poor, all the nuns there having died of the plague, leaving only one left, and she went to Stamford.

At the Dissolution the monastery was valued at £65.19.0

Stixwould (Stykeswold)

W. F. Rawnsey in *Highways and Byways*, Arthur Mee in *the King's England* and the Monastic Map all give the nunnery as belonging to the Cistercian Order, but Dugdale says it was a Benedictine nunnery.

Rawnsey says it was founded in the reign of King Stephen (1135–1154) by Lucia, the first wife of Ivo Taillebois. Taillebois was a native of Angers and nephew of William I, and he carried his standard at the battle of Hastings.

Dugdale mentions an inquisition taken in the reign of Edward I (1272–1307), in which it was found that the nuns held several lands of the gift of Lucy, mother of Ranulph de Meschines, Earl of Chester (who died 1128), which they had so held for the space of 100 years. So the nunnery must have been founded not long after the Cistercians came to England.

There is nothing to say whether the nunnery prospered, but it lasted until the Dissolution, but there is a document about the value of the property of the nunnery which says, "All which Premises were Extended to the yearly Value of £152.10.5. and no more . . . and for the Yearly Rent of £15.5.1 to be paid into the Court of Augmentations, that being the true Tenth of the aforsaid Manors, Rectories, etc."

The nunnery having surrendered, then Henry VIII did what was for him a most unusual action, quite out of keeping with his general practice: he founded a new monastery on the site of the old Nunnery of Stixwould. Not only did he do this but he got Thomas Cranmer and Thomas Cromwell to witness the charter, both being great enemies of the Religious Houses, and only too willing to pull them all down.

Dugdale gives the charter, and I quote from him:

"The Charter of the 29th of Henry VIII sets forth, That he had thought fit to found a Monastery of Premonstratension Nuns, in the same place where the Mon: of Stix-or Stykeswold, in Lincs, suppressed by Parliament, had stood, for them to perform the Divine Office there, for him and his Queen Jane, whilst they lived, and for their Souls when dead; which Mon: he did accordingly found to last for ever, and to be called the New Mon: of Henry VIII at Stixwould –

Therefore that this Foundation might have full Effect, he granted and gave to Mary Missenden, Professed Nun of the aforesaid Order, by him appointed Prioress of the new Mon:, for ever the Place etc. . . . . of the old Mon: with all the Houses etc. He also made the said Nuns a

Body corporate . . . and as such to be capable of receiving any Possessions, of having a Common Seal, and of suing or being sued . . . He further granted them . . . all things belonging to Stixwould as the same had come into his hands, on Pretence of the Act of Parliament begun the 3rd of Nov;, in the 21st year of his reign."

As I said this charter was witnessed by Thomas Cranmer, Archbishop of York, and by Thomas Cromwell, Lord Privy Seal.

Of the old nunnery at Stixwould, very little remains. In the churchyard there are the stump of an old cross, a medieval floorstone and several broken coffins. In the church, which was rebuilt in 1831, an old stoup has been preserved and a finely carved 14th century font. In the church at Woodhall Spa, which is not far from Stixwould, there are set in the chancel two medieval stones which are said to come from the old nunnery at Stixwould. One is a floor stone with an engraved cross and the other a stone with a deep recess and a man peeping out from the recess.

What happened to the monastery which Henry VIII built, Dugdale does not say, but I believe it did not last for long and was in the end dissolved like the rest of the monasteries.

Stone

The priory at Stone in Staffordshire was said to have been first inhabited by Augustinian canons, and then they disappeared and nuns took over the priory. Whether the legend of its foundation contains any truth is not certain. King Wulfhere, son of Penda of Mercia, married Ermenilda, daughter of the King of Kent, and he is supposed to have murdered his two sons, Wulfad and Ruffin. He did this deed while they were praying in the cell of St. Chad, who had converted them to Christianity. Queen Ermenilda persuaded her husband, as a penance, to build the priory at Stone. This was in the year 670.

At the time of the Norman Conquest, Lord Robert of Stafford owned the land, and there were then only two nuns with one priest. All three were slain by Enyson de Waltoue, and he destroyed the priory also.

Robert of Stafford restored the building and again placed canons there. The priory was dedicated to St. Wulfad. It was dissolved in 1536, and little remains of it at the present day. The site is at the bottom of Abbey Street, where there is a house called Priory House, and it contains vaulted cellars, which are probably the original cellars of the old priory.

Stratford

A Benedictine nunnery of the 11th century, dedicated to St. Leonard. Bishop Tanner says it was founded by William, who was Bishop of London from 1051–1075. In the reign of King Stephen, Christiana de Sumery and her sons donated much land to the nunnery.

It was situated near the Bow Bridge and was sometime called Stratford Bow.

At the Dissolution of the monasteries Dugdale says it was valued at £108.1.11.

Studley (Stodely)

A nunnery in Oxfordshire of the Benedictine Order.

It is difficult to say who was the founder, except it was probably one of the Walerico family, as many of them seem to have been donors to this nunnery during the thirteenth century, so it was established sometime early in that century.

The following lines I quote from Dugdale:

"Bernard de Santo Walerico granted to the Church of St. Mary of Stodely, to the nuns there serving God, half a Hide of Land at Horton, which is confirmed by his son William, with leave to choose their own Priests, with his approbation, or that of his Steward, if he happened not to be in England, and at his return the Prioress was to appear before him at his court at Oxford to pay the homage she owed him.

Thomas de Santo Walerico gave these nuns three shillings a year at Bechly, Anno 1257, also a load of Wood weekly for fuel out of his wood at Horton.

Robert, Lord of St. Walerick gave them the Church of Bechly, Anno 1227.

Richard, King of the Romans (2nd son of King John) granted them the Breadth of 12 Feet in land quite round the Priory.

Godfrey de Craucumb bestowed on them all his Manor of Craucumb, with the Advowson of the Church."

A futher quotation from Dugdale:

"The Charter of the First of Richard II says, this Church was founded by Thomas St. Waleric, and that the Honor of Studley, of which that Church was a part, being escheated into the Hands of his Progenitors, and of course the Advowson of that Church, he had approved of the choice made of Elizabeth Fremental for Prioress there."

Swine

A Cistercian nunnery near Beverley in Yorkshire, founded by Robert de Verli in the reign of King Stephen. Dugdale mentions the name of Eronbrock de Burtona; he may have been a donor.

The last Prioress was Dorothy Knight, who when the nunnery was suppressed was given a pension of £13.6.8 p.a., and her nuns received from £3.6.8 to £2 p.a. Dugdale says the nunnery was valued at £82.3.9, but Speed says £13.6.9.

Syngthwaite (Sinningtwait)

A Cistercian nunnery near Bilton, 4 miles from Wetherby in Yorkshire, founded by Bertram de Haget about 1160. His son, Geoffry was also a donor. The nuns at one time felt they were not being treated properly and they appealed to several of the Popes, Alexander II, Gregory VIII and Lucius III during the 12th century.

Catherine Forster, the 14th and last Prioress surrendered the nunnery in 1553. This was much later than many of the other Houses, as the Prioress was left in charge until that date, being paid out of the Revenues 10s. in annuities and Carrodies.

There are the remains of several walls and arches, with decorations of leaf motifs and zigzags on the wall surfaces. A perpendicular window and part of the main gateway are showing.

Syon

A monastery of the double Order of Bridgettines. This Order had been founded in Sweden about the year 1375 by Queen Bridget of Sweden. Lord Fitzhugh, a nephew of Archbishop Scrope told the Community that he wished to found a convent in England near Cambridge and Henry IV, having murdered Archbishop Scrope, encouraged the idea, and a priest was sent by the Abbess of Vadstena to take possession of the property near Cambridge, but the design came to nothing.

When Henry V came to the throne, he laid the foundation stone of a monastery at Twickenham. It was dedicated to The Holy Saviour, St.

Margaret and St. Bridget, and was a double monastery of men and women, ruled by an Abbess and Confessor, which was the title of the head of the Brethren. When it was opened there were only four consecrated sisters, and three brothers, but in 1420, twenty seven sisters, five priests, two deacons and four lay brothers took their vows.

William of Alnwick was appointed Confessor and Matilda Newton, Abbess. She became an ancress at Barking in 1417, and Joan North, who had been a nun at Markyate succeeded her. In 1420, Thomas Fishbourne became Confessor.

In 1431 the monastery moved to Isleworth, and then finally settled at Syon. In its last days the number of nuns was sixty, with thirteen priests, four deacons and eight lay brothers, all of which when reckoned up amounted to as many persons as the thirteen Apostles, and seventy two Disciples of Christ.

At the Dissolution the Bridgettines departed to Sweden.

The site was given to the Duke of Somerset by Edward VI, who built the building, known as Syon House. Then the Dukes of Northumberland occupied it. When Mary came to the throne, she restored it to the Bridgettines, then Elizabeth expelled them, and in 1604 it was given to Henry Percy ninth Earl of Northumberland.

Tarrant

To the north east and south of Blandford in Dorset there are a number of parishes all lying by the banks of the Tarrant a tributory of the Stour. At one of them, Tarrant Crawford, the church occupies the site of an old Cistercian Abbey of nuns. It was founded by Ralph de Kahaynes in the reign of Richard I.

Tarrant had very close associations with Richard Poor, whose name is spelt in several ways — Poure, Poore and La Poor. Even after he left the south for the north he took an interest in the nuns at Tarrant. He had an interesting career; he was Dean of Old Sarum in 1197, elected Bishop of Chichester in 1214 and translated to Salisbury in 1217. In 1219 he removed the see of Old Sarum to the present site of the town of Salisbury among the marshes where several rivers meet. After having consecrated the High altar in the Lady Chapel in 1225 and laid out the plans for the new town, he was transfered to Durham far away in the north, in 1228.

After he had been Bishop of Durham for two years, in 1230 he refounded the convent of nuns at Tarrant in Dorset, and they adopted the Rule of the Order of the Cistercians. He wrote a book called the "Ancren Riwle" which he addressed to the Ancresses at Tarrant, and drew up originally for three young women for their guidance. These women had had their cell for retirement at Tarrant Keynston.

An interesting donor to this convent was Johanna, daughter of Edward II of England. She married David II, King of Scotland, in 1328.

Thetford

A Benedictine nunnery in Norfolk, dedicated to St. Gregory. In 1072, Thetford became the See of the Bishopric of East Anglia until Bishop Herbert Losinga removed the See to Norwich in 1094. In the reign of Edward III there were eight religious houses, including the nunnery. The last Prioress's name is given as Elizabeth Hothe, and when the nunnery was suppressed, she was given a pension of £5 p.a. until she died in 1553 at the age of a hundred.

Thicket (Thikehead)

A small Benedictine nunnery in the East Riding of Yorkshire, founded in the reign of Richard I by Roger FitzRoger. It was dedicated to the Blessed Virgin.

Dugdale gives the name of the nunnery as Tykehead, and says that Robert Ashe was the founder; but he was probably a donor. He did give the nuns 7s.4d. to pray for the souls of himself, his wife and his children on the anniversary of their deaths.

At the Dissolution the value of the nunnery was given as £20.18.10. by Dugdale, but Speed gives £23.12.2.

Trentham

A nunnery in Staffordshire, founded in Saxon times by St. Werburga, the daughter of King Wulfhere and Queen Ermenilda of Mercia. St. Werburga founded many houses, and her uncle King Ethelred helped her to endow them, but Trentham always remained in poor circumstances.

It was to Trentham that Werburga retired when she was getting on in years, and it was there that she died.

The nuns left Trentham to escape from the Danes, and took the body of St. Werburga and translated it to Chester. About 1251 the nunnery became a priory of Austin canons. It was suppressed in 1536.

The Church at Trentham occupies the site of the old nunnery, and there is a niche in the Church for a statue of St. Werburga.

Tynemouth

High on the sandstone crags at the mouth of the river Tyne stand the ruins of Tynemouth Priory. A small wooden Chapel was first erected on the site by King Edwin, who died in 633, and in it his daughter Rosella took the veil. King Oswald, his successor rebuilt it of stone, and it was called the Oratory of the Virgin. A great many of the illustrious dead were buried there, including King Oswin, the royal martyr, Henry, the hermit of Coquet Island, Malcolm Canmore, King of Scotland and his son Prince Edward. It was destroyed by pirates, who may have been Danes, but refounded by King Ecgfrith in 671. In 876 the Dane Halfden reduced it to ashes and massacred all the monks and nuns.

The nuns from Hartlepool are said to have fled to Tynemouth for refuge, but they were all martyred, and for years the place was left in ruins.

The remembrance of St. Oswine was entirely forgotten until the time of Earl Tostig, who married the Conqueror's niece, Judith. There was still a sexton who looked after the graves, and his name was Edmund. One night he had a dream in which the saint came to him and revealed to him his burial place. The dream was told to the Countess Judith, and she made a determined search for the grave of St. Oswin, and when it was discovered, she had the body recommitted to the ground with great ceremony.

According to Leland Earl Tostig rebuilt the priory. Then his successor gave it to the monks of Jarrow in 1075, including the body of St. Oswin; but the monks of Jarrow were not really interested, and left the place deserted.

In 1090, Earl Mowbray refounded the priory and filled it with black canons. There were no longer any nuns there. It became a cell of the Abbey of St. Alban's in Hertfordshire. The body of St. Oswin was returned to Tynemouth from Jarrow and became its patron saint.

The priory was dissolved in the 16th century, and its beautiful ruins can be seen at this day, but they probably show nothing of the old original priory; its remains will be buried in the dust.

Wallingwells

A small Benedictine nunnery built and endowed by Ralph de Chevrolant in the reign of King Stephen, shortly before 1247. It was situated in the north of the County of Nottinghamshire.

Dugdale says that de Chevrolant "gave to St. Mary, the Mother of God, for ever, A Place in his Park at Carlton. To be called St. Mary of the Park, there to build a religious House, and with it the Brook to build mills, and pasture in the Park for cattle and swine, with lands for free passage."

It was called originally "St. Mary in the Park", but changed its name to Wallingwells because of it being surrounded by wells, fountains and streams.

At the Dissolution it was valued at £59, and the last Prioress, whose name is given as Margaret Guldsmith, was given a pension of £6 p.a., and the three nuns, who were all that were left, received the same.

Waterbecham (Waterbeach)

A nunnery of the Order of St. Clare, called Minoresses, in Cambridgeshire. The Minoresses were originally founded by St. Francis. Dionisia de Monte Canisio, Lady of Anesty, gave her Manor of Waterbeche to build this nunnery in 1294, and Joanna de Nevers was made the first Abbess.

Mary of St. Paul, Countess of Pembroke during the reign of Edward II, transferred the nuns of Waterbecham to the Nunnery of Minoresses at Denney.

Watton

A very ancient nunnery situated about seven miles north of Beverley in Yorkshire. Bede calls the place Wetadun, the name meaning a wet place among water and marshes. It was built about the year 686, and no founder's name is given.

When John of Beverley became Bishop of York upon the death of Bishop Bosa in 705, he visited the nunnery. The Abbess was named Hereburg, and she had a daughter, whom she was training to succeed her; a practice of one member of a family succeeding another until that time being usual, but was now beginning to be frowned on by those in authority, as they thought the nuns should be given the choice to choose their own Abbess. Bede tells of a miracle when Bishop John was asked by the Abbess to cure her daughter, who was evidently at the point of death. He prayed at her bedside, and soon she was cured.

The old nunnery is not mentioned again, and was almost certainly destroyed by the Danes.

Sometime before 1149 or 1150, Eustace FitzJohn, who married the daughter of Ivo de Vescy, gave the site of the nunnery to build a priory for nuns and canons of the Gilbertine Order. It was dedicated to the Blessed Virgin.

The reputation of the Gilbertine Houses had always been very high, but the Priory of Watton is the one instance where there occurred any scandal.

Henry Murdoc, Archbishop of York from 1149, had entrusted a young girl of four years of age to be cared for by the nuns at Watton, so that she should eventually become a nun herself. But she began as she grew older to be found most unsuitable for the life in a convent. She fell in love and formed an attachment to one of the young canons, and she became pregnant.

The nuns of the convent were livid at the affront to their reputation, and filled with horror; in their indignation, they took the girl and punished her severely, beating her and clapping her feet in iron fetters. The young canon, meanwhile, had fled, but the rest of the canons decoyed him by disguising one of their members as a nun, hiding his face with a veil, and the youth was thereby caught and his brethren gave him a thrashing. The nuns, who appear to have been a most vicious lot, persuaded the canons to hand over their victim to them, and then they dragged him into the prison with the offending nun, and thrusting a knife into his hands, they forced him in front of the girl to mutilate himself.

The Archbishop, Henry Murduc, had died before this incident occured, but he appeared to the girl in her sleep, and told her to recite psalms. At this point to the amazement of all the community, the pregnancy disappeared, and one of the fetters fell off.

Then the prior, sorely perplexed, decided to ask advice, and probably at the suggestion of St. Gilbert, the Master of the Order, called in the great Abbot of Rievaulx, St. Aelred, who was known for his great wisdom.

St. Aelred examined the iron fetter that had fallen, and decided that it could only have happened by the Power of God; no human agency could have loosened it — and when the nuns asked him if they should replace the fetters with others, he forbade them to do so.

A few days later, the Prior wrote to St. Aelred and told him that the second fetter had fallen off, and asked him what they should do. He replied "What God has cleaned make not thou common; and do not thou bind the woman whom He absolves."

In its early stages the priory had 140 nuns and 70 brothers. In 1326, William Melton, Archbishop of York consecrated 53 nuns at one time. At the Dissolution the priory was valued at £360.16.10.

Langdale, writing in 1822, says that the site of the priory belonged to the Bethells of Rise, who made every exertion to preserve what little remains.

Weedon

A very early nunnery of the 7th century in Northamptonshire, originally built and founded by St. Werburga, daughter of King Wulfhere and Queen Ermenilda of Mercia. St. Werburga spent a great deal of her life after she became a nun in this nunnery, and from this centre she visited other convents which had been placed under her control by her uncle, King Ethelred. It was from Weedon that the story is told of the farmers complaining of the wild geese eating all their crops of corn. Werburga is said to have banished the geese, and to this day no wild geese have ever been seen there.

Nothing more is heard of this nunnery after the Danes arrived; it was most certainly destroyed by them. In the reign of Henry II a priory was built on the site, which was under the control of the Abbey of Bec in Normandy, hence it got the name of Weedon Bec. On the south side of the churchyard there was formerly a chapel dedicated to St. Werburga.

Weeks (Wikes, Wix, Wicks)

A priory for nuns in Essex, of the Order of St. Augustine. I have found the name of the place spelt differently, by three separate authorities, but I am presuming they all mean the same priory. Each one says it was in Essex and built in the reign of Henry I. Dugdale calls it Wikes, and says it was founded by Walter Mascherel and that Henry II confirmed all the nuns' possessions.

Welles

A Gilbertine priory in Lincolnshire. No nuns are mentioned, but most of the Gilbertine priories consisted of nuns as well as canons.

Dugdale says, "King John, by Charter of the 5th of his reign, confirmed the Foundation of this Priory by Ralph Havil, and the grants . . .For which the Canons to say one Mass for ever for the Soul of the said King John's Queen Ellenor . . . "

Wenlock (Much Wenlock)

A double monastery of men and women founded about the year 680 by St. Milburga, who was one of the daughters of King Merewald and Queen Domneva of Mercia. In the building of this monastery she was greatly encouraged by her father Merewald and her uncle Wulfhere, who were both sons of King Penda.

She was inspired by the example of St. Botulph and his famous Abbey at Icanhoe in East Anglia, and to assist her, a nun named Leobsynde came over from Chelles in France.

St. Milburga was much reverenced for her sanctity, and she soon had a large community of monks and nuns, and was given gifts of land not only from her native Mercians but also from among the Welsh, who gave her monastery property at Llanfillo, north east of Brecon, and the church there was dedicated in her name.

It was at Wenlock that one of St. Milburga's monks had a vision of heaven and hell beyond the grave. The monk had been thought to be dead, but was raised to life again. He had been terrified by what he had seen, and revealed the whole occurrence to his brethren. The story had been told to Hildelith, Abbess of Barking, presumably by Milburga, herself, or one of the inmates of Wenlock. Hildelith repeated the story to St. Boniface, who wrote in a letter to the Abbess Eadburga, Abbess of Thanet, and remarked on this wonderful happening and described to her the experience of this monk in detail.

When the Danes came the monastery was destroyed, and from the 10th century the site was deserted, until about 1084 Roger de Montgomery, Earl of Shrewsbury, restored the building and filled it with Cluniac monks.

Quite accidentally the tomb of St. Milburga was found; two boys were playing when they fell through a pavement. The hole where they fell was examined and a tomb was found. William of Malmesbury says a most fragrant odour came from it and many diseases were miraculously cured at the spot.

There are still ruins of the Abbey church to be seen.

N

Wherwell

A Benedictine nunnery in Hants, built by Elfrida (Aelftheyth), after the death of her husband, King Edgar in 975, and the assassination of her stepson, Edward in 978. The rumour that she built it as an atonement, was not thought of at the time but started up in the 12th century many years afterwards. William of Malmesbury gives another explanation, he says that her conscience was stricken and that it was in expiation of King Edgar's cruel act in killing her former husband. When the nunnery was built both Dunstan and Ethelwold trusted her, and put all the nunneries under her care, which they would not have done if they thought she were a murderer.

Her son, Ethelred endowed the nunnery well as an offering for the soul of his mother. In 1008 he gave the nuns of Wherwell land and property in Winchester consisting of twenty nine houses. Later on this grant was confirmed by Henry III. In 1221 Pope Gregory VIII took an interest in the nunnery. He confirmed all grants and forbade any nuns to leave without the consent of the Abbess.

This is the nunnery to which St. Wilfrida, the mother of St. Edith of Wilton, fled while fleeing from King Edgar, and she was received there by Wenfleda, an aunt of King Edgar.

Another notable woman who retired there in 1048 was Queen Edith, the widow of Edward the Confessor.

D. M. Knowles makes two statements about Wherwell: one, that the gross income in Domesday was £52.4., and two, that the nunnery was burnt by William de Ypres as it gave support to the Empress. During the dispute between the Empress Matilda and King Stephen, William de Ypres, who was made Earl of Kent, was accused of burning Wherwell because the nuns had harboured some of the partisans of the Empress. Restitution was made when peace was restored.

Whitby (Streanaeshalch)

An abbey of monks and nuns situated on a cliff overlooking the north sea in Yorkshire. In Saxon times its name was Streanaeshalch, the meaning of which, according to Bede is "the Bay of the Lighthouse". The name of the place was changed to Whitby after the Danes settled in the district.

The abbey was one of the most famous abbeys of Saxon times. It was built about the year 657, and St. Hilda was the first Abbess. She may have been the founder. Baptised when she was very young by St. Paulinus in 627 at the same time as her uncle King Edwin of Northumbria. The building of this abbey was said to be because of a vow that King Oswy made before the battle of Winwaed in 655. Oswy vowed that if he gained the victory, he would benefit the church, and give twelve small estates on which to build some monasteries. He was successful, and in 657 with the consent of St. Finan, who was then Bishop of Lindisfarne, he recalled Hilda from Hartlepool, where she had been Abbess, and where the king had placed his daughter, Aelfflaed, under her care, and made her the first Abbess of Whitby.

Under her rule the community became a great centre of culture and learning. Many famous men took advantage of the knowledge they could gain there. Five of them afterwards became bishops:- Bosa was consecrated Bishop of York; Ætla, Bishop of Dorchester; John of Beverley first Bishop of Hexham, then of York; Wilfrid Bishop of York; and Oftfor, who after studying with Archbishop Theodore in Kent and paying a visit to Rome, became the Bishop of the kingdom of the Hwicce.

It was at Whitby that England's first great poet was discovered, his name was Caedmon. Bede claims that this poet was the first to use the old heroic metrical verse and convert it into a form for Christian poetry. He tells how Caedmon had a dream and was told to write about the Creation. St. Hilda received him into the Community and probably taught him to write and gave him some sort of education; but his poetry was perfectly natural to him and came spontaneously.

Both King Oswy and the bishop, Finan, owed allegiance to the Celtic Church, originating from Iona, but in 644, when Colman had succeeded Finan as Bishop of Lindisfarne, was held the famous Synod of Whitby. The abbey was chosen for the meeting place because of its great importance, and there it was decided to acknowledge the supremacy of Rome and to be disciplined by its Church and to follow the same date for the celebration of Easter.

The abbey had a cell at Hackness, which was intended as a retreat for the nuns, and there was another cell at Osingadun, whose site is unknown; the historian Colgrave suggests that it might be Kirkdale, where there are some very early Saxon remains.

St. Hilda died in 680 after a long lingering illness, which lasted for six years. She was succeeded by Aelfflaed, the daughter of King Oswy, who was assisted by her mother Eanflaed.

After the battle of Nechtansmere, Trumwine, Bishop of the Picts with his monks migrated to Whitby, and was a great help to the Abbess in the running of the abbey.

While Aelfflaed and her mother were at Whitby they had the relics of St. Edwin translated there, and a shrine was built to contain them; King Edwin was the father of Queen Eanflaed. In the Abbey there was a chapel dedicated to St. Gregory, where his name was deeply revered, and one of the monks of Whitby wrote the earliest known Life of St. Gregory.

The Abbess Aelfflaed corresponded with a number of people, and there is a letter still existing written about 700 to Adolana, Abbess of Pfalzel near Treves, in which Aelfflaed asks the Abbess to take care of one of her friends, who wished to travel abroad.

William of Malmesbury says the abbey was destroyed by the Danes about 867, and then the name of Streanaeshalch was changed to Whitby. The abbey remained a deserted ruin until in the 11th century, three monks from the south came north to seek the places that they had read about in the Ecclesiastical History of Bede. Reinfrid an ex-soldier of William I, settled at Whitby with a few fellow monks, and once again a monastery rose from the site of the old abbey.

In 1833 memorial name slabs were found with the names of both men and women carved on them, and they dated from the 7th century. Excavations to the north of the ruins of the 11th century abbey revealed a plan of a typical Celtic monastery, with a rampart and buildings of wood and wattle for domestic use with a church in the centre. The cells were probably of a beehive shape.

Wiggenhall (Wigehal)

In the parish of St. Mary Magdalene, Wiggenshall, there was a nunnery of Cluniac nuns. It was founded in 1181.

William de Lisewis granted the land to the Nun Lene, daughter of Godfrey de Lenna. In one deed, William de Lisewis says the land is to be held of him and his successors, without any subjection, paying yearly twelve pence acknowledgement to the Church of St. John at Reinham. Reinham was a priory in Norfolk, and was a cell to the great Cluniac abbey of Castle Acre.

Reginald Fitzbaron was another donor to the nunnery, he gave the gift of Arahetin containing 1 acre & 8 oves in the field of Torpelond and after placed one of his daughters there as a nun.

Wilberfoss

A Benedictine nunnery, situated about eight miles from York. It was founded in 1153 by Helias de Catton and endowed with lands by her son Alan de Catton, and dedicated to the Blessed Virgin Mary. There are no remains to be seen.

Wilton

A Benedictine abbey for nuns in Wiltshire, three miles from Salisbury, founded during the 9th century. During Saxon times it was always under royal patronage. There is some confusion as to who was the founder. King Egbert, who reigned from 803–839, is said to have founded the Abbey of St. Mary at the request of his sister Elburga. Dugdale does not give the site of St. Mary's, but the "Book of Saints" compiled by the monks at Ramsgate mention the sister of King Egbert, and says that she founded Wilton Abbey, near Salisbury, whither she retired and took the veil in her widowhood.

In 854, King Ethelwulf, father of Alfred, was at Wilton, where he signed a charter which benefited the clergy of the time.

Dugdale then says that King Alfred, Egbert's grandson, founded a new abbey at Wilton and placed in it twelve holy virgins under the Abbess Radegundis, and that he transferred twelve nuns from King Egbert's Abbey of St. Mary to the new Abbey at Wilton, making the total number of nuns there, twenty four. The new building was dedicated to St. Mary and St. Bartholomew.

The succeeding kings, Edward the Elder, Athelstan, Edmund were all benefactors to the nuns, and King Eadred, reigning from 939–940, put a curse on anyone who disturbed the possessions of Wilton.

We do not have a complete list of the Abbesses, but several are mentioned: Radegundis, whom King Alfred first appointed as Abbess; St. Wilfrida who retired to Wilton, after she had been courted by King Edgar, and she had had a daughter by him, and became a nun, having received the veil from Ethelwald, Bishop of Winchester, and then afterwards, she became the Abbess. Her daughter, Edith, who became the famous saint of Wilton, assisted her mother in the running of the Abbey. While the two were in charge, the relics of Edward the martyred king were translated to Wilton in 979. Edith died while she was quite young in 984, at the age of twenty two.

In 1066 at the time of Domesday, the income of Wilton was £256; it was clearly one of the richest of the women's monasteries.

D. M. Knowles says that Queen Edith, daughter of Earl Godwin and wife of Edward the Confessor, rebuilt the church at Wilton, having retired there for a time about 1072.

There were several well known nuns who sought the veil there:- Gunhild, daughter of King Harold; the poetess Muriel; Eve, whose original home it was, and who later became a recluse and went abroad with Goscelin; and Alice, who became one of the spiritual daughters of Archbishop Anselm. Knowles also says that the nuns contributed copies of hexameter verses to the "Bede Rolls" which were circulated at the time.

In spite of many vicissitudes, such as being plundered and burnt by the Danish King Sweyn in the reign of Ethelred II in 1003, but recovered, and then ravaged by Robert Fitzwalter in 1140, and then King Stephen trying to turn the Abbey into a fort, it survived.

At the Dissolution of the Monasteries it was given to William Herbert by King Henry VIII, and on the site of the old Abbey he built a beautiful mansion.

Wimborne

A double Benedictine monastery known as Wimborne Minster in Dorset, founded about the year 705, although Dugdale mentions the year 718. King Ine of Wessex sent for his sister Cuthburga to organise the monastery and she was assisted by her sister Queenburga.

Cuthburga had at one time been Queen of Northumbria, wife of King Aldfrith, and had spent a year as a nun at Barking under Abbess Hildelith.

The name Wimborne has been said to be derived from "the Fountain of Wine" because of the fertility of the land on which it was built. It was one of the most strict of the double monasteries; the men and women were completely separated, high walls surrounding the two parts, and each having their own church. The Abbess only, was allowed to communicate with the men and then only through a window. One of the later Abbesses, Tetta, denied entrance even to priests and bishops, except a priest who came to administer the Sacraments. Even so, the Abbess had complete control over the whole Community.

St Cuthburga died in 725. It is not stated who succeeded her, but Tetta became Abbess soon afterwards, and there were five hundred nuns under her rule. It was in her time that nuns were sent abroad from Wimborne at the request of St. Boniface, to assist him in his missionary work in Germany. At first Tetta was not at all keen for her nuns to go so far afield as they had been brought up in such great seclusion, and she feared for their safety and conduct. St. Boniface persuaded her, and at last she consented, and several nuns were sent and became great successes; almost certainly due to her training. Among those who went were Lioba and Thecla, and they both became Abbesses in Germany.

The second in command under the Abbess was called the Prioress, and one of these was very unpopular and made the lives of the younger nuns very unhappy. This tale comes from Lioba herself, who long remembered with humour the conduct of these nuns, which was not always perfect, and they were very often given to jesting, and she probably joined in herself in some of their misdoings. There they were, enclosed within high walls, and it was not surprising that they occasionally gave way to their natural feelings. When the Prioress died, the nuns were overjoyed and gathering round the grave, they stamped it down flat with their feet.

The Abbess Tetta, when she discovered what had happened, and looking at the grave and seeing that it was lower than the surface of the ground, was horrified and calling all her nuns into the Chapter house, she preached at them and made them fast for three days, and offer prayers for the soul of the departed Prioress. At the end of the three days they gathered round the grave, chanting litanies and prostrating themselves, and then the ground over the grave slowly rose.

Another tale relates how the Sacristan lost the keys of the church after she had locked up after Compline. She went and confessed to the Abbess, who thought the nuns were up to their practical jokes again. The night Offices had to be held in one of the cells, and when they were ended the nuns found a fox at the door with the keys in its mouth. The Abbess, being wise, said it must have been the devil again.

Although there was never any real scandal told about Wimborne, there is a story about the nephew of Alfred the Great, Ethelwald, eloping with one of the nuns, but it is not mentioned in any of the Chronicles. The monastery was eventually destroyed by the Danes.

Winchcombe

There appears to have been a nunnery here founded by King Offa in 787. The authority for this mention of a nunnery is Dugdale. William of Malmesbury says that King Kenwulf built a monastery there in 798, and placed in it 300 monks. There is no further mention of any nuns, so they must have been there only eleven years.

Winchester

A nunnery in Winchester in Hampshire, founded by Ealswith, wife of King Alfred the Great. King Alfred came to the throne in 871, and he and his queen found the country in a desolate state. The Danish invasions had swept nearly all the old monasteries away, and ignorance and ruin prevailed almost everywhere. The royal couple were anxious to revive the religious communities as soon as they could obtain sufficient peace in the land to carry out their purpose. To quote D. M. Knowles — "The traditions of the early monasteries, old sites and names of saints lingered on, and moulded the minds of Alfred . . . ", and other great men of the 9th and 10th centuries.

The nunnery in Winchester was called Nunnaminster, and was dedicated to St. Mary. After King Alfred's death in 898, his widow retired there. All Alfred's sons and grandsons who succeeded him on the throne became patrons of the nuns. King Edward the Elder sent his daughter, Eadburga, there to be under the care of Queen Ealswith, her grandmother.

When King Eadred died in 955, he left a will, in which he endowed the Winchester Nunnery with money and estates; I quote from the will:- "To the Old Minster at Winchester and to the New Minster and to the Nunnaminster there, he gives three estates each: and to the three nun Minsters, at Winchester, at Wilton by Salisbury and at Sherborne, Thirty pounds each."*

At a meeting held at Winchester in 972, in King Edgar's reign, all religious Houses both for men and women were put under the direct patronage of the king and queen.

When Ethelwold became Bishop of Winchester in 963, he set about reforming the monasteries, making them keep more strictly to the Benedictine Rule, and he translated into English the "Rule of St. Benedict" especially for all the nuns.

The standard of all the monasteries went down during the troubled times of Cnut (1016–1035) and fresh Danish invasions, but the nunnery at Winchester still managed to produce some great work, several of them masterpieces, such as "The Book of Nunnaminster".

By 1066 at the time of the Norman Conquest there appear to have been only nine fully organised religious houses for women and Winchester was one of them. The annual value of this nunnery at that time was £65.

During the reign of Stephen, the quarrel between the king and the Empress Maud caused great devastation to a large number of the churches. Henry of Blois, brother of King Stephen, was then Bishop of Winchester, and unbeknown to him the empress sought refuge in the castle at Winchester, and he found the place in a state of siege. In his wrath he determined to smoke her out and to burn the city to the ground. Whether he really meant to harm the nuns is not known, but on 2nd August 1140 he reduced to ashes the Nunnery of St. Mary's and all its buildings and treasures.

This great house of Benedictine nuns, the Nunnaminster, must at some time after the disaster of the fire have been restored, because at the time of the Dissolution it had become a place of education for the daughters of the nobility, and there were twenty six of them then. Their names are given, and the first name on the list was Bryget Plantagenet. The house was well spoken of by the Mayor and the whole city, and Henry VIII accepted a bribe of £333.6.8. from the nuns to save the place, but it was of no avail, and the nunnery was dissolved in 1538.

*The Pre-Conquest Church in England by Margaret Deanesly.

Winteney (Wintney, Hartley Wintney)
On Wintney Moor some distance from the modern Parish of Hartley Row in Hampshire there stood a priory of Cistercian nuns, (Dugdale calls them Benedictine). It was founded in the 12th century. Richard Mayerel granted land to God and these nuns, and the grant was confirmed by Richard de Heveard, and later by King Edward I. The priory was dedicated to the Blessed Virgin and St. Mary Magdalen. The first church was built of wood, but in 1234, the nuns were given enough to replace the wooden structure with one of stone. The Bishops of Winchester made frequent visits and the nuns came under their control.

The priory never seemed to have had much in the way of sacred or worldly goods; an inventory taken in 1420 states:- "their refectory or hall . . . in addition to two worn tapestry hangings at the back of the high table and certain linen, a worn basin at the lavatory, a pewter salt-cellar and two latten and one pewter candlestick", and that is all they appeared to possess.

At the Dissolution it was valued at £52.5.8. Where the priory once stood there are now two cottages and some old barns which are pre-Reformation.

Wroxhall (Wroxall)
A Benedictine priory in Warwickshire, founded in the 12th century, by Hugh, Lord of Hatton and Wroxhall. There is quite a romantic story about the foundation of the priory. The Lord of Hatton had gone on a pilgrimage to the Holy Land, where he had been taken prisoner, and he had not been heard of by his family for seven years. He remembered his home and the church there, which had been dedicated to St. Leonard. One night as he was sleeping St. Leonard appeared to him, and told him to escape and that when he reached home he was to build a priory for nuns of the Order of St. Benedict. The saint then vanished but appeared to Hugh when he was fully awake and made him vow to build the priory.

Then by some strange means the Lord Hugh found himself wafted away and found himself back in England in Wroxhall Wood. He asked a shepherd, who happened to be passing where he was, and about his family. The Shepherd did not recognise him; neither did his family when they saw this strange man. It was only when he produced half a ring which he had broken with his wife when he had parted from her all the years before that she realised who he was. They went together to the church of St. Leonard to give thanks to God, Our Lady and St. Leonard.

The Lord Hugh built the priory where stones miraculously appeared to show where it should stand. Henry I confirmed all the grants. Two of the founder's daughters, Cleopatra and Editha, became nuns there. The first Prioress's name is given as Ernborow, and it was at this priory that one of the nuns built a Chapel at the bidding of Our Lady. Her name was Dame Alice Croft.

Wykeham (Wickham)
About six miles to the west of Scarborough in Yorkshire in the

grounds of a mansion known as Wykeham Abbey is the site of an old Cistercian nunnery. This nunnery was founded by Paganus de Wykeham in 1153, and dedicated to St. Mary or St. Michael. Theobald de Wykeham, son of the founder, added more lands, and King John confirmed the grants.

The church belonging to the nunnery was demolished in 1853, but the north wall of the original church is still standing, and a cross marks the site of the altar.

At the Dissolution the nunnery was valued at £25.17.6.

Wythorp (Wothorpe)

Dugdale calls this place in Northamptonshire Wyrthorp, but I think he means the place now called Wothorpe, where there was a small Benedictine nunnery. Thomas de Holland and his wife Jane in 1355, being patrons of the nunnery, finding it so poor and decayed and only one nun left, because the rest having died of pestilence, annexed it for ever to the nunnery at Stamford; the one nun removing there as well.

There is no date as to when the nunnery was originally founded, nor who the founder was.

York – The Bar Convent

This convent is situated by the Micklegate Bar in York. It was founded in 1686, at a time when it was very difficult for Roman Catholics to live in England. Sir Thomas Gascoigne gave and endowed the house. He wrote to Frances Bedingfield to come to England to found a school for girls. Frances Bedingfield was one of the nuns who lived in Paris and belonged to the Institute of the Blessed Virgin Mary. This Institute was founded by an Englishwoman, who had originally lived in Yorkshire, named Mary Ward. In 1609 she formed a group of nuns who were free to work among the people and were not in an Enclosed Order.

Forty years after Mary Ward's death, Frances Bedingfield arrived in England and first formed a school in Hammersmith, but later she removed the convent to York with the help of Sir Thomas Gascoigne.

At that time, 1686, the Roman Catholics were not looked upon with any favour, and Mother Bedingfield was several times sent to prison. The surrounding people in York were not generally aware that the "Ladies of the Bar" were of the faith which was condemned during that period; they were presumed to be just running a school and interested in education.

The nuns were said to be under the protection of St. Michael, and there was one occasion when the furious mob were about to break down the door of the convent; Mother Bedingfield was clasping in her hands a picture of St. Michael, praying for help. Then there was a sudden silence, and the mob dispersed. It is said that they saw an angel on horseback appearing over the house coming to its defence.

It was not until the 19th century that the nuns appeared in a religious dress.

The school which is now a day school is still flourishing and is recognised by the state, by being given a direct grant in 1929. In the great Parlour hang portraits of Mary Ward, the originator of the Order, Francis Bedingfield, the first Mother Superior, Dorothy Bedingfield, the second Superior, and Anne Aspinal, who was responsible for the present building.

York — Clementhorpe Nunnery

A small Benedictine nunnery dedicated to St. Clement, founded by Thurstan, Archbishop of York, about 1130. In 1192, Archbishop Geoffrey wished the nunnery to be given to the Abbey of Godestow, but the nuns of St. Clement's objected; they had always been free, and they appealed to the Pope, who supported their complaint.

There were several donors of land to the nunnery:— about 1217 Peter Percy gave them a grant and Archbishop Walter Gray confirmed it. Another donor was Nicholas, son of Ermsius de Walmgate. The Prioress at that time was Agnes de Wyten.

The last Prioress at the time of the Dissolution was Isabell Warde, and she received a pension of £6.13.0 in 1553.

Ruins of the church of the nunnery were still standing in the 18th century but were swept away in 1873, except a small portion of the Precinct Wall, which is on the south side of the street of Clementhorpe. In 1745, some of the stones of the old wall, which was the boundary wall of the nunnery were used to repair the city walls, about 85 feet, 9 feet high.

York Museum contains some fine worked stones from the site and a fine though mutilated figure of the Virgin and Child.

BOOKS OF REFERENCE

Bede, St., the Venerable
The complete works in the original Latin . . . parts of it accompanied by a new English translation . . . By J. A. Giles. 12v. London 1843.

Bede, St., the Venerable
Ecclesiastical history of the English people; ed. by B. Colgrave and R. A. B. Mynors. Oxford 1969.

Colgrave, Bertram
Two Lives of St. Cuthbert: a life by an anonymous monk of Lindisfarne and Bede's prose life; tr. and notes by B. Colgrave. Cambridge 1940.

Cuthbert, St., Bp. of Lindisfarne
The life of St. Cuthbert written anonymously about the year AD 700 . . . ed. by W. Forbes-Leith. Edinburgh 1888.

Dugdale, Sir William
Monasticon anglicanum, sive pandectae coenobiorum . . . digesti per R. Dodsworth & G. Dugdale. 3v. Londini, 1655–73.

Easson, David Edward
Medieval religious houses: Scotland, with an appendix on the houses in the Isle of Man. London 1957.

Knowles, David
The monastic order in England: a history of its development from the times of St. Dunstan to the fourth Lateran Council. Cambridge, 1940.

Knowles, David
The religious orders in England. 3v. Cambridge 1948–59.

Ramsgate, St. Augustine's Abbey
The book of saints: a dictionary of servants of God canonised by the Catholic Church . . . . compiled by the Benedictine monks of St. Augustine's Abbey, Ramsgate. 3rd ed. London 1934.

Butler, Alban
The lives of the Fathers, martyrs and other principal saints. 2nd ed. 12v. Dublin 1779–80.

Baring-Gould, Sabine
The lives of the saints. New edition. 16v. London 1897–98.

Simeon of Durham
Opera omnia; ed. T. Arnold. 2v. London 1882–5.

Bravonius (Florentius) Wigorniensis
Chronicon . . . ed. B. Thorpe. 2v. Vaduz 1964.

William of Malmesbury
De gestis pontificum anglorum libri quinque. Ed. . . . by N. E. S. A. Hamilton. London 1870.

Reginald, monk of Durham
Libellus de admirandis beati Cuthberti virtutibus quae novellis patratae sunt temporibus. ed. J. Raine. London 1835.

Giraldus [de Barry] Cambrensis
Opera. 8v. London 1861–91.

Anglo-Saxon Chronicle
The Anglo-Saxon Chronicle . . . ed. by B. Thorpe. 2v. London 1861.

Felix, Hermit of Crowland
Life of St. Guthlac, ed. B. Colgrave. Cambridge 1956.

Jones, Charles William
Saints' lives and chronicles in early England, together with first English translations of the oldest life of Pope St. Gregory the Great, by a monk of Whitby, and The Life of St. Guthlac of Crowland by Felix. Hamden, Conn. 1968.

Eddius
The life of Bishop Wilfred. Text, translation and notes by B. Colgrave. Cambridge 1927.

Aelred, St., Abbot of Rievaulx
The life of Ailred of Rievaulx (and the letter to Maurice) tr. . . . by F. M. Powicke. London 1950.

Juliana, Anchoress of Norwich
Revelations of divine love, recorded anno domini 1373 . . . ed. by Grace Warrack. London 1940.

Nennius, Abbot of Bangor
Nennius's 'History of the Britons' . . . ed. by A. W. Wade-Evans. London 1938.

Duckett, Eleanor Shipley
Anglo-Saxon saints and scholars. New York 1947.

Duckett, Eleanor Shipley
Saint Dunstan of Canterbury: a study of monastic reform in the 10th century. London 1955.

Duckett, Eleanor Shipley
The Wandering Saints. London 1959.

Whitelock, Dorothy
English historical documents. Vol. I: c500–1042, ed. D. Whitelock. London 1955.

Blair, Peter Hunter
An introduction to Anglo-Saxon England. Cambridge 1956.

Blair, Peter Hunter
The world of Bede. London 1970.

Deanesly, Margaret
The pre-conquest church in England. London 1961.

Lingard, John
The history and antiquities of the Anglo-Saxon church . . . 2v. London 1845.

Lappenberg, Johann Martin
A history of England under the Anglo-Saxon Kings, tr. . . . by B. Thorpe. 2v. London 1845.

Hutchinson, William
The history and antiquities of the County Palatine of Durham. 3v. Newcastle 1785–94.

Mackenzie, Eneas
A historical and descriptive view of the county of Northumberland. 2v. Newcastle upon Tyne 1811.

Ridpath, George
The border-history of England and Scotland, deduced from the earliest times to the union of the two crowns. London 1776.

Mayr-Harting, Henry Maria Robert Egmont
The coming of Christianity to Anglo-Saxon England. London 1972.

Anson, Peter Frederick
The call of the cloister. London 1964.

Encyclopaedia Britannica
30v. London 1974.

Burke, Sir John Bernard
A genealogical and heraldic history of the extinct and dormant peerages and baronetcies of England, Ireland and Scotland. London 1841, repr. 1964.

Crockford's clerical directory
London, various editions, 1860–present.

Timbs, John
Abbeys, castle and ancient halls of England and Wales. 3v. 2nd ed. 1872.

Jameson, Anna Brownell, Mrs. Robert
Sacred and legendary art. 2v. London 1890.

Cutts, Edward Lewes
Scenes and characters of the middle ages. London 1926.

Hole, Christina
Saints in folklore. London 1966.

Morton, Henry Canova Vollain
In search of England. 35th ed. London 1946.

Morton, Henry Canova Vollain
In search of Scotland. 18th ed. London 1933.